Praise for *Borderlands*

"*Borderlands* is an amazing book, and Ken Salazar is one of the great storytellers needed to heal our nation's divides. In this memoir, he demonstrates the old adage that to tell the story you need to live the life. He describes the full sweep of his family's Mexican American history, starting more than a century before Pilgrims saw Plymouth Rock and insists on America's diversity as our superpower. Ken describes the way forward for a New North American Alliance with Mexico and Canada. He tells many real stories in this remarkable book with the color and drama that only lived experience can provide. *Borderlands* is a must-read for Colorado and our nation!"

—Senator John Hickenlooper

"*Borderlands* is a gripping and deeply personal journey through the fault lines of identity, power, and belonging. Ken Salazar not only brings readers inside the moments that shaped his own life as a public servant, diplomat, and son of the Southwest, but his memoir is an urgent account of some of the most complex immigration and national security challenges we face. At such a pivotal moment, Ken Salazar challenges us all to lead with both strength and principle."

—Congressman Jason Crow

"From the ranch to the Senate and the president's cabinet, Ken lived the American dream and had a career defined by hard work and selfless public service. *Borderlands* offers every American insight into what our country can be at its best, and how we must overcome divisive politics to solve the hardest challenges we face together."

—Senator Mark Kelly

"Ken Salazar's *Borderlands* is both a testament to the importance of effective public service and a powerful tribute to the diversity that built America."

—Senator Catherine Cortez Masto

"*Borderlands* is a powerful reminder that the story of America cannot be told without the story of the border and the people who live there. Ken Salazar brings dignity, truth, and a reminder that diversity is America's superpower to a conversation our country urgently needs.

Ken has spent his life telling the truth about the border and the people who call it home. *Borderlands* honors the history, culture, and resilience of Mexican Americans and reminds us that our stories are essential to the story of America."

—Eva Longoria, actress, director, and entrepreneur

"Ken Salazar has long been revered for his devoted and distinguished public service—as a United States senator, secretary of the Interior, and diplomat—and for his countless contributions to our country. His compelling retelling of the uniquely American journey that shaped his trailblazing career is deeply profound, and offers vital lessons to citizens of all ages. And his bone-deep commitment to our country's best ideals, and the many insights that he provides on how we can recommit ourselves to achieving them, will inspire generations to come."

—Congressman Joe Neguse

"*Borderlands* is more than an elegant, evocative recounting of Ken Salazar's extraordinary life, his service to our nation and his fight for a country that can live up to its promise despite its history of injustice. It is more than an homage to the majestic West, our culture, the land, and her people. He beautifully captures our landscape, the triumphs and failures of government, and the possibilities that come with those lessons.

At its core, *Borderlands* is an urgent plea to reckon with the painful, tragic moment we are in; it is a celebration of diversity and a clarion call for unity and understanding. There's never been a more urgent moment in our lifetime to heed Ambassador Salazar's powerful message, his warning, his hope, and his optimism."

—Congresswoman Veronica Escobar

"Ken beautifully expresses and captures what it means to be part of America today. By blending his own personal story with history, he brings to life a broader narrative about identity, migration, and the communities that shape this country. *Borderlands* is a thoughtful reminder that the story of Latino communities is not separate from the American story: it sits at the heart of it."

—Luis A. Miranda, president of 5000 Broadway Productions
and chairman of the Miranda Family Fund

BORDERLANDS

BORDERLANDS

My Fight for an Inclusive America

KEN SALAZAR

BENBELLA

BenBella Books, Inc.
Dallas, TX

The events, locations, and conversations in this book, while true, are recreated from the author's memory. However, the essence of the story, and the feelings and emotions evoked, are intended to be accurate representations. In certain instances, names, persons, organizations, and places have been changed to protect an individual's privacy.

The opinions and characterizations in this piece are those of the author and do not necessarily represent those of the US government.

BENBELLA

BenBella Books, Inc.
8080 N. Central Expressway
Suite 1700
Dallas, TX 75206
benbellabooks.com
Send feedback to feedback@benbellabooks.com

BenBella is a federally registered trademark.

Printed in the United States of America
10 9 8 7 6 5 4 3 2 1

Library of Congress Control Number: 2026013752
ISBN 979-8-90268-021-5 (hardcover)
ISBN 979-8-90268-022-2 (electronic)

Special Writing Advisor: Nils Johnson-Shelton
Editing by Claire Schulz
Proofreading by Lisa Story and Mary White
Indexing by WordCo Indexing Services
Text design and composition by PerfecType, Nashville, TN
Cover design by Kara Klontz
Author photos (cover and interior) by Tami A. Heilemann
Back cover photo by Kenneth Lane
Printed by Lake Book Manufacturing

For Hope, Melinda, Andrea, Mireya,
Selena, and Amelia.

And for my beloved mom and dad, brothers and
sisters, all their children and grandchildren,
and our ancestors along the Borderlands.

CONTENTS

PART IV–EVERYONE MATTERS

PART V–THE PINNACLES OF POWER

The United States Senate

Eighth in Line to the Presidency

PART VI–THE AMBASSADOR

A New Beginning

The Borders

PREFACE

This book was written during a period of national strife that, as of publication, remains ongoing. This period has pitted regular Americans against each other; law enforcement officers against the people they are meant to protect; undocumented and documented migrants against the power of the state; the rule of law against the rule of man; and, in a perhaps dire foreboding, the rights of states against the policies and whims of the federal government. It is cleaving the country into warring camps. It feels as if we are already engaged in a domestic cold war about where the country came from and where it will go.

In June 2025, when I was about halfway through this manuscript, federal Immigration and Customs Enforcement (ICE) officers conducted sweeps at a Home Depot in Westlake, Los Angeles. The main targets were undocumented day laborers, nearly all Hispanic men. These actions spurred mass protests by incensed Angelenos.

Many commentators on the political right called these protests "riots" or "rebellions," even though they were overwhelmingly peaceful. Unfortunately, some agitators among the protesters acted out, and many of the images coming out of LA were violent and disturbing. In response, President Trump called in four thousand National Guard troops and seven hundred US Marines. This was against the will of both California's governor and the mayor of Los Angeles and strained legality.

For some, the president's actions were easy to comprehend. The news showed tear-gassed crowds, burning vehicles, riot officers clubbing protesters, people hurling stones at police officers, and law enforcement trying to respond. The city was in turmoil, and President Trump took advantage, accusing the protesters of being "people who hate America" and calling them "animals" and "a foreign enemy."

For others, the situation was not so black and white. Despite the rhetoric leveled against them, the people of Los Angeles were *not* acting like animals, and this city of immigrants was *not* under siege by foreign enemies. Other images of the protests showed peaceful, diverse groups marching and dancing through the streets, people facing off against police officers without incident, and countless examples of nonviolence on the part of the protesters and professionalism on the part of local law enforcement.

And many showed people waving American flags—as well as Mexican flags.

These Mexican flags, along with the presence of the United States Marines, seemed to be "proof" that Trump's social media posts about a "migrant invasion" were true and accurate. But when reporters asked the people waving the Mexican flags if they were siding with Mexico over the United States, they said no. They said instead that they were simply expressing their solidarity with migrants and celebrating their cultural heritage as Americans. The red, white, and green tricolor with the golden eagle in the center was not a symbol of foreign invasion, but a symbol of our inclusiveness. Of our history. Of our unique American diversity.

Many forget or possibly do not even know that California, as well as all of the American Southwest, was part of Mexico fewer than two hundred years ago. As I write, a plurality of California residents is Hispanic American, and the vast majority of these are Mexican American. Some are recent immigrants. But some have even deeper roots: These Mexican

Americans have lineages that go back to the first Spanish and Mexican settlements in California, whose major cities still bear the names of Spanish and Mexican religious figures. San Francisco. San Bernardino. Santa Barbara. San Diego. El Pueblo de los Ángeles—the Town of Angels.

These original Mexican Americans have lived across the American Southwest for centuries. They have been in what is now the United States for longer than any other group—longer than the English, French, or Dutch—with the obvious exception of Native Americans. These Mexican Americans became citizens of this country not by choice but by conquest when, in 1848, the United States won a bloody two-year conflict it had waged against Mexico.

The history of this war goes a long way toward explaining how we got to where we are today. It partially explains why Trump can get away with calling Mexicans "foreign enemies," and it completely accounts for why so many Americans dismiss Mexico and so many Mexicans distrust Americans.

It's generally accepted that the United States' "original sin" is the institution of chattel slavery. And it is true that this was a moral sin of the highest order. But I see three American "original sins": slavery, the intentional and systemic eradication of Native tribes and peoples, and the war against and conquest of the original Mexican Americans and the land on which they lived. All three are connected.

In the mid-1800s, American pro-slavery Democrats—intent on westward expansion and establishing more slave-holding states—set their sights on northern Mexico. And they had their champion in President James Polk.

In late 1845, following the US government's failed attempt to purchase what is now the American Southwest from Mexico for $50 million, Polk dispatched General Zachary Taylor and four thousand US regulars across the disputed Nueces Strip to the modern city of Brownsville, Texas. Their orders: Establish a fort there—which Taylor did. The fort's guns were squarely pointed across the Rio Grande at the Mexican town of Matamoros to ward off any unwanted incursions.

The problem, which Polk exploited, was that the newly constructed Fort Texas had been built in borderlands that were claimed by both countries. The United States viewed its territorial boundary as the Rio Grande, but Mexico maintained that the boundary was 150 miles *north* of the Rio Grande at the Nueces River. Fort Texas was therefore a provocation to the Mexican government and could not be countenanced.

Mexico deployed a force of 1,600 soldiers to deter any further unwanted US incursions. General Taylor caught wind of this on April 24, 1846, and sent a platoon of seventy of his finest dragoons to investigate. The next day, this reconnaissance party met the Mexican troops and were swiftly routed. Eleven US soldiers were killed, and nearly all the rest were taken prisoner. Less than one month later, with Mexico appearing to have fired the proverbial first shot, President Polk made his case to Congress, which overwhelmingly approved a resolution to declare war.

The rest, as they say, is history—which, as we know, the victors get to write. The Mexican-American War, as it's known in the United States, saw thirteen thousand American and as many as twenty-five thousand Mexican casualties, many of them civilians. Most of the American deaths were due to illnesses like dysentery, smallpox, and malaria rather than musket fire or the cold steel of a bayonet.

Overall, the Mexican-American War enjoyed broad support in the United States—but not universal support. Many abolitionists were opposed to the war since they viewed it as an attempt to secure more slave states for the Union. Henry David Thoreau was so opposed that he refused to pay a Massachusetts poll tax and ended up being arrested. This would help inspire his famous essay "Civil Disobedience," which, over a hundred years later, would inspire another activist, by the name of Martin Luther King Jr.

Another prominent critic of the war was Abraham Lincoln, at the time a congressman from Illinois. He viewed the war as immoral, pro-slavery, and totally anathema to our country's republican values—and he let Polk know it in a famous and controversial speech from the floor of the House of Representatives. This caused Lincoln some temporary political trouble—but, as we know, the lanky man from Springfield would eventually be remembered as the greatest president in US history.

Ulysses S. Grant, another future president, had the dubious distinction of being a lieutenant under General Taylor and was stationed at Fort Texas when the war began. Though Grant was only twenty-four years old at the time, he was clear-eyed. He later wrote, "We were sent to provoke a fight, but it was essential that Mexico should commence it" in order to justify a declaration of war against a sovereign neighbor. In his memoirs, he would call this war "one of the most unjust ever waged by a stronger against a weaker nation."

The Treaty of Guadalupe Hidalgo, ratified in 1848, set the terms of Mexico's defeat. It addressed remuneration and various debts and established specific rights for the newly absorbed Mexican Americans, such as the right to practice Catholicism, the right to become full US citizens, and the right to retain the land grants that had been handed out by the Mexican government. Of course, these rights were routinely violated or unenforced, but the original intent is there in black and white. This treaty is still on the books today.

As a result of this treaty, Mexico ceded to the United States roughly 55 percent of its territory, an area that now comprises all of California, Nevada, Utah, Arizona, and New Mexico, as well as much of Colorado and a small portion of Wyoming. Mexico also relinquished any claim to Texas, and the treaty established the Rio Grande, not the Nueces River, as the dividing line between Texas and Mexico. This treaty created today's border, which stretches nearly two thousand miles from Brownsville–Matamoros to El Paso–Juárez to San Diego–Tijuana. Article XI of the treaty stipulated that the United States, not Mexico, was responsible for policing this border.

These are the same borderlands we live with today.

The Mexican flags on display in Los Angeles in June 2025 fit squarely in this long, misunderstood, and mostly forgotten history. And while some may argue whether waving Mexican flags was politically shrewd at a time when Trump and his disciples were searching for any "anti-American" symbols to vilify, waving them nonetheless made perfect sense. Mexican pride, especially in defense of rights, is no different than the pride felt by other people with different national origins, such as Italians, Irish, Japanese, Germans, Ethiopians, and so on.

The Mexican American contributions to our shared story—past, present, and future—have made and will continue to make the United States an economic and cultural global powerhouse. Mexican Americans are a vital part of that powerhouse.

John F. Kennedy once observed that America's diversity is what makes our country so great. As he wrote, "There is no part of our nation that has not been touched by our immigrant background." This is as true today as it was then. All the people of the United States, regardless of where they come from, whether they're rich or poor, rural or urban, white or Black, women or men, are part of our nation's incredible diversity.

As President Ronald Reagan said at his farewell address in January 1989:

> The past few days when I've been at that window upstairs, I've thought a bit of the "shining city upon a hill." The phrase comes from John Winthrop, who wrote it to describe the America he imagined. What he imagined was important because he was an early Pilgrim, an early freedom man. He journeyed here on what today we'd call a little wooden boat; and like the other Pilgrims, he was looking for a home that would be free.
>
> I've spoken of the shining city all my political life, but I don't know if I ever quite communicated what I saw when I said it. But in my mind, it was a tall, proud city built on rocks stronger than oceans, wind-swept, God-blessed, and teeming with people of all kinds living in harmony and peace; a city with free ports that hummed with commerce and creativity. And if there had to be city walls, the walls had doors and the doors were

open to anyone with the will and the heart to get here. That's how I saw it, and see it still.

Today, about fifty million Mexican Americans live in our country. Some came to the United States after the war with Mexico, riding the ebbs and flows of labor needs and shifting migration policies. But other Mexican Americans have been here for a long time, like those whose ancestors founded the nation's oldest state capital, Santa Fe, long *before* the Puritans landed at Plymouth Rock. The lives of Mexican Americans are deeply rooted in stories of struggle, marginalization, and the triumph of the American dream.

I am from one of these older families. I am Mexican American, and I am proud of it. I am even more proud to be a citizen of the United States of America. Like many people, my life has encompassed struggle, marginalization, and triumph. My life has been a testament to the American dream; it was all made possible precisely because of the opportunities available to people like me in the United States. These same opportunities belong to all good and hardworking Americans.

I was fortunate to have been raised with the hallmark values of faith, family, and community, and to have had exceptional mentors throughout my life. These mentors have been friends and spiritual advisors, men and women, white and Black, brown and Native. They have taught me to insist on respect from the rich and the powerful who are "in the mainstream," not only for myself but for anyone who is considered "different." They have taught me to fight for a diverse and inclusive America.

And now is the time to fight.

Donald Trump's policies are harming families, communities, cities, states, and the nation. They are hurting our national security and needlessly making adversaries out of our closest allies. They are pulling us away from our never-ending and exceptional project of creating a more perfect union. And his anti-diversity policies are designed to further divide the American people, not bring us together, all so he can lay claim to more power and wealth and monuments for himself.

As Lincoln reminded us, "A house divided against itself cannot stand." Today, our nation is more divided than at any other time in modern history. In this time of despair, we must make a covenant to use every nonviolent tool available to combat Trump's project of erasure. We must urgently strive for more unity so that we do not stand "divided against" ourselves. We will not get past this moment peacefully if we do not work to understand each other.

And so: Take my hand, come with me down to the borderlands, and see what this Mexican American's life has been like. Have a cold Tecate or a tequila and some home-cooked food. See the mountains and the prairies, the land and the water. Come and meet your neighbors.

PART I

THE BREAKUP

1

THE DOOR CLOSES

On the afternoon of July 25, 2024, a Beechcraft King Air turboprop descended into the small Doña Ana County Jetport in New Mexico, just west of El Paso, Texas. As reported, the plane had originally taken off from an airstrip near Culiacán, Mexico, and disappeared on flight tracking systems before reemerging near the US–Mexico border. A call was put out to US law enforcement. Three men were aboard: the pilot and two others, both high-value targets in Mexico's Sinaloa Cartel. One of these passengers was making the journey voluntarily. The other most definitely was not.

The FBI field office in El Paso scrambled to send an arrest and SWAT team to the airstrip, which met the Beechcraft as it touched down. The plane made the short taxi to the waiting team, and after the pilot cut the engines, the door opened. A Mexican man in his late thirties emerged, his hands raised high. The agents' weapons trained on him, he identified himself as Joaquín Guzmán López, one of the sons of the infamous drug lord Joaquín "El Chapo" Guzmán, then serving a life sentence at the federal supermax prison in Florence, Colorado.

Guzmán López was cuffed. The agents then carefully boarded the aircraft and found a heavily sedated figure zip-tied in his seat. To their surprise, it was Ismael "El Mayo" Zambada García—the legendary cofounder of the Sinaloa Cartel, a man who had evaded capture for more than thirty years despite being one of the FBI's most-wanted criminals and carrying a $15 million price on his head. At seventy-six years old, El Mayo was the last of the old guard, a living monument to the cartel's ruthless rise to power. And here he was, being served up as a prosecutorial bargaining chip by his godson in what appeared to be a monumental act of betrayal.

Indeed, it was a betrayal, fit for a TV narco-thriller. We eventually learned from Mexican government officials that Guzmán López had lured El Mayo to a meeting in Culiacán earlier that morning, ostensibly to resolve a dispute about funding for the University of Sinaloa. Mexican Congressman Héctor Cuén was in attendance. When El Mayo entered the conference room, its table set with flowers and a breakfast banquet, he was ambushed, wrestled to the ground, cuffed, hooded, and forcibly sedated. As the kidnappers carried him outside to a waiting truck, they were confronted by El Mayo's security detail, a highly trained group of ruthless killers. All of these men were shot dead, as was Cuén, who had formerly served as both mayor of Culiacán and president of the University of Sinaloa. It remains unclear why Cuén ended up dead.

As the US ambassador to Mexico, I received word of these arrests later that afternoon. As for every other US official, they came as a complete surprise. For years, I had been asking the Mexican government to capture and extradite these and many other high-value cartel figures to the United States to face justice in US courts. With a few notable exceptions, the Mexican government had slow-walked these efforts.

Now, all of a sudden, the United States *did* have two of these high-value targets in custody—not thanks to the Mexican government but rather to what appeared to be a hostile action taken by one cartel member against another.

I immediately recognized both the triumph and the peril of this development. Triumph, because El Mayo and Guzmán López were finally in US custody; peril, because the strangeness of these arrests would send the Sinaloa Cartel into a spiral of violent internecine retribution. Many would die in the war that soon erupted.

I also knew these arrests could greatly upset the outgoing Mexican president, Andrés Manuel López Obrador—or AMLO, as almost everyone called him. I suspected that he would have a hard time accepting that the US government had not been directly involved with these arrests in any way. I also suspected that AMLO might not view them the way I did: that they had come about as a result of larger-scale cooperation between the United States and Mexico in dismantling the Sinaloa Cartel; that the joint pressure our governments had put on the cartel had caused one faction to turn on another.

After a short phone briefing from other US officials, I composed a message to AMLO. He had to understand that the United States had no prior knowledge of this abduction, and that under no circumstances had we conducted an unsanctioned operation on Mexican soil, which would have been a grave violation of their sovereignty. I immediately sent it to AMLO.

That evening, US Attorney General Merrick Garland and I prepared a more formal response to the Mexican government. "It was not our plane, not our pilot, and not our operation," we stated explicitly. I again sent this communication directly to AMLO and offered to meet to discuss the operation.

I waited for his reply. Hours passed. Nothing.

I tried again the next day. I knew AMLO often took the weekends to travel to his ranch in Tabasco or to tour the country and meet directly with everyday Mexicans. But wherever he was, he did not respond. For the sake of thoroughness, I sent additional letters to the Mexican attorney general, Alejandro Gertz, and again to AMLO. AG Garland also sent a memo to his Mexican counterpart. Then, in an unprecedented move, we offered to display the evidence including the Beechcraft plane and its contents to Mexican authorities and to convene US and Mexican law enforcement officials directly at the landing site. AG Gertz agreed. I later met with law enforcement teams from both countries in El Paso and at the Doña Ana airport in New Mexico to jointly inspect the evidence including the plane. From all appearances, the meeting of US–Mexico law enforcement officials was successful and I hoped the Mexican government would agree. I informed Washington and Mexico City, including AMLO and Mexican Attorney General Gertz, about the meeting.

But still there was only silence from AMLO.

By Monday, it was clear that something was seriously wrong. Though I was still the US ambassador to Mexico, the open door I'd enjoyed with the Mexican president appeared to have been slammed shut.

2

THE PALACIO NACIONAL

On July 21, 2024, four days before the arrests of El Mayo and Joaquín Guzmán López, I was in Oaxaca, Mexico, at the annual Guelaguetza festival. I'd just attended mass at Oaxaca's cathedral with my daughter Andrea and granddaughter Selena when my trusted colleague Zeppa Kreager approached me with tears in her eyes. Careful not to say anything, she held out a Post-it. I scanned it quickly—President Biden had just ended his campaign for reelection and, in the coming hours, would throw his weight behind Vice President Kamala Harris to run against Donald Trump.

This was a sad moment for many reasons. Politicians never like giving up in the middle of a campaign. Adding insult to injury, President Biden was succumbing to pressure that he was too old and feeble to do the job. You can agree with what President Biden did—some days I do, others I don't—but it was still painful and unfortunate.

It was made even more unfortunate, at least where the border was concerned, because President Biden was finally succeeding in bringing the border and migration flows under control. Biden had issued an executive order on the US–Mexico border and encounters there had dropped by 50 percent, and over fifty thousand migrants had been repatriated on over 175 flights back to their home countries. This should have been a moment of vindication—after all, American voters were demanding action on the border—but it was too late, and images of an out-of-control border would dominate the closing months of the presidential election. With President Biden now bowing out, the media, spurred on by his opponents, would just run with that story, blaring it across the airwaves and internet. I had little hope that Americans would learn (or even believe) that the border had finally gotten under control, and I knew that Trump would continue to lie and gleefully exploit this very real crisis to his advantage.

That evening, I returned to Mexico City and immediately requested a meeting with President López Obrador in his office at the Palacio Nacional. The seat of power in Mexico, the Palacio consists of a conglomeration of interlocking four-story buildings that take up an entire city block. It is on the eastern side of Zócalo, Mexico City's historic central plaza, catty-corner to the famous Mexico City Metropolitan Cathedral, which is visited by millions of people every year.

As I had so many times before, I entered the Palacio through the highly secured Corridor Eight, which was used by all visitors heading to AMLO's chambers. The uniformed military guard gave me a crisp salute, and a staffer accompanied me on the five-minute walk through the hallways to the president's wing. The sound of our footfalls echoed off the walls, adorned with Diego Rivera murals and priceless Aztec relics.

AMLO greeted me warmly in his office's doorway and ushered me inside. His own political life was coming to an end—Mexican presidents can only serve one six-year term—and so he must have felt some camaraderie with President Biden, whose respective political life was ending in a much less noble way. AMLO told me that he admired President Biden's decision, saying it was "something few politicians would have the courage to do, to step away from power." It was clear that he'd hoped President Biden would win, and that the last thing he wanted was for

Trump to be president again. I tried to assure him that whatever happened, the United States and Mexico had crossed some sort of Rubicon in our economic integration and our cooperation on issues like security, energy, and climate policy. I had drafted a letter from AMLO to President Biden setting forth the vision for a durable North American alliance, which AMLO asked me to read to him. He listened attentively, nodded in agreement, and said he would send the letter in a few days. He again spoke favorably of President Biden and asked that I deliver a short letter of his own that he had prepared for him. This letter also assured Biden of AMLO's continued cooperation with the United States.

"Con gusto, señor presidente. I will do so immediately," I said.

We exchanged a warm abrazo and I walked back through the Palacio corridors. I exited the building, climbed into my armored SUV, and returned to the bustle of Mexico City.

I didn't know it then, but this would be the last time I met or spoke with the Mexican president.

3

PERSONA NON GRATA

In addition to President Biden's decision to end his reelection campaign and the arrests of Guzmán López and El Mayo, I had recently made public statements about my concerns over a set of controversial judicial reforms AMLO was pushing for. These changes would require all Mexican judges to be elected rather than appointed. For comparison, this would be like the GOP or the Democrats in the United States demanding that all federal judges, including Supreme Court justices, be voted into their respective offices. It doesn't take much imagination to see how easily some judges could be corrupted if campaign funding and political clout were prerequisites for taking office. This would consolidate political power across supposedly coequal branches of government, effectively doing away with checks and balances.

I had written several private notes to AMLO stating my concerns and suggesting alternatives to his judicial reforms, but like my other communications around this time, they went unanswered.

And of course, in Mexico, there was a wrinkle to this issue that went beyond politics: organized crime. It was well known that Mexico's powerful transnational criminal cartels had compromised many government officials. An elected judiciary would unquestionably grant the cartels more power. This squared with another criticism I had been making as the US ambassador: that AMLO's policy of "abrazos, no balazos"—"hugs, not bullets"—was insufficient for combating the cartels.

To be clear, AMLO was not proposing to hug the cartels into submission, but rather to use his platform of economic populism to help poor Mexicans get educations and jobs so that they didn't feel so compelled to work for the cartels. I was very supportive of these types of programs, but I insisted that they occur alongside, and not in place of, security enhancements. I'd said it often, and AMLO had heard it many times: "Sin seguridad, no hay prosperidad"—without security, there can be no prosperity. It was clear that the Mexican people, as well as American visitors, did not feel safe, and for me, that was all that mattered.

On August 22, I spoke at a press conference from the ambassador's residence. I answered questions about the arrests and the US–Mexico trade relationship and addressed AMLO's proposed judicial reforms. I said, "Based on my lifelong experience supporting the rule of law, I believe that popular direct election of judges is a major risk to the functioning of Mexico's democracy. Any judicial reform should have the right kinds of safeguards that will ensure the judicial branch will be strengthened and not subject to the corruption of politics."

AMLO's reaction was swift. The next morning, in his daily press conference, he spent nearly an hour attacking me personally for interfering with Mexico's sovereignty and announced a "diplomatic pause"—not against the United States, which the Mexican government continued to work with, but against *me*.

"The ambassador is a person who has good intentions, but he does not know Mexico," AMLO told the assembled reporters. AMLO knew that of course I was not Mexican, but he also knew my family's story and its deep roots in lands that had once been Mexican. He was fully aware that I had worked tirelessly—often traveling ten thousand miles a month within Mexico and between Mexico and Washington—to advocate for the people of both our countries and for the necessity of closer ties with Mexico, its people, and its culture.

AMLO continued his diatribe against me: "It is not for him to make comments on our constitutional reforms. Mexico is a free, independent, sovereign country. We are not a colony of any foreign country."

I was not speaking up to infringe on Mexico's sovereignty—far from it. I was speaking about the rule of law both in the United States and Mexico. But there it was: that old, shared history of our two countries—and not the good side of it, but the embittered side, the side that hunkered down and dug in.

Right around this time, I heard from a friend I called "the Whisperer." He was a prominent Mexican businessman who occasionally whispered advice in my ear, but mainly he was the AMLO whisperer, someone who was a friend and confidant to the Mexican president.

The Whisperer almost always had something nice to say about me that AMLO had relayed to him in some casual, offhand manner. But not this time.

"AMLO is a changed man," he warned. "He can't let go of power. And he is very concerned about the information the United States will get from El Mayo," he said, as if the powerful and entrenched capo might spill the beans on any number of Mexican public officials.

As painful as this diplomatic rupture was on its own, it also mirrored another sad reality: my disillusionment with my own government's repeated failure to fix our border and immigration system.

I found myself caught between worlds, in a kind of borderland of the mind. In Mexico, I had been frozen out by a president I had worked persistently to understand and deemed an intruder in a country where my own ancestors had deep roots. In Washington, I had spent years warning about the border crisis and the need to fix our broken immigration system, only to be ignored until it was too late. Like the original Mexican Americans of 1848, I existed in a diplomatic limbo—my identity, experience, and expertise rendered invisible by the very powers I served.

And then, a couple of months later, Trump won the presidential election. My time in Mexico City would soon draw to a close.

Even if Vice President Harris had beaten him, I intended to resign. I needed to get back to my family and life in Colorado. But during this lame-duck period, I grew reflective.

How did I get to this point in my career? What did my story have to say about the larger saga between our two countries? How would our relationship unfold going forward? Would we continue to heal the scars between Mexico and the United States, as I had worked so hard to do during my time as ambassador, as United States senator, and as secretary of the Interior? Or would the old wounds along our borderlands be reopened in a new and bitter era under the incoming Trump administration?

One day in late November, sitting in my office at the embassy in Mexico City, I found myself looking at the photos on my desk. One showed me standing next to President Biden in front of the *Resolute* Desk in the Oval Office. Another captured a moment with AMLO during a tour of the border in early 2022, when the possibilities for our two countries felt endless and full of optimism. And there, between these photos, stood a small clay figure of a campesino—a Mexican farm laborer. It was a gift from an Indigenous artisan I had met in Oaxaca. To me, it represented the ordinary people caught between powerful forces.

I picked up the figure and turned it in my hand. The border. Migration. Security. Economics. Politics. Dignity. Respect. Understanding. History. Diversity. All of it swirled in my mind, opportunities squandered through inaction, mistrust, and what I could only call political malpractice.

At that moment, I felt like a man with no country.

PART II

ROOTS

4

THE VALLEY

But here's the thing: I know exactly where I'm from. Come on, hop in my pickup, and let me take you on a ride through my home: my very own corner of Colorado's San Luis Valley.

We pull out of the Ohkay Ranch, our adobe single-story house with foot-thick walls, a Spanish tile roof, arched windows, and a ground-mounted solar array off the garage. Like most homes in the Valley, the house is surrounded by a patchwork of cattle, hay, and alfalfa fields, some irrigated by a network of ditches, others defined by scaffold sprinklers that spray water pumped from a deep aquifer as they slowly sweep the fields, creating great, 130-acre circles when viewed from high overhead.

Off to the south of our ranch are some rounded desert rock formations and mountaintops called Los Cerritos—a rise in the land I regularly take in from my kitchen table over morning coffee. A short distance to the east are the hills that make up Los Rincones—"the corners"—where I grew up in the 1950s and 1960s, and where several of my family members currently live. It is a proud place. The home of my ancestors and family since the 1850s, the first non-Native settlement in Colorado.

The Valley is right up against the Continental Divide. In the distance to the west are the snowcapped peaks of the San Juan Mountains and to the east are the Sangre de Cristo Mountains. These great ranges, boasting several summits over 14,000 feet, define the valley floor, which is overwhelmingly flat despite having an average elevation of over 7,600 feet.

The Valley is not a narrow strip like other valleys you might envision, but rather a kind of long, uneven oval surrounded by towering mountains. It is huge—at over eight thousand square miles, it is the largest alpine valley in the world—and is bisected by the Rio Grande, also known as the Río Bravo del Norte, the Fierce River of the North. This great river wends through the Valley to New Mexico and ultimately along the entire Texas–Mexico border on its way to the Gulf of Mexico.

The Valley is defined by many things: wind, dust, faith, cattle, rivers, ditches, fence lines, churches, sun, snowpack, sacrifice, headgates, basketball, track and field, pickup trucks, tractors, brown and white in the winter, green and blue in the summer—land, water, people. My people.

We pull out of the driveway and onto County Road 19. There, off to the right, is a stand of mature cottonwood and willow trees. On this exact spot stood a house that once belonged to my great-grandparents on my father's side, Eusebio and Amada Salazar. The house was neglected and eventually razed, never to be replaced—at least, until we built our home on the Ohkay Ranch just down the dirt road. Like many things in the Valley—water, the seasons, crops, calves—what goes around comes around.

We drive west past more fields and homes, mostly single-story and set back from the road. We soon come to the town of Manassa, population 961, birthplace of the heavyweight champ Jack Dempsey, "The Manassa Mauler." Nowadays, it is a struggling place with only one gas station and shuttered storefronts. It's like much of the rest of rural America I have traveled through. But when I was a child, this was the big city. Manassa was where I first went to school. It was where we got our used trucks repaired, where my dad, Henry, bought gas and diesel and kerosene for our adobe home, which had no telephone or power lines. The only power we ever had came from a small generator we called "la planta," the plant. It powered a few lights in the house, a washing machine Dad had bought for Mom, and a water pump. This meant that technically we had lights and running water, but the generator was so chronically broken that we usually had to pump water and read by the light of kerosene lamps. Los Rincones didn't get full power until 1981.

Henry was born in 1916. He never worked fewer than fourteen hours a day, seven days a week, tending to sheep and cows, growing potatoes and alfalfa. He worked so hard because he knew he was lucky to be alive. Five of his siblings had died before they reached the age of five, and Henry himself had survived several bouts of childhood pneumonia.

Our ancestors had been given land grants when this area was part of Mexico—but then they were taken away. Following the Mexican-American War, our ancestors went about acquiring land in the Valley, and at one time they owned thousands of acres—almost all of the land along the five miles from Manassa to Los Rincones. Then, during steep economic downturns in the late nineteenth century, they lost practically all of their property to banks and speculators. Since then, the Salazar family has been engaged in a project of reclaiming that land—collectively, we now own several thousand acres close to Los Rincones. We have built on efforts undertaken by my grandfather Juan Bautista Salazar, who went to the gold mines in Telluride in 1900 at the age of sixteen in order to save enough money to repurchase the forty acres of the Ohkay Ranch his parents had once owned.

From Manassa, we turn south and soon cross the Conejos River, the tributary that gives the county its name. This stream is one of several veins of a riparian system that crisscrosses the Valley, bringing water to fields and cattle and sheep and horses and people. Every spring, we work to clear ditches and headgates of downed limbs, mud-caked brush, and beaver dams before allowing water to flow freely into the fields. It is a tried-and-true system, using ditches—"acequias" in Spanish—that are over 175 years old, designed to create seasonal ponds and watering holes, to literally soak the land in cold meltwater cascading down from the surrounding mountains.

We pass through more fields, and see stands of cottonwoods here and there, leaves flickering in the breeze. In the Valley, wherever there is a stream, there are cottonwoods, as well as gangs of reedy willows. We cross through several more fields with tall, open-sided shade structures for storing baled hay. We pass equipment sheds, some of which are ours, housing tractors and balers and brush hogs and ditchers and trailers and drag harrows.

After a mile or so, we turn back east and soon pass my younger brother Elliott's house along the San Antonio River. A retired IRS field agent who used to work around Durango and across the Southwest with a gun and a badge, Elliott returned to the Valley (many Salazars return to the Valley) to take up ranching once more. He loves horses and tractors and has an iron grip and a freewheeling cackle of a laugh. He likes to laugh.

We head east, back toward the Rio Grande. We are driving alongside the black ribbon of the San Antonio River now, which is off the right side of the road. This is Elliott's land. Elliott is a master conservationist who has been recognized by the Colorado Cattlemen's Association for his efforts. He restored his section of the San Antonio to its present beauty by cordoning the river from cattle and engaging in a practice called rotational grazing. Cattle can do a number on the sand and stone riverbanks, causing erosion and, over time, a complete degradation of the flora and fauna that make up the waterside ecosystem. Of course, cattle must drink, but they don't need to damage the river to do it. That's what ditches, ponds, wells, and carefully managed access to the river are for. Here, the cottonwoods thrive and the red, arrow-like stalks of willow bushes reach skyward. The cattle make their own paths through the dense foliage as they graze native hay, which simply grows year after year without being planted. The birds twitter, and the bugs buzz.

But look over here, out on the left side of the truck, and you'll see something else. Here is a neighboring ranch with its absentee landowners, a feeding ground dedicated to cattle and little else. This vast expanse of ranch is not an example of stewardship but of exploitation. It is a landscape put under pressure, where the riverbed of the San Antonio has suddenly been sucked dry, where thirsty, hundred-year-old cottonwoods crack and wither in the sun, where cows trample and eat everything, where the Valley transitions to something more akin to barrenness. There is no reason for this mistreatment. When land is treated sustainably, it can be both healthy and productive. There is no need to sacrifice one for the other.

But we continue on, hoping that one day the San Antonio will not be emptied like this, and that it will once again support the land, the trees, the animals, the people.

On the road between Manassa and Los Rincones, we crest a low swell and pass the Mormon cemetery on the right and, a short while later, the Catholic cemetery on the left. The Valley is a very devout place. The Spanish population is largely Catholic, and the Anglo folks are mostly Mormon (but also Mennonite and Amish).

My father, Henry, and mother, Emma, are both buried in the Catholic cemetery, as is my oldest brother, Leandro. We stop there to visit the gravesites and the timeless tombstones of my grandparents and great-grandparents, the oldest among them born in 1827. Leandro's tombstone—showing his birthday, August 31, 1949—has the famous eagle of the United Farm Workers etched into the stone. Leandro was my parents' firstborn, the only one of my siblings not given an anglicized name. He died tragically in a farming accident in 1992, which deeply affected our entire family. My parents' strength and faith supported us through the agony of our loss. I remember Leandro as a man before his time, insistent that we do not forget the Spanish language of our ancestors and that we fight for social justice and for the cause of the United Farm Workers.

White crosses stand all around us here, marking reserved plots for family members. Leroy, the next-eldest son of Henry and Emma, purchased a dozen plots in the center of the family burial site which he reserved for each of us. "So we can be together forever," Leroy joked when he told us about the plots one evening at his home in Los Rincones.

We get back on the road and continue. All around us now are endless tracts administered by the Bureau of Land Management, a federal agency I oversaw when I was secretary of the Interior Department. The landscape here is dominated by low scrub and wild grasses, a favorite slithering ground of prairie rattlesnakes, which scared me to death when I was a child. All over the Valley are pronghorn, elk, loggerhead shrikes, meadowlarks, coyotes, kangaroo rats, least chipmunks, and ground squirrels, among many other animals big and small, including several herds of wild horses. Scan the hills to the east and you can probably spot them grazing and playing in the afternoon sun.

Soon we come to a 130-year-old steel truss bridge spanning the Rio Grande. The bridge is black and worn, its timber-wood roadway splintering and creaky. This is now a recreation area where rafters and kayakers, bikers and hikers, and hunters and anglers come year-round. The bullet-scarred signs you see in the parking area make me grimace: I worked on projects to restore and celebrate the Rio Grande during my time as state attorney general, US senator, and Interior secretary. I haven't just brought you here to this great river; I've also come to this spot with governors, senators, members of Congress, state lawmakers, county commissioners, ranchers, and environmentalists.

We turn off the hard-packed dirt road and bump along rutted four-wheel tracks. This exact spot is where the river deepens from a shallow, prairie-level waterway into the black volcanic basalt gorge it has carved over millennia. Here, on the Lobatos Bridge, the gorge is only twenty or thirty feet deep, but fewer than fifty miles downriver, near Taos, New Mexico, the gorge dives a dizzying eight hundred feet. If you know where to look, both here and down in Taos, you'll see prehistoric petroglyphs, some of which date back thousands of years.

We came to this section of the Rio Grande near our home many times as kids. We would have rock skipping contests and yell at the top of our lungs for the echo that spoke back to us as sound bounced from one gorge wall to the other. Every August, Dad, my brothers, and I would come here carrying empty five-gallon buckets and follow the riverbank to a wild and ancient chokecherry orchard, where we'd pick berries to our fill. We'd take them to Mom, who would preserve and pack them into jars. Chokecherry jam was often the only fruit we had over the winter. Dad would use the rest to make chokecherry wine. Henry was practically a teetotaler, but he made an exception for the red concoction that flowed from his little still, a barrel-like contraption tucked behind our wood-burning stove. If you came by and he was in the mood, he'd offer you some of his home brew to sip as you watched the sun drop over the mountaintops.

Back in the truck, we turn around. It's dinnertime at my brother John's house, and we're running late. We head back over the section of federal land, right at an intersection that has no name, and continue more or less straight for several miles. Look to the left, and you can see the afternoon haze of dust blowing off the fields, beginning its airborne journey to the basin in the northeast where it has gathered and settled for millions of years, creating the Great Sand Dunes. Much closer to us, the hills just off on our right form one side of Los Rincones—promontories that I have hiked countless times—and soon we are on land that is all owned by Salazars. Here we grow hay, graze cattle and sometimes raise sheep or pigs, and farm seed potatoes. Leroy—who served as an agricultural engineer for many years and knows as much about water and aquifers as any other person in Colorado—is nationally renowned for his seed potatoes, which are used to cultivate crops across the United States.

We pull into John's driveway, crossing over a spot where an old house once stood, now long gone. We know the exact room in that spot where Henry was born in 1916. It was the same room in which his mother, our Grandma Tita, Maria Antonia Cantu Salazar, was born in 1884. This is a spiritual place, which John and his family walk over and through many times a day. Our old family home still stands near here too, just off to the right and toward the hills—a white adobe ranch with forest green trim. Nowadays, my sisters, Elaine, Margaret, and June, are restoring the house to make it a sanctuary of celebration of our parents' memory and our living family.

John and his wife, Luz, greet us and pass out drinks, inviting us inside. Leroy and his wife, Michelle, are here—they live a short walk away in a passive solar home Michelle designed—as are my sister Margaret and her husband, Marvin, both retired high school math teachers. My wife, Hope, is here too. Luz and John are great cooks, and smells fill the kitchen: rice and homemade pork sausage, pinto beans and fresh tortillas, and Marvin's signature red chile. John, once a US congressman, is laughing and telling a story about how he took a beating for me from Dad for some trouble I'd gotten into at school. Of course, that's not how I remember it—I got a whupping too.

We sit and eat, surrounded by history, love, faith, friendship, ancestors, and land that we know as well as anyone knows any land, anywhere in North America. We're people who live with rather than just off the land. People who give more than they take, and in many different ways.

I sip my beer, and I think: In order to truly help and fight for a place—whether it's the Valley, Colorado, the United States, or Mexico—you first have to understand a place. This is a fact too many so-called leaders have either forgotten or have willfully remained ignorant of. Point being: We understand the Valley, and therefore, we understand the country writ large.

The Valley is our home. It is our America.

5

INNOCENCE

Growing up, I knew the Valley was my home. I knew I was Mexican American, and I knew our family to be proud American citizens, but I didn't know how other people—Anglos, mostly—thought about us. Until, that is, I started attending school.

Like many children, my innocence (and my ignorance of the wider world) was still intact when I started school. Funny how school both educates you and quickens you to the world's problems, isn't it? I vividly recall one day in 1960, when I was just four. It was afternoon, and I was in the kitchen with Mom while she cooked and took care of my newborn sister, Elaine. The comforting smells of fresh bread and popcorn filled every corner of our home. I was perched on a table, acting silly and cooing at Elaine, which made her smile. But I was also keeping one eye on the window, eagerly waiting for any sign of the big yellow school bus that would return my brothers to me. Finally, I spotted it in a cloud of swirling dust. It was the first day of school for my three big brothers, and I couldn't wait for them to come back. The house had felt empty while they were away.

As the bus pulled to a stop, I slid from the table and hustled outside, running as fast as I could to the cattle guard separating our yard from the main road. Leandro got out first, followed by Leroy and then John, the youngest of the three. I jumped into Leandro's arms. He gave me a big hug, put me back on the ground, and patted my head.

"Tanto que te quiero," he said, meaning "I love you so much." We often used it as a greeting and a way of asking what one of us had been up to.

I replied excitedly in Spanish, "Esperandolos . . . Mom has popcorn and fresh bread for you. She is waiting for you!"

"Que bueno," Leandro said. He was only ten years old, but to me he already seemed like an adult.

John, who—as the closest to me in age—would be my brotherly partner in crime once I started school, skipped past me with a high five and then broke into a run for the house. Over his shoulder, he shouted, "You can't catch me!" I didn't accept his challenge that time, though I often did.

Leroy put his arm around me, and we walked together up the dirt road to the house. "Look at this, little brother." He pulled something out of his bag, which I recognized as his *Weekly Reader*. "A man named John Kennedy is running for president against someone named Richard Nixon," he said. The names were meaningless, but he flipped through the reader to show me a picture of each. I liked the look of Kennedy—he was handsome, had a joyful smile, and "Kennedy" sounded like "Kenneth." (Later, my grandfather in New Mexico began calling me Kennedy instead of Kenneth.) I have no clear recollection of Nixon that isn't mixed up with images of either his 1968 victory or his national disgrace following the Watergate scandal, but I do remember not being impressed.

I pointed at Kennedy. Leroy explained, "He's a Catholic from Massachusetts, and he's a Democrat. People think he won't win, but I'm supporting him." This was a funny thing for a nine-year-old boy to say given that he couldn't vote, but there were other ways to support candidates, then as now.

I looked at Leroy, his bright eyes glinting in the afternoon sun, and asked, "Do you think I could be president one day?"

"Of course, if that's what you want," he said without a hint of insincerity.

I have no doubt that Leroy already knew my chances of being president were low. But to Leroy's credit, he didn't let on. I was his four-year-old brother; who was he to crush my dreams?

That afternoon, as we checked on our flock of seventy sheep and our small herd of cows, making sure they had enough feed and water and that they were safe from stray dogs and coyotes, I did like many young boys in those days and pretended to be president of the United States. Little did I know that, many years hence, I would be in the Oval Office countless times, not as president but as a US senator and, later, as the secretary of the Interior, serving in the cabinet of the first Black president, Barack Obama.

But in 1960, all of this was far off. Of course, John F. Kennedy beat Nixon that fall, and would serve as the nation's first Catholic president until his assassination in 1963. Many years later, when I was in college in Colorado Springs, I would read portions of his book *A Nation of Immigrants*. In it, Kennedy wrote, "Every American who ever lived, with the exception of one group, was either an immigrant himself or a descendant of immigrants." Kennedy mostly wrote about European immigrants in his treatise, but his main point was that our diversity is what makes America strong.

6

THE TOWN WITH LIGHTS

I started school one year later. Our elementary school was a three-story red brick building in the bustling downtown metropolis of Manassa, which then had a population of 831. Manassa was like a different world. For one, it had power, and the town was full of lights. This is where my life away from Los Rincones began.

The first floor of the school housed the kindergarten; the second floor the first, second, and third grades; and the top floor had fourth- and fifth-grade classrooms and a fire escape slide that was the longest slide I'd ever seen. From time to time, a mischievous kid would pull the fire alarm so all the children on the top floor could escape (joyfully) to safety.

Pretty much from the moment I stepped into Manassa Elementary, I was in trouble. I wanted no part of school, so I decided to make it so that school would want no part of me. Maybe, if I made enough trouble, I would get kicked out, and once that feat was achieved, I could stay home and work on the farm at Los Rincones forever.

Of course, this was not an option. Henry and Emma drilled into all of us that getting an education was crucial. "They can take your land away, but no one can ever take away your education," Henry repeatedly proclaimed. Getting an education was imperative, whether we liked it or not. So, despite my many misgivings, I went to school. It was not easy.

On the first day of kindergarten, I jumped out the ground-floor window and ran to my aunt's house in Manassa, almost a mile away, because it pained me so to be trapped in a classroom. In first grade, I destroyed another kid's rubber snake because I was taught that snakes represented evil, and also because I was terrified of the rattlesnakes that could surprise you anywhere in the Valley, day or night.

In second grade, my teacher, Mrs. Jackson, caught me and a friend playing tic-tac-toe on the blackboard during lunch hour when we were supposed to be outside. She gave me a whupping and sent a note home with my brothers that I had been disobedient.

In third grade, a friend and I cut class to buy a candy bar with his birthday money. My teacher was livid, and the principal threatened to kick me out of school "if you don't want to be here," sending another letter home. And throughout all my years at Manassa Elementary, I fought with Anglo kids who made fun of the Spanish kids who brought tortillas instead of bread to lunch.

Being singled out for being a "dirty Mexican" was something all of us Spanish kids had to put up with as a fact of life. It was odd: At home, we spoke Spanish and referred to ourselves as "Mexicanos," and it sounded right. But when someone called us "Mexican" in English, it was pejorative. The non-offensive term used back then was "Spanish"—we had ancestors who'd originated in Spain, after all—which helps explain why most white people in the Valley were called "Anglos." (This was long before labels like "Hispanic" or "Latino"—terms that were invented to categorize people—were applied to those of us with Spanish heritage.) Back then, we weren't taught anything about our Mexican ancestry in school, nor did we learn anything substantive about the Mexican-American War, but this derogatory usage of "Mexican," which continues to the present day, is a direct consequence of that war and its legacy of animosity and misunderstanding.

This singling out didn't just come from the kids, either—it also came from the adults.

The treatment we got from some of our teachers would not fly today. If we were caught speaking Spanish, which was strictly forbidden, we would get called out and, if we persisted, punished. I'll never forget Leandro's stories about teachers washing his mouth out with a bar of white soap for speaking Spanish. When I asked him later how it tasted, he grimaced and said, "Horrible. They are cabrones to do this to us."

Fourth grade brought some changes to my educational life. On the upside, we had a brand-new school on the south side of Manassa, a sparkling, single-story red brick building, which my dad had helped build. The whole community was proud of it. On the downside, my fourth-grade teacher was Mrs. Joyce.

Mrs. Joyce had a reputation throughout the school as a tough disciplinarian with a mile-wide mean streak. She was slightly built with curly gray hair and had piercing blue eyes that could make you jump out of your seat. On the first day of fourth grade, she paced at the head of the room holding a thin wooden ruler, which she slapped into the palm of her hand for emphasis. "Class," she announced, "I am Mrs. Joyce. I run a tight ship. Ours will be a no-nonsense classroom. Do you understand?" She paused.

"Yes, Mrs. Joyce," we called in unenthusiastic unison.

"There are to be no hijinks, shenanigans, or outbursts. Order will rule, or you will get the ruler." She slapped her hand so hard it must have hurt. She spun and looked at all of us expectantly.

"Yes, Mrs. Joyce," we repeated, this time with even less enthusiasm.

"You will be obedient and pleasant, and if you are, then we will all be able to learn. Understood?"

"Yes, Mrs. Joyce."

Indeed, Mrs. Joyce did run a tight ship that, like all tight ships, was built on routine. Every single morning, she had us place our hands palms down on the desk in front of us as she prowled the aisles. At least two-thirds of the kids at Manassa Elementary, Spanish and Anglo, lived on farms and worked every day after school and every weekend milking cows, feeding horses, collecting eggs, shearing sheep, checking fence line—you name it. Nearly all of us had dirt under our nails, even after we bathed. If she stood over you for more than a few seconds then you knew what was coming: a tap on the shoulder, her silent order to go to the bathroom to wash up. When you returned to class, you had to hold out your hands for reinspection. If she wasn't satisfied, you were sent back to repeat the process.

One morning, she had me wash my hands three times. When she finally released me to my seat, my friend Ernest Sisneros looked at me from across the room and chuckled quietly. I smiled back. Mrs. Joyce, who was writing on the blackboard, whirled around and caught us looking at each other. She calmly placed her white chalk on her desk and said, "Kenneth, Ernest. Come here, please." As we stood, she leaned over and opened the drawer in her desk that contained the one thing we were all terrified of: her paddle.

Mrs. Joyce loudly called out to the neighboring classroom for Mr. Ornelas, who would be her witness for the thrashing that was about to occur. It was not the first such punishment I got and, I'm sorry to say, it would not be the last. She picked Ernest to go first, which, if you ask me, is the long straw. It hurt just as much to go first, but at least you were spared the agony of watching someone else suffer, knowing full well that you were next.

I stood there, contemplating my own lashing, as Ernest bent over the side of her desk, grabbing the sides for support. Mrs. Joyce said, "I wish I didn't have to do this," and then she got to work. Time after time, she wheeled back with her one-inch-thick paddle, drilled with holes for aerodynamic speed, and administered her punishment. I watched Ernest's round face, his eyes welling with tears, but he didn't start to cry until the fifth whack. Satisfied she had inflicted enough authoritarian pain, she stopped, told him to go back to his desk, and summoned me to the lashing spot.

I bent over the desk in the same manner, my face turned toward my classmates. Many of them couldn't bear to look me in the eye, and I couldn't blame them. I silently hoped they were praying for me and that I would quickly be relieved of the pain that was about to come. She whacked me once, twice, three, four, five times. It was excruciating, but I didn't cry or beg for mercy.

After the fifth strike, she asked quietly, "Have you had enough, Kenneth?"

To which I responded, "I didn't do anything wrong, Mrs. Joyce."

She resumed her onslaught.

After the eighth or ninth paddling, I lost track of how many times she hit me. Finally, perhaps because she was physically spent from the exertion, Mrs. Joyce stopped and told me to return to my desk. I stood, hobbled back to my chair, and tried to sit in such a way that didn't put any weight on my tender backside. It was very awkward. I looked to the front of the room to see Mrs. Joyce thank Mr. Ornelas. She then calmly returned the paddle to her desk drawer and wiped her sweaty forehead with a white embroidered handkerchief. Before resuming her lesson, she told me, "Kenneth, you are to stay after school today." She didn't elaborate, but I feared the worst.

Since we had no telephone at the ranch, the only way for teachers to communicate with our parents was through written notes. Fortunately, I was not subjected to more punishment that afternoon, but instead I was handed a letter addressed to my father. She read it to me first. According to her, I was "sassy and most disrespectful," and she was requesting he come to school to discuss my behavior.

She folded the note back up and, at that moment, my brother John entered her classroom. "To ensure that this note gets to your father, I am asking you, John, to deliver it to him. Understood?" I was not a trustworthy mailman, it seemed.

"Yes, Mrs. Joyce," John said dutifully.

As soon as we were safe outside, John told me there was no way he was going to hand that note to Dad. I'd already gotten one beating; there was no sense in getting another. "I'll figure something out," John said. "Just try to forget about it."

I did try. And for a week or so, I succeeded. John couldn't hold on to the note—it was evidence of his disobedience as well as my impertinence—so he gave it to our Grandma Tita, our dad's mom. This ruse worked for a little while, but eventually Dad did learn of the note. And, as expected, John and I both got whupped. Once again, I went second.

The next day, Dad drove me to school so he could meet Mrs. Joyce, hat in hand. He apologized and told her it would never happen again, but if it did, he wanted to know right away.

"Of course, Mr. Salazar," Mrs. Joyce said, clearly happy she was speaking to another staunch disciplinarian.

"Besides," Dad added, "he won't be any trouble for the school next year. We're headed to Idaho Springs for the year, where Kenneth will attend school. With the triplets and all, I need another job to make ends meet. But we will be back as soon as we can. I can't leave the ranch."

This was not entirely news to me, but it still came as a shock to hear it out loud. It was strange to think that I would be going to a different school in a town to which I'd never been. But even though I was only ten, I understood.

Four years earlier, in 1961, Mom had given birth to triplets. At that time, she had four boys and Elaine, my baby sister, who had been the family prize since coming home from the hospital. Mom was looking forward to having one last baby to make our family one with half a dozen children.

Late in her pregnancy, Dad moved Mom to the truly big city of Alamosa, population 6,500, to be close to the hospital. When her water broke, he rushed her to the ER. They admitted her and directed Dad to the waiting room (fathers weren't allowed in the delivery room back then). When the first triplet, Margaret, was born, the nurse came in to announce to Dad that he was the proud father of a baby girl. He was elated. Dad went to the phone and started to call the people in the Valley who had phones to spread the news. But then, a short while later, the nurse returned, a little paler than before. "Mr. Salazar," she said, "I'm happy to tell you that you are also the proud father of another baby. A boy!" This was Elliott. Dad started making more calls to announce the improbable news. Emma, a petite, 120-pound woman who stood at a proud five feet, two-and-three-quarter inches tall, had had twins!

Then, not long after, the nurse reappeared. This time she was ashen. "Mr. Salazar," she said, "I'm happy to inform you that you are a father again. To another baby girl!" This was June, a tiny, beautiful girl weighing only three pounds.

Dad couldn't believe it, but it was true. They had expected one child but ended up with three. The triplets were so small and fragile that the medical staff were unsure if they would survive. All three were given emergency baptisms, just in case.

But of course, all three did survive, and our family now had eight children, not the six they'd expected. Eight children that needed to be provided for. So Dad and Mom had to hustle to make ends meet.

By 1965, when Los Rincones teemed with the energy of a five-year-old and three four-year-olds, Henry's need to seek employment elsewhere was more than understandable. "I'll come back on weekends to work the ranch," Dad explained to Mrs. Joyce.

"Well, I hope you're back soon," she said, although I don't think she cared either way. "And Kenneth is a smart boy. He's learned a lot. He just needs to learn to be obedient."

These last words came as a surprise. I'd rarely gotten any indication that Mrs. Joyce thought anything about me besides that I was a dirty kid and a nuisance who needed regular punishment. Certainly, she didn't care about me like Dad did.

Nevertheless, Mrs. Joyce and I were both relieved to be rid of each other. I had no idea what awaited us in Idaho Springs. But as I left school with Dad that day, I couldn't help but let a small, surreptitious smile break out across my face. Next year, I would be free of Mrs. Joyce.

7

IDAHO SPRINGS

Idaho Springs was a small mining town nestled in a canyon along Clear Creek, thirty miles west of Denver. Only about 1,500 people lived there, but it was one of Colorado's original mining towns. When they moved, Mom and Dad brought me, my little sister Elaine, and the triplets, while John—who was always lucky—was chosen to stay with our Grandma Tita in Manassa. My father had sent Leandro and Leroy to a seminary school in Cincinnati, Ohio, hoping to fulfill his dream of raising a family of Franciscan priests.

Idaho Springs, where we spent the 1965–66 school year, was a different world. Dad used a VA loan to purchase a small home on Miner Street for $8,500. The town was in the mountains, and had only one other Mexican American family. Everyone else was white, as far as I could tell. But aside from that, it was the first time we lived in a "city." There were traffic lights, a Safeway, a library, and a category of people I'd never encountered before: tourists. Sometimes they stopped in town, and sometimes they continued on deeper into the Rockies to go hiking or hunting or skiing.

The other thing we had was power. At Los Rincones, we still used kerosene lamps and pumped our own water. News from the outside world came to us over a battery-operated radio that lived in the kitchen, if it came to us at all. But now, we had something totally novel: a television.

Dad had gotten a job working for the Colorado Department of Revenue as a port of entry officer. Basically, he was assigned to a roadside weigh station to check long- and medium-haul trucks as they headed west over the Rockies or east to the plains and points beyond. When we moved into town, his boss surprised us with the gift of a used black-and-white television. For the first time in my life, I was able to watch shows that I'd only heard of before: *Gunsmoke*, *The Rifleman*, *Bonanza*—and the nightly news. This was how I came to learn of the war in Vietnam and the Civil Rights Movement. The war seemed to be escalating daily as the news reported the number of Americans and North Vietnamese killed and wounded every day in Southeast Asia. Dr. King had delivered his "I Have a Dream" speech two years earlier in 1963, and now the Civil Rights Movement was in full swing and also featured regularly in the news.

Another new thing was that, for the most part, we were accepted in Idaho Springs. Mexican Americans made up roughly half of the Valley, whereas white people dominated Idaho Springs, but it was the latter place that was more accepting of us. To this day, I have no idea why. Maybe we too were a novelty; maybe it was because of the hardworking miners in town; maybe the townspeople also felt looked down on by the people who lived in the nearby city of Denver. Whatever the reason, instead of being met with apprehension or hostility, we were welcomed. For me, it was a revelation. My fifth-grade teacher, Mr. Sabin, was about as far from Mrs. Joyce as you could get. He was a middle-aged white man with thinning hair and large-framed glasses, and he seemed to care for all his students, even new arrivals like me. He was someone who I wanted to do good for, not someone I was terrified of, and so, under his tutelage, I dedicated myself to learning. That year, and for the first time in my life, I got straight As, scoring highly even in the subjects I wasn't particularly good at or fond of. This newfound academic determination took root in me and, from that moment forward, never ceased to grow.

And yet, this is America, and kids are kids. There was one girl at school, Pamela Blankenship (funny how certain names stick in one's memory), who would stoke up trouble. She took a needling pride in telling my classmates that I was a "dirty Mexican" and that the Salazars did not belong in Idaho Springs. She and two of her friends got off the school bus at the same stop as me, and they would pelt me with insults, calling me a "turd with glasses" and saying that my family lived "like mice" in our "tiny house." For several weeks, I'd call them out and fight back, and more than once I threw rocks at them and threatened them, hoping they would leave me alone. Somehow, I managed to avoid getting in any serious trouble for fighting with them in their hometown, and they eventually got the message.

We left Idaho Springs in the summer of 1966 and returned to Los Rincones. I would miss this town in the mountains, but I was overjoyed to be returning to the place that I was beginning to recognize as my ancestral home: the San Luis Valley.

8

ALMOST A PRIEST

When I was thirteen, my father arranged for me to follow my brothers to the faraway land of Cincinnati so that I could become a future Franciscan priest too. At the time, Leandro and John were still students there, while Leroy had left after three years. Of the four of us, only Leandro would graduate—he would stay with the Franciscans for about ten years, but he didn't make it to the priesthood. Instead, he went to California and, in 1973, fell in love with a young woman named Loretta while they organized with the United Farm Workers of America.

Although Leandro, Leroy, and John had all gone to the seminary because they wanted to, I had not. I loved the church, and I still do, but I didn't want to be a priest. I wanted to be a farmer and rancher like Dad. I also did not want to leave the Valley.

As with my brothers before me, I'd need to take an IQ test—administered at home by a regional representative of the Franciscan order—to see if I qualified for admission. I wasn't sure when he would show up, but I knew it would be sometime in late spring. And sure enough, one April morning, as I was in the corral feeding our milk cows,

I spotted a rooster tail of dust rising along the road, a sure sign of a car headed our way. The hay I pitched over was fresh with a green tint, preserved in bales from the previous year's harvest, and our cows were gnashing it up. Somehow, I knew who was in the car before I saw him: Father Barry Finbar, the Franciscan scholar who'd been sent to determine if I was intelligent enough to serve God professionally.

As soon as the car pulled into our driveway, I ducked behind one of our cows, hoping she would save me. She didn't. Dad had a gift for always knowing where we were, and he came around the corral calling out, "Ken, ¡ven aquí! ¡Ven aquí!" Come here! Come here! I emerged from behind the cow's haunches to find Dad standing next to a middle-aged white man wearing a long, black frock, his hands laced together at his waist. The frock came all the way to the dusty ground; I couldn't see his shoes. I briefly wondered if he was barefoot.

Father Finbar held out his hand as I approached. I took it. He had a strong handshake, a broad smile, and a kindly twinkle in his eye. "You must be Mr. Kenneth Salazar," he said.

"Yes, Father," I said, fully aware that the test had already begun.

"It's a pleasure to meet you and," he turned to Dad, "to be back at Los Rincones."

We walked together back to the house. Within a few minutes, we settled in the living room, which had rainbow-painted walls and was reserved for only the most special of occasions. Father Finbar went over the test's instructions and I opened the packet and got to work. He watched me for a few minutes and then went into the kitchen to chat with Mom and Dad.

The test was unlike any I'd seen. It had a lot of visual questions, which were more like little puzzles, and word problems that seemed to have multiple answers. I answered the first two pages very quickly and, in that moment, decided I would simply fly through the test as a way to ensure a poor result. This would be my escape route from the seminary. I was confident I could pull it off. About thirty minutes later, I called out, "I'm done, Father."

Father Finbar reappeared, a surprised look on his face. "Did you answer all the questions, Kenneth?"

"Yes, Father."

"Very well then," he said. "Let's have your answer sheet." I passed it to him and followed him back to the kitchen, where he resumed his visit with my parents. I'd been in a hurry to finish but apparently he was in no hurry to grade it. As I ate Mom's cookies, Dad gave me a sidelong glance that was not encouraging—he probably suspected what I was up to—but I tried to ignore it.

After a while, Father Finbar took out his grading grid and set it next to my answer sheet. It only took him a few minutes to go through the exam, and when he was done, he put down his pencil, looked me square in the eye, and said, "Congratulations. You passed. Considering how quickly you took the test, your result is very impressive. We would be happy to have you at St. Francis Seminary, Mr. Salazar."

Dad stood and gave my shoulder a tight squeeze that felt equal parts proud and admonishing. I was not smiling. Now I had to find some other way of not going to Cincinnati.

Throughout that summer, I pleaded with Mom and Dad to let me stay in the Valley and go to Centauri High School. I was a good student, and I didn't want to leave home. But they weren't having it. Dad had a longtime dream of fielding a legion of Father Salazars, a dream rooted in our family's Catholic faith. We'd each been baptized at La Iglesia de San Francisco, the church a mile or so up the road from our house, which my own great-grandparents had helped build in the mid-1800s. All of our family's baptisms, weddings, and funerals had taken place inside that large white adobe church with its green roof and aproned gables. I'm sure Dad hoped that, if he somehow raised five ordained Franciscan priests, one of them would end up in the Valley, leading a flock of friends and family for decades to come.

Despite my pleas, it was decided. I would leave on a bus at the end of August. But I still made one final appeal to my Grandma Tita. One August evening at her bedside, I told her simply, "Mama Tita, no quiero irme a Cincinnati." She had lived with us most of my life, and at eighty-four, she was in her last years. She blessed me and comforted me, holding my head gently in her arms, then took a deep breath and said, "You should go. It will make your father happy. And you will see the world beyond the Valley."

I almost told her that I'd already seen that in Idaho Springs and on our TV set, but I held my tongue.

"Besides," she added, "you don't have to stay if you don't like it. You can always come home like Leroy."

And so, I went to Cincinnati. John and I rode the Continental Trailways bus, which picked us up in Walsenburg, a hundred miles from Los Rincones. As we crossed the country, America's demographics changed before my eyes. In Denver, the bus was boarded by a group of Black people. If you can believe it, these passengers were the first Black people I had ever seen in real life. By the time we got to Indianapolis a couple of days later, half the bus's passengers were Black. Finally, we pulled into Cincinnati, where a shuttle bus took us to Mount Healthy, Ohio, the home of my new school, St. Francis Seminary.

I stayed there for two years, for ninth and tenth grade. Leandro had already graduated, but besides me and John, there were about a dozen other Mexican American students, all of whom had been recruited from New Mexico or Colorado. Academically, I did well at the seminary, earning mostly As and getting on the honor roll. I learned Latin and German and played basketball every chance I got, making the starting lineup on the varsity squad.

But I was never happy at the seminary. And when John stopped attending St. Francis after my first year, I was both unhappy and alone.

After my second year, I heeded my grandmother's words—she had since passed away—and told Dad I wanted to come home. He wasn't angry, which surprised me, but he was disappointed. His dream of a family of friars was fading before his eyes.

Later in life, when Dad was about eighty-five, we were driving together around the banks of the Rio Grande in my green Ford Ranger pickup, and I asked, "Daddy, ¿por qué nos mandó al seminario?" Why did you send us to the seminary?

In just a few words, he said softly, "Era lo mejor para ustedes." Because it was best for you.

It was just the two of us. I was then the Colorado attorney general, and he was in his last years of life. We drove mostly in silence, passing the places we knew like the backs of our hands. The San Antonio River, the Rio Grande, Manassa, the endless fields, Los Rincones. He never said more. But I knew that in his quiet way he was proud of his children. I suspected that, as a World War II soldier who had seen far-off places like Washington and Hawaii, he viewed the seminary as the best way to expose his older children to the United States and the larger world. Or maybe, with the Vietnam War raging during much of our childhoods, he thought it best that his boys might become priests. But I'll never know for sure. Leroy and John enlisted in the Army, Leandro stayed in the seminary, and I registered for the draft but was never called. Elliott, who never went to the seminary, was too young.

Regardless of Dad's reasoning, his persistence allowed us to experience the wider world for the first time.

9

NATIONAL HONOR SOCIETY

My last two years of high school saw me finally back in my home. One good thing about going to the seminary: It put me way ahead of my peers at Centauri High. I excelled at school. By my senior year, I had a 4.0 GPA, I was on the student council, I was an all-conference point guard who led our basketball team in scoring, and I'd qualified for the state finals in track and field for the 880-yard dash and the long jump. In the fall, I was headed to Colorado College in Colorado Springs. I was a Spanish kid from the Valley, and I was making good.

The night before graduation, Centauri High held its baccalaureate ceremony. All the seniors filed into the auditorium wearing caps and gowns, ready for the culmination of twelve years of schooling. As we entered, faculty members distributed the graduation programs and presented gold cords to the National Honor Society inductees—cords that would drape over their shoulders during the following day's commencement, signifying their academic achievement.

I scanned the program, flipping through the pages in search of my name among the new National Honor Society members. But it wasn't there.

This made no sense. I was the salutatorian at Centauri High.

The ceremony proceeded with prayers, speeches, and songs, but I barely registered any of it. My mind kept circling back to my missing cord and my absent name. Had there been some mistake? An oversight? The gold cords gleamed on other students' shoulders, a visible marker of achievement and acceptance that had somehow been denied to me.

We filed out of the auditorium after the ceremony. It was dusk, and the sun had just dropped over the snowcapped mountain peaks in the west, tipping them with pink and orange light. I exited through the south doors and was making my way to Dad's truck when I felt a hand gently grip my arm.

It was Coach Frank White, my civics teacher and the school's wrestling coach. Everyone just called him "Coach."

He guided me out of earshot of the other students and their parents and said in a low voice, "Ken, I want to apologize to you."

I was puzzled. Coach had always been kind to me and in my corner. "For what, Coach?"

"You should have one of those gold cords. You're one of our best students," he said. "But some people didn't want that."

The words landed like stones in still water. My snub was *not* a mistake.

"What happened?" I asked, half hoping he wouldn't tell me.

"Let's go for a walk," he said, looking over his shoulder. We headed toward the parking lot as Coach White explained that my eligibility had been the subject of a heated debate among the faculty over the previous days. The decision to induct students into the National Honor Society required faculty approval, and while he had argued forcefully on my behalf, one teacher had blocked my admission.

"Who?" I asked.

"Mrs. Franklin," he said. "She said you weren't National Honor Society material because you hung around the wrong kids."

There it was. My friends were mostly kids in vocational classes—the kids from families like mine who couldn't afford instruments for band or the fancy clothes worn by the more affluent students. Kids with "dirty hands" and soil permanently lodged under their fingernails. Many of them were Mexican American, but not all. Mrs. Franklin may have been racist in that moment, or she may have been biased against poor kids, or she may have been a bit of both, but whatever the case, she'd scuttled what should have been mine.

I stood there for a moment trying hard not to let my anger bubble over. I was angry not just for me and my mistreatment, but for my friends who might not have gotten as good grades or who had not been so successful at athletics or who were never going to go to college. Kids who would, in all likelihood, never leave the Valley. Finally, I said, "Thanks for telling me, Coach."

"Of course, Ken," he said, gently grabbing my arm again. "I argued as hard as I could. You deserve to be in there." He gripped my arm harder for emphasis and added, "Ken, this is why you need to come back here. So you can help change these things."

That night, I went home to write the speech I was due to give at commencement. I might not have made the National Honor Society, but Mrs. Franklin couldn't disqualify me from being salutatorian. I sat at the same typewriter desk where I'd tried and failed to flunk my IQ test for St. Francis Seminary and wrote it out by hand.

I wish I still had that speech. I remember writing about closing one chapter and beginning the next, about our futures stretching before us—the usual commencement fare. What I don't recall is whether I managed to express what I truly felt: that the system that was supposed to recognize merit had revealed itself to be focused on something else entirely. I'm sure I didn't say anything about Coach White and his suggestion that, someday, I come back to the Valley to help fix these things.

But I'll never forget Coach White and his advice. It held a place in my mind next to my grandmother's words: "You can always come home." It would take me a while, but I would heed them both.

PART III

DISCOVERY

10

THE VALLEY AND THE AMERICAS

Most people don't have a good understanding of who they are until they leave home and strike out on their own. Like every high school graduate, I still had a lot of growing to do, but I had a pretty good grip on who I was—or so I thought.

I was in the fields the day I left for college, driving a tractor and baling alfalfa in a part of our ranch known as La Florida. On a good day, I'd make a thousand seventy-pound bales, some of which would feed our cows and the rest of which we'd sell to ranchers and hay stores in New Mexico. Dad pulled up in his beat-up green Ford pickup, hopped out, and waved high over his head. I cut the tractor's growling engine. It was a hot August morning, late in the dry season, and a scrim of tan dust blew across the Valley in the distance to the south.

"Hey, Dad!" I called.

"Kenneth! Ya es tiempo! No quiero que llegues tarde a donde vas." More softly, he said, "It's time to go, mi hijo."

I stepped off the tractor and jumped to the ground, the jagged little stalks of cut alfalfa crunching under my cowboy boots. There was still a lot of work to do in the fields that day, but Dad would have to finish up.

I walked up to him, taking off my wide-brimmed Stetson and wiping my forehead with the back of my sleeve. "Ya mero acabo. I got as much done as I could, Dad."

"Bueno. Yo acabaré. Ya es tiempo que te vayas a Colorado Springs." He looked quickly from me to the ground. I could already see tears welling in his eyes. "Mom's waiting for you."

"OK, Dad."

He took my arm and guided me into the shadow of the tractor, out of the sun.

Whenever one of us left for college—and by then, all of my older siblings had left for college, which in the Salazar family was mandatory and regarded as "thirteenth grade"—Dad gave us a blessing. (In truth, he did this whenever we left home. I wouldn't have been surprised if he did it every day, silently, when we got on the school bus and headed down the road to Manassa.) He held both my hands and lowered his head, saying quietly and almost automatically, as if someone else were speaking through him: "La bendición de Dios Padre, todo poderoso, y La Virgen María Santísima, y de todos los santos, vayan siempre contigo, que Nuestra Señora de Guadalupe, la madre de Dios, te cubra siempre con su manto azul, que te lleven por buen camino y que no te pase ninguna contigencia. En el nombre del Padre, y del Hijo, y del Espíritu Santo. Amén."

"Amén," I whispered with him.

"Tanto que te quiero, mi Kenny. I'm going to miss you," Dad said, wrapping me in a tight hug.

I hugged him back and gave him a kiss on the cheek. "Tanto que lo quiero, mi papa." Then I bounded off toward home while he stayed to work the fields.

When I got back to Los Rincones, I found that Mom had packed up my stuff in the same footlocker I'd taken to seminary a few years earlier. I hopped in the shower to wash off the fields and put on fresh clothes, then I went to find Mom in the kitchen. She'd prepared a little home-cooked lunch for me, wrapped in a cloth napkin. I thanked her and gave her a kiss, and then we went outside to the weathered blue Volkswagen Beetle that was mine to take to school. I opened the door and flipped the front passenger seat forward, and somehow Mom and I managed to wedge the footlocker into the diminutive backseat. Before I left, Mom gave me a hug and the same benediction that Dad had given a short while earlier. With my parents and God firmly on my side, I hit the road. Destination: Colorado College, nearly two hundred miles north in Colorado Springs.

Believe it or not, I'd never visited the school. I'd only applied there because a friend from high school, Mike Espinoza, who was a couple of years older than me, went there and told me I should give it a shot. So I did, along with the University of Colorado, Colorado State, and the Colorado School of Mines. Obviously, I did not want to go far from home. Despite my time in Cincinnati, I had a hard time conceiving of the world beyond my home state, and I wanted to be close to the Valley so I could continue to ranch with Dad and my brothers and sisters during weekends and long breaks. Ultimately, I chose Colorado College not because I knew much about it, but because I knew it was small and that, as a result, I could probably make the basketball team. Also, CC gave me a good financial aid package.

As I made my way north on I-25 in the VW Beetle, which barely went over sixty miles per hour and whose engine ran with that distinctive Beetle gurgle, my nerves began to build. I wasn't just wary about what I'd find once I got there—I was nervous because it suddenly occurred to me that I had no idea where Colorado College was.

It was in Colorado Springs, that much was certain. So once I got there, I followed the first sign I saw for Colorado College. I got off the interstate at the Uintah Street exit and headed east, looking for a college campus, whatever that happened to look like. I kept driving and driving through what felt like the biggest metropolis I'd ever navigated and eventually reached East Colorado Springs. Clearly, I was lost. I had a map in the car—this was decades before smartphones—but those were used to get you to general places, not specific ones. So I did what we all did back then: I pulled into a gas station and asked for directions.

"Oh, yeah, you missed it, man," the attendant said. "Take this street all the way back toward the freeway, then go right on Nevada for a couple miles. You'll see signs."

"Thank you, sir," I said.

"Not at all," he said.

I followed his directions to a T, and sure enough, I soon found myself on a college campus. Only, it was the wrong one. He'd directed me to the Colorado Springs campus of the University of Colorado.

I went into their admissions office and told a kid with long scraggly hair my conundrum, and he set me straight. South for a stretch on Nevada and then right on Cache La Poudre. I couldn't believe it. I had gone right past CC and ended up at the wrong university. I was embarrassed but determined to find my bearings. Soon enough, I reached my new home away from home: Slocum Hall.

The registration process was straightforward—they gave me a packet and told me I was assigned to room 132. That evening, our resident advisor, Dudley Mendenhall, called all the freshmen on our wing to meet in the hallway. He was a junior, tall with brown hair, and he seemed genuinely interested in who we were and where we'd come from. We chowed on pizza, and he asked us to introduce ourselves. There were a lot of kids from all over, and even a few from as far away as New York. When it came around to me, I told everyone my name and said matter-of-factly, "I'm from the Valley," as if there were only one valley in the world.

The other new students were confused. Finally, a white student with dark curly hair said, "Like the Rio Grande Valley in Texas?"

I felt suddenly foolish and must have turned a little red. "Oh, no. I'm from here. Colorado, I mean. I'm from the San Luis Valley south of here. I live on a ranch, and I like to play basketball." I was the only Spanish kid there, and I was shy to begin with, so I didn't say more than that.

A little while later, while the other students were mingling and I was busy keeping to myself, Dudley approached. "Hey, Ken."

"Yessir."

"Yeah, man. I was wondering—you planning on joining MEChA?"

I gave him a perplexed look. "MEChA?"

"It's the Chicano student organization," he said. He didn't explain it then and I didn't know, but it stood for Movimiento Estudiantil Chicano de Aztlán—the Chicano Student Movement of Aztlán.

"I don't think so. I'm not Chicano. I'm Spanish."

"Oh, well," he said, trailing off. "Check them out. You might get along." He sauntered off, clearly confused.

And truthfully, so was I. It was funny and somewhat ironic that I would learn about a Chicano student organization from a well-meaning white kid, but that was one of the great things about Colorado College in 1973. The school was changing in those days, trying their best to bring diversity into their student body so that the people who went there more closely mirrored the demographics of the state of Colorado and the United States. Even though I wasn't fully aware of it at the time, I was part of that change.

The next morning, while I sat on my bed unsure of what to do, I heard a loud knock at my door. "Something out here for you, Ken!" one of my hallmates yelled. It was a Friday, and I wasn't doing anything, so I hopped up and opened the door. Someone had left me a note. I picked it up off the floor and opened it. Scrawled across it was, "Call me—Manassa" and a phone number. Of course, this was Mike Espinoza, my friend from the Valley, whom everyone at Colorado College called "Manassa." I'd always looked up to Mike, not just because he was older and cooler than me but because he was a phenomenal basketball player. He wasn't tall, but he was quick and a knockdown shooter. This was before the three-point line, but if Mike had played with one of those, he would have been like a Chicano Steph Curry. At least in my eyes, he would have been.

I went down to the dorm's community phone—kind of like a pay phone but with no way to feed it coins—and called the number. Mike picked up almost immediately. I didn't even say it was me before he blurted, "Hey, Ken! Whatcha doing? Why don't you come on over to Mathias Hall?"

"Uh, OK. But I don't know where that is."

"Don't worry. I'll come get you. Sit tight."

Five minutes later, Mike bounded into the common area, his hand outstretched. I gave him a high five, and he gave me a warm hug. "How're you getting settled?" he asked.

"Fine, I guess. It's a little weird. I'm not sure that I've ever had nothing to do before. Although I am supposed to go to some orientation thing this morning." I was so used to working all the time on the ranch, or going to school, or playing basketball, or running track, or helping with the housework—the list seemed endless. Of course I'd had idle moments in life, but not like this. It felt like I was waiting for something, but I wasn't sure what.

"Ah, don't worry," he said again. "It'll all sort itself out. Schoolwork can get hectic, but the truth is there's a lot of downtime here. So what do they want you to do?"

"I think there's a tour somewhere. And I need to go to the financial aid office. Hey, where's the gym?"

"I'll show you, no sweat. But look, you don't need to do any of that stuff."

"I don't?"

He waved his hand dismissively. "Heck no. Look, I'm going to Pueblo tomorrow to see my friends Randy Serna and Tom Autobee. They're here at CC and Mexicanos like us. You should come along."

"But I—"

He laughed and said, "You don't need to do any of that stuff. It's not that important. Come on!"

"O-OK," I said. And that's how the next day I found myself heading forty-five miles south to Pueblo with Mike. We stayed with Randy's folks in East Pueblo, and his mom made Tom, Mike, Randy, and me a big home-cooked dinner that night. I learned that they came from old Spanish families like mine and had joined MEChA as part of the Chicano Movement. After dinner, we headed out to a bar on Union Avenue where Randy was playing his horn with a Chicano band called the Orange Sunshine. We stayed there for hours, playing pool, drinking beer, listening to rock and Tex-Mex music—música tejana—and just hanging around until the early hours of the morning. The next day, we went to a huge outdoor parade ground west of Pueblo to see the Nitty Gritty Dirt Band. There were thousands of people there, more than I'd ever seen in one place, and I witnessed things I'd never encountered in my sheltered life in the Valley: topless women with big boa constrictors draped around their necks and shoulders, people smoking marijuana openly, people dancing, making out, sneaking off. It was the hippie era in full bloom, and my eyes were suddenly open.

Not that I became a hippie or anything like that. Vietnam was ongoing but would soon draw to a close, and the draft had ended in January of 1973, meaning there was no chance I or any other American man would be conscripted into what was then the longest war in US history. It also meant that the era of protest was waning.

Not long after that first weekend of off-campus college orientation, Mike took me to my first MEChA meeting, an organization that was trying to change Colorado College as well as countless other campuses across the country. MEChA was more than a student organization—it was a community. We were joined by many others, like Pat Garcia, Dolores Atencio, and Manuel Martinez—all from Pueblo. We met regularly in a house on campus called the Political Action Committee Center, which we shared with the Black Student Union. We brought speakers to campus, including Dolores Huerta of the United Farm Workers of America. We organized social events, including dances where we played Tex-Mex and northern New Mexico music like Roberto Griego's "Ojitos Verdes." We were joined by "honorary Chicanos"—Anglo students like Hank Worley, Ed Joyce, Ted Swan, and Jack Pottle—who believed in our civil rights cause, and who liked our music and food. Each would become close and lifelong friends.

It was awesome and life-altering to meet so many Mexican Americans from places beyond the Valley. I had been taught so little about my heritage in primary and secondary school that I naively presumed most of the country's Mexican Americans were actually in the Valley, plus some other areas in New Mexico, where we often visited my mother's family. But no. There were Mexican Americans all over the American West, in places like Texas and California. Even in Utah.

But my real transformation happened in the classroom. I didn't get great grades the first couple of years—it took a while for me to learn how to write for college—but in the middle of freshman year I took a course called The Chicano Experience, taught by Professor Juan Chavira, who hailed from the Rio Grande Valley in South Texas.

And there, for the first time, I began to learn the history of what it meant to be Mexican American. I had to leave home to truly learn who I was and where I had come from. This was the early 1970s, and the primary and secondary educational systems were not keen on teaching students about diversity at all. Diversity was barely even a concept. Like so many Americans, I had been denied a deep understanding of my own heritage. Maybe this denial was intentional, but I suspect it was more often reflexive. Teachers in the Valley were not taught about the history of Mexican Americans, so how could they be expected to add this to their curriculum? But whether it was by design or not, the net effect was the same: I and literally millions like me did not know about our own history.

For me at least, learning it was life-changing.

In Professor Chavira's class, we read books like *Occupied America* by Rodolfo Acuña. We learned about the Mexican-American War and the 1848 Treaty of Guadalupe Hidalgo. We studied the Chicano Movement, which was opening doors for Mexican Americans and instilling pride in us for our Native American, Mexican, and Spanish ancestry. We read about the leaders of the movement: Cesar Chavez and Dolores

Huerta of the United Farm Workers; Rodolfo "Corky" Gonzales leading the Crusade for Justice in Denver; José Angel Gutiérrez founding the La Raza Unida Party in Crystal City, Texas; and Reies Tijerina fighting for the Mexican land grants in New Mexico.

I learned that my family and I weren't outsiders who had somehow made our way to southern Colorado, like some of my teachers in the Valley presumed. We had been there longer than any other group except Native Americans—certainly longer than the Northern European Americans who sometimes treated us as foreigners in our own land. I realized that even though I was sometimes made to feel like an outsider growing up, Mexican Americans had been on those lands for centuries.

Colorado College works on what's called a "block" schedule. Instead of taking three or four courses over a semester, students take one class at a time for about a month. The idea is to immerse yourself in a subject and get to a place, quickly, where you can think deeply and critically about any given topic. For one of the blocks in the fall of my junior year, I was lucky enough to do a study abroad in Costa Rica.

For that trip, I chose to research President Kennedy's Alliance for Progress, a program that had promised to transform Latin America through economic cooperation and development. When President Kennedy announced the initiative in March 1961, he called it "a vast cooperative effort, unparalleled in magnitude and nobility of purpose, to satisfy the basic needs of the [Latin] American people for homes, work and land, health and schools."

The program was intended to serve as a kind of Marshall Plan for Latin America. The United States would provide $20 billion over ten years, combined with $80 billion in internal Latin American investment, to achieve annual economic growth rates of 2.5 percent. The goals were ambitious: eliminate adult illiteracy, establish democratic governments, and create economic prosperity that would make communist revolution unnecessary. In those days, many Latin American countries were attracted to communist models. This was the Cold War, after all, and the USSR was busy throughout the Western Hemisphere, trying to gain a foothold in the United States' backyard. And so, like many well-designed aid programs, such as the now-defunded US Agency for International Development (USAID), American altruism was both morally laudable on human rights grounds and strategically important as a matter of national security.

My visit to Costa Rica was an experience I would never forget. In San José, the capital, I lived with an elderly small businessman and his wife. It was the first time I'd lived anywhere with maids and a cook.

Then I traveled to the Caribbean coast in the state of Limon and stayed for weeks at a banana plantation in a primitive guest house—really just a shack with mosquito netting draped over the bed. While there, I interviewed members of agricultural cooperatives that had been formed with Alliance funding. That money had dried up by 1973, but evidence of the Alliance still existed in 1975. One visceral remnant was a relatively new John Deere tractor that my dad would have loved to own. But it was out of commission and sat dusty and neglected in a corner of the packing warehouse. When I asked one of the workers why they weren't using the tractor, he said they needed to fix the carburetor, but that there was no way they could do that so far away from a John Deere shop. If I'd been home and had access to our tools and spare parts, I thought I could easily have fixed it for them. But I wasn't, and so an otherwise fine tractor sat idle, for want of only about a hundred dollars' worth of parts and labor.

Many of the workers at the banana plantation were descendants of Black immigrants from Jamaica who spoke perfect Spanish and an English patois I could barely understand. They echoed what the Alliance's boosters and administrators had stated: The Alliance had been somewhat successful but ultimately had fallen short, mainly for lack of resources. Though farming cooperatives like theirs had been formed with great fanfare, a variety of factors had kept the benefits from reliably reaching the workers. Especially after President Kennedy's assassination, the Alliance's vision of lifting people out of poverty had not been properly supported, and the whole project slowly burned out. The expensive, fixable but unusable John Deere was a perfect representation of the situation.

During long afternoons on the banana plantation, I often headed to the beach to write notes in my journal. I jotted down snippets of conversations I'd had with the workers or with the local priest, whom I often walked with in the morning as the jungle woke from its humid, sticky slumber. I wrote about the Jamaican men and women I met, and the hostility and racism they sometimes experienced from Ticos (as many Costa Ricans called themselves). To some of the Ticos, the Jamaicans were "dirty," "thieving," and "untrustworthy." It was all nonsense, of course, but I learned in Costa Rica that racism is not the exclusive provenance of blond-haired, blue-eyed white people. Far from it.

Too soon, my time in Limon came to an end. I'd gotten tired of eating bananas but loved the jungle and the monkeys and the colorful birds, as well as the blue Caribbean Sea. Following a walk along its shore for what might have been the last time, I wrote in my journal about the failure of the Alliance for Progress. The Alliance was supposed to represent the United States at its best, using its wealth and power to lift up its neighbors, to create a hemisphere of prosperity and democracy. But what I witnessed in Costa Rica bore little resemblance to this aspiration. Instead, I saw American idealism constrained by lack of commitment and corroded by Cold War fears and accommodations with corrupt elites.

In 1969, President Nixon commissioned Nelson Rockefeller to produce a study on the state of Latin America. His report was damning—there was "general frustration over the failure to achieve a more rapid improvement in standards of living," and "the United States, because of its identification with the failure of the Alliance for Progress to live up to expectations, is blamed." By 1973, the Organization of American States disbanded the permanent committee established to implement the Alliance. Already riddled with problems, the Alliance at that moment effectively died.

As I prepared to leave Costa Rica and return to Colorado College, I realized that the Alliance for Progress suffered from the same kind of institutional failure I was discovering everywhere: good intentions undermined by a lack of understanding and/or an unwillingness to commit fully to a cause.

During the spring of my junior year, I would take another trip for one of my blocks. While the destination wasn't as exotic as Costa Rica, it was still exciting. I was headed to Chicago to study at a private research institution called the Newberry Library.

A group of MEChA Chicanos rented a van to drive the thousand miles from Colorado Springs to Chicago. I'll never forget passing through Omaha, Nebraska, late one afternoon and discovering a Mexican section of town teeming with restaurants and stores, nearly all of their signage in Spanish. Even at that stage in my awakening, it had barely occurred to me that any Mexican Americans lived *east* of Colorado. In my mind, everyone on that side of the country was either white or Black. Little did I know.

And then, Chicago. This was my first time in a true melting pot of a city. At the Newberry, a grand pink granite Romanesque building built in the late 1800s, I got lost in the stacks. The library specialized—then and now—in the humanities, and it held tons of maps, manuscripts, and original genealogical information from throughout the United States. I wanted to see if the library had any information about my family, which I had only recently come to understand had been in the Americas for at least four hundred years (and much longer, if you included the Native American part of my ancestry). And so, I went about searching for the names Salazar, Cantu, Montoya, and Garcia in their vast archives.

None of this kind of thing existed in the Valley back then, or if it did, I had no idea where to find it. But at the Newberry, I easily found an old Colorado census from the 1880s. And there, in black and white, were my great-grandparents, Felipe Cantu and Refugio Salazar, and their latest child, my grandmother Mama Tita, Maria Antonia Cantu Salazar, listed as age one. This was the same Grandma Tita who had helped raise me with so much love and wisdom, a woman who would birth eight children but only see three reach adulthood. This was the same woman who had consoled me when I was so resistant to go to seminary school in Ohio: "You can always come home."

Outside the walls of the Newberry, I was hit with another revelation. One day, one of my classmates said we should go check out Little Mexico, or La Villita, as it was commonly called. This neighborhood near the South Side, and principally along a section of West 26th Street, teemed with Mexican businesses and cultural institutions like churches, dance halls, and rec centers. I soon learned that more than a million Mexican Americans lived in Chicago alone—more in this one Midwestern city than in all of Colorado and New Mexico combined. It was in Chicago—well over a thousand miles from the Valley—that I finally learned that Mexican Americans were everywhere in the United States.

When I returned to Colorado College, I felt like a full battery itching to power my own education and further my growing cultural awareness. I threw myself into my studies and into MEChA with the same vigor and work ethic I'd learned on the ranch. I became president of MEChA and a capable student activist. I was getting straight As, shedding my innate shyness, and becoming increasingly comfortable with public speaking and meeting with older figures in the school administration. At MEChA, our work centered on recruiting new Hispanic students and faculty. Now that I was beginning to understand how prevalent Hispanic people were across the country, we cast a wide geographical net, going anywhere and everywhere we could find qualified candidates. Beyond recruitment, we also lobbied for changes in what was taught. It was imperative that Chicano students knew themselves and had the opportunity to get to know themselves.

I had heated debates with Professor Rudy de la Garza, a brilliant political scientist who had come to CC from the University of Texas. While he supported our efforts, he argued that there were limits to how far we could push. "There are only so many resources in a private school like this," he would say. "What's the limit on the resources that can be applied to this program? When do we know we have enough Chicano and Hispanic students and teachers?"

Whatever the "limit" was, my response was always the same: We had just started and surely hadn't yet gone far enough. By the time I graduated Colorado College, about 6 percent of the students were Hispanic, and that was progress. But it wasn't reflective of Colorado's demographics, let alone the country's. We needed more. Today, roughly 10 percent of Colorado College's student body is Hispanic, and over 35 percent is non-white. Back in the 1970s, MEChA and other student organizations like the Black Student Union were laying the groundwork for that future.

My experiences in Costa Rica and Chicago were much more than just academic exercises. The Costa Rica trip especially would permanently shape my view of what real progress looked like. It wasn't enough to create programs that sounded good on paper. You had to be willing to challenge the systems that kept people marginalized—and to keep challenging them. You had to insist on genuine inclusion and concrete support, not just the appearance of it. The failure of the Alliance for Progress also became another piece of evidence that real change required confronting uncomfortable truths about who held power and how it was used. These were lessons I would carry with me throughout my life as a lawyer and rancher and that I would bring with me to the US Senate, the Department of the Interior, and the US embassy in Mexico.

11

THE RANCH AND THE DREAM

In May 1977, I graduated Colorado College with a political science degree and returned home to Los Rincones. My dream was still to be a rancher and farmer in the Valley, helping Mom and Dad and my siblings. But I needed to pay off my student loans, and to do that, I needed a career that paid better than ranching. I'd also be able to help out on the ranch by using the money I earned to buy more land and equipment for the ranch.

I'd arrived at a fork in the road: graduate school or law school. It was not a straightforward decision. If money were the only consideration, then the obvious choice was law, yet I remained ambivalent.

I decided to take a year off from my education and toil in the fields alongside my dad and the other Salazars. Maybe the manual labor, the sky and grass, the water and the land, would help clear my mind.

During this interregnum, my friend Hank Worley—one of MEChA's "honorary Chicanos"—contacted me. He and I both wanted to see more of the world. We'd talked about traveling through the Americas after graduation, maybe all the way to Tierra del Fuego, using a guidebook that promised we could get by on a dollar a day. And now was as good a time as any to make those plans a reality.

After getting permission from Mom and Dad, I left the ranch after the 1977 haying season, taking a bus with Hank to El Paso, Texas. There, we crossed into Juárez and caught a different bus to Mexico City. We spent a few days there, visiting the Zócalo, the Basilica, and the National Museum of Anthropology, eating at cafés and sleeping in youth hostels.

From Mexico City, we took a bus to the state of Veracruz, where we entered the jungle on the Yucatán Peninsula, the second-largest tropical jungle in the Western Hemisphere. "This place makes the Valley look like the Sahara," Hank said one afternoon, staring out the window of a bus as the never-ending green scrolled by.

We soon came to the crossing into Guatemala at El Ceibo. Traversing Guatemala was a risk—the country was in the midst of what would be a thirty-six-year-long civil war—but it was one we were willing to take to see more of the hemisphere. At the border, Mexican officials in military garb waved our bus through, and on the other side, the Guatemalan officials briefly boarded. They looked everyone over, including Hank and me, smiled, and told the driver to keep going.

We continued through the jungle. It was more of the same: the same trees, the same monkeys lazing in the midday heat, the same birds flitting back and forth, the same sky above and ground below. Or so we thought.

After an hour or two of bumping down the two-lane road, the bus pulled to an abrupt stop. Hank and I leaned into the aisle to see what was going on. The road was blocked by a platoon of heavily armed soldiers, their truck-mounted machine guns pointed directly at the bus.

"Shit," Hank said quietly.

I remained silent.

Just then, the bus door opened and a pair of soldiers jumped aboard. I assumed they were Guatemalan military, but it was difficult to tell. They easily could have been aligned with one of the groups fighting the government and were only pretending to be the Army—especially here, deep in the Selva Maya.

One soldier stayed by the door while the other moved down the bus, his rifle pointed at the floor. He yelled in Spanish for everyone to put their hands up and move outside. Of course, we did as we were told.

There were more soldiers on the road. They separated the men from the women and children. The bus driver was pulled to the side by himself. All of the men were lined up and ordered to face the bus, to place our hands on its side, and to spread our feet out wide. I quietly told Hank what to do since he didn't completely understand Spanish, but it wasn't necessary—it was obvious what was going on.

The men roughly searched all of us and then ordered us away from the bus to stand in a patch of sunlight with our hands above our heads. Everyone was terrified. There was a chance, however slim, of us all getting shot right there, or kidnapped and held hostage for God knows how long. We watched as the soldiers tossed our luggage onto the road and searched through it haphazardly. To this day, I'm not sure if they were looking for something specific, doing this as an exercise, or simply hunting for money or things to steal.

Our arms ached from holding them above our heads for so long. After what seemed like an interminable wait, a soldier who appeared to outrank the others ordered everyone back on the bus. The luggage was thrown into the cargo area as he yelled, "Don't stop again! We will radio ahead to let them know you have been searched. The jungle is dangerous. You can all be killed here."

He didn't have to tell any of us twice. After maneuvering around the military vehicles, the bus driver floored it, not making another stop until Guatemala City, which was still hundreds of miles away.

We only spent two nights in Guatemala City before traveling to the tiny Colombian island of San Andrés, and then to Cartagena, Colombia. Hank and I were thrilled to take our first steps on the northernmost point of South America.

In Cartagena, I decided to call home to check in and let my family know all was well before continuing south. I found a place where I could make cheap international calls and managed to reach Dad at his port of entry job. Dad was happy to hear my voice, and not only because he missed me. "Kenneth, ya es tiempo de volver al rancho," he said. "I really need you here. We have all this hay that we need to haul and sell. It is time to come home."

Dad knew I was a good son who rarely argued. Besides, he probably thought of me as blowing in the wind, having fun. There was nothing wrong with that, of course, but in his eyes, it made me available.

"Sí, Daddy. I'll be home as soon as I can. Might take a few days, though."

"Thank you, mi hijo lindo."

"Of course."

I returned to Hank, who was outside sipping a beer, and told him my trip was over. He was sad to see me go, but he carried on solo.

I would have liked to have kept going, but I was also happy to return home, on our land and with my family in Los Rincones. The Valley was unchanged outwardly. But to me, it had completely transformed from the place it was before I'd gone away to college. I now knew why my people were there, and I knew how far they had come to be there. I knew why they had been given land and then had that land taken away. I knew what it meant to be Mexican American, not just in my home in the San Luis Valley, but in the country at large. And I was beginning to understand the relationship of the United States to the rest of the Americas.

As I drove tractors across fields for endless days, and in restful dreams at night, I would think to myself, *How could I have lived for eighteen years in a place that was half Mexican American and yet never learn about the Treaty of Guadalupe Hidalgo? Why was I never taught that my Mexican ancestors became United States citizens through conquest, not choice? How could US schools have failed so completely to teach students about their own history and heritage—not only mine but everyone else's too? Why didn't we have a better understanding of the Americas, from Mexico to Central and South America? Could it be possible to unite the Americas to create better opportunity for the people of the Western Hemisphere? Could we work together to deal with poverty, security, violence, and corruption throughout our shared half of the globe?*

These interminable questions became a dream of what could be. I wasn't sure how to do it, but I always remembered this dream. Ultimately, it would guide my journey—all the way to the highest pinnacles of power in the United States.

12

THE HALLOWED HALLS OF MICHIGAN LAW

Ultimately, I chose the law. I applied to law schools at the University of Colorado, the University of Denver, Stanford, Harvard, and Michigan. Stanford was the dream, but I didn't make the cut. I chose Michigan—mainly because they gave me the best financial aid package.

I left home in August 1978. The road to Ann Arbor was over 1,200 miles, and I made the trip in one stretch in Leroy's Chevy LUV pickup, only stopping for gas, snacks, and two or three short naps at truck stops. I had to be there by a certain date, but I also didn't want to leave the truck alone for any extended period of time. After all, it was loaded with everything I owned: a couple of packed suitcases, some books, a basketball, and the dreams of a kid from Los Rincones.

The plains rolled endlessly by, corn and soy and fallow fields, punctuated here and there by dark rolling hills and lines of trees marking streams or canals. As I drove over this open expanse, my mind reeled with possibility and trepidation—and with recent events that connected closely to my decision to go to law school. Only two months earlier, in June 1978, the headlines were dominated by the Supreme Court decision in *Regents of the University of California v. Bakke*. This was *the* case that established affirmative action as justifiable where it concerned higher education admissions practices (until 2023, at least, when the Roberts Court effectively overruled *Bakke*). In the case, Allan Bakke, a white applicant to the University of California Davis School of Medicine, had claimed reverse discrimination, contending that he'd been denied admission because "less qualified" minority students had been accepted ahead of him.

The Court's ruling was complex, even contradictory if you squinted at it. Racial quotas were unconstitutional, the justices said. But affirmative action—the practice of considering race for school admissions—was not illegal. As Justice Powell wrote in the majority opinion, achieving diversity in the classroom was "a compelling state interest," and therefore doing what was practical to achieve this was fully above board as far as the Constitution was concerned.

As the country passed by outside Leroy's truck, I thought about what this decision meant for someone like me. Had I gotten into Michigan because of affirmative action? Possibly. My grades at Colorado College were solid—I graduated with a B-plus average—but not spectacular. Ditto my LSAT scores. In a pool of applicants where many must have had 4.0s and near-perfect test scores, what had pushed me over the line? My heritage?

Perhaps. Michigan, which had had virtually no Black or Hispanic law students just ten years earlier, was known as a place actively putting an emphasis on diversity. And if I had benefited from affirmative action, it made me only more determined to succeed.

For the next thirty-six hours, as I drove across the country, I pondered this and other, less heady things—like whether I could make it to the next service station without running out of gas or if I wanted a ham sandwich for dinner. The middle part of the country went by in a blur, and before I knew it, I pulled into Ann Arbor, the sun setting behind Leroy's dependable little truck.

That's when I saw it for the first time.

Hutchins Hall rose in front of me on State Street like a Gothic cathedral, its limestone tower stretching to the sky above. There was no danger of getting lost this time, like there was in Colorado Springs five years earlier. I could barely believe it. I was actually here to attend one of the nation's most prestigious law schools—top five, everyone said. If I made it through, this would be my home for the next three years. It would be the center of my world.

I parked the truck and went inside. The person in the main office welcomed me and said I couldn't get into my apartment for another couple of days, so I checked into a small hotel near campus. That first night, lying on the narrow bed listening to the familiar sounds of a college town, I felt the full weight of how far I was from home. No mountains on the horizon. No scent of alfalfa or cut hay, no sound of water running through ditches, and no Mike Espinoza to help me get my bearings.

Classes started a week later. It was early September. Of the roughly 350 first-year students, there were maybe thirty Hispanic students—for Michigan Law, a dramatic increase from only a few years earlier. The law school had clearly made diversity a priority.

The academic demands were unlike anything I'd experienced. It felt a bit like getting the wind knocked out of you, over and over and over again. All first-year students, called "1Ls," took the same four classes—Criminal Law, Torts, Civil Procedure, and Property Law. The workload was crushing. Six to seven days a week, I was either in class or parked in the library, studying until I was ushered out by a quiet librarian at closing time. Most nights, as soon as I got home, I sat at my small kitchen table and kept reading, kept taking notes, kept learning. Or trying to learn.

Two facts of Michigan Law were particularly anxiety-inducing. One was what I'll call the "sink-or-swim" mandate placed on all students. "Look to your left," my Criminal Law professor Yale Kamisar announced during the first week. We were all still terrified, so we did as we were told. "Now look to your right." The class audibly whispered as heads swung around. "Some of you won't be here next semester. That might be you or anyone sitting next to you."

The 350 of us would be whittled down significantly at the end of the first semester. It was do or be done.

The other discomfiting feature of law school involved figuring out how to deal with the Socratic method, the millennia-old teaching technique that required students to speak authoritatively with other students and professors across a range of topics. For someone like me, who preferred not to talk in class, it was a real struggle.

Of all my professors, Kamisar scared me most. He was a tall, mostly bald white man with a few dark hairs combed over the top of his head, and his glasses seemed always to be balanced on the tip of his nose. He had piercing eyes, and whenever he called out, "Mr. Salazar?" my heart jumped. I was not used to this way of learning in the classroom, and it didn't help my nerves that Kamisar himself was a legend. He was a bona fide expert on criminal law and procedure and a key figure in developing the Miranda warnings that inform defendants of their legal rights. How was it possible to debate someone like that?

How? Through practice, and through all the studying I was doing. Through dissecting facts. Through analyzing legal issues. Through defending my reasoning in front of my peers. Through doing the work of becoming a lawyer.

But the pressure didn't just come from academics; the social atmosphere could be oppressive too. Especially given the *Bakke* decision, affirmative action seemed to be on the tip of everyone's tongues. I often wondered what the white male students felt about folks like me, or about the Black students, or the female students. Walking the halls of the castle-like Hutchins Hall was like strolling through a veritable parade ground of whispers and surreptitious glances.

And occasionally, plainspoken words.

"I know someone who should be here instead of you," a white male classmate told me one day as we sauntered out of Torts.

He stated his words like an observation, as if he'd said, "Sure is cloudy today." But it pissed me off. I lifted my finger and called him an asshole. Then I laid into him: "You're only here because your parents are rich. They sent you to the best schools and they dropped you off here themselves. You're privileged and we are not. You've probably never had to work a day in your life!" Apparently scared I was going to punch him, he scrambled away.

As I walked along State Street toward my apartment for yet more studying, I fought the urge to turn and find him, to make him understand, to tell him about the Valley, about what it was like growing up as a Mexican American there, about Mrs. Joyce, about being frozen out of the National Honor Society because some Anglo teacher thought I hung out with the wrong crowd. I wanted to show him my hands and tell him why they were so calloused and worn. I wanted to show him the dark band across the back of my neck and the nearly white skin that covered my back just below it, set apart by a distinct line that marked the collar of my shirt. These things came from countless hours of hard work in the fields—which I doubted this person had any experience with. I wanted to set him straight. But I slowly decided to let the anger go. What did I know about his life? Perhaps he was one of those white kids from a hard-working family who himself had been a beneficiary of affirmative action. Maybe my reaction was unfair.

I wasn't the only one who heard this kind of thing. A sort of "third world coalition" took shape in the bowels of Hutchins Hall. That was where the La Raza and the Black Law Students organizations each had small offices, the former providing support and services to Hispanic students, the latter giving the same to Black students. We found strength in numbers, and we made a quick community that would grow in the years and decades that followed, not only at Michigan Law but at other institutions across the country. We often commiserated over the kind of thing that white student had said to me, drilling down on a seemingly infinite number of ways other people called our qualifications into question. It was not always pleasant, but it built community.

Fortunately, Michigan itself was fully supportive of our organizations. They saw us as necessary partners in their quest to make the legal profession more representative of the United States. But this support didn't make the grind any easier.

As the first semester wore on, it hit all of us that we would not be able to avoid the first marking period. It was widely understood that no matter how hard we worked, most of us would receive Cs. Getting a B would be a major accomplishment. An A was like rainfall in August in the Valley—practically unheard of.

One of my La Raza friends, Ray Avila, a thirty-something 2L from a Texas border town, said to me one day in the library, "Don't stress about it, Ken."

"How could I not stress about it, Ray? This is my future. You already made the 1L cut last year."

He shrugged. "My mom has a saying: 'Don't worry. All that guarantees is that you suffer twice.'"

I chuckled. "Wise words."

"Yeah. Look, you should always do your best, but don't worry. If you only get Cs, so be it. You'll be in good company." At this, he pinched his shirt at the shoulders and puffed it up, like a modern-day basketball player tugging proudly at his jersey. "Just do the work, show up to class, and you'll be fine."

As October passed into November, I threw myself into my studies with an obsessive intensity. Whenever I lay down at night, exhausted from sitting all day, my head swimming with words that sometimes began to lose meaning, I would picture Mom and Dad. Cooking. Cleaning. Haying. Calving. Slaughtering. Driving. Cutting. Planting. Looking all of us kids in the eye, boy or girl, young or old, and saying, "Get educated. Get educated. Get educated." In 1978, Leroy was already an agricultural engineer, and John had a business degree. Elaine was at Colorado College, and the triplets were finishing up high school. Leandro had graduated college with a philosophy degree and had already worked with the United Farm Workers in California's San

Joaquin Valley. Work, work, work. Failure is not an option. Work. That's what Salazars do. We work.

When I finally drifted off to sleep for a few hours, I dreamed of nothing.

Sometimes, I woke to the sheer volume of noise just outside my apartment or to the sound of the Michigan band warming up.

Because if there's one thing the University of Michigan is really famous for, it's football. My apartment on Packard Street was practically right next to Michigan Stadium, which in 1978 wasn't yet known as "The Big House." While other students went to games—the Wolverines were really good that year, boasting a 10–2 record behind a defense that allowed just over seven points a game—I studied. Every Saturday, the stadium would roar to life, and every Saturday I would not be a part of it. I would be in the law school, heeding Henry and Emma Salazar, working.

It was during one of these quiet working sessions that I made a significant discovery. Like many law schools, Michigan decorated its halls with portraits of distinguished alumni—judges, politicians, diplomats, advocates, academics—lawyers who had shaped American jurisprudence. Hundreds of faces looked down from the walls on us, day in and day out.

Nearly all of them were white and male.

But then, one day, I found an outlier.

In Room 120 was a portrait of a young, handsome man with curly dark hair parted to the side, intelligent eyes, and prominent, attentive ears. His was not like the other portraits of white men. I leaned closer. The nameplate read: "J. T. Canales, Class of 1899."

I scurried off to the library and looked him up. I learned that José Tomás Canales was born in 1877 on a family ranch in Nueces County, Texas. After graduating from Michigan Law, he moved to Brownsville—the site of the beginning of the Mexican-American War—to work as a lawyer. He eventually rose to become a Texas state judge and would serve five terms in the Texas House of Representatives, where he was the only Mexican American.

Canales seemed larger than life—not just in the legal and political positions he held, but also in his particular accomplishments. In 1918, he brought nineteen charges against the Texas Rangers, who had been acting as vigilantes along the border and terrorizing people of Mexican descent, both US citizens and not. This was a somewhat lawless time, a bridge between the era of westward expansion and the modern US government. The investigation that followed heard testimony from eighty-three witnesses—Anglo, Mexican American, Mexican, Black—as it took pains to document the 1918 massacre of fifteen unarmed ethnic Mexicans at the hands of the Rangers. In the end, it was determined that the Rangers had killed somewhere between three hundred and five thousand people of Mexican descent between 1914 and 1919, a finding that had lasting effects.

This was a trying time for Canales, who came under direct threat from prominent Rangers, including one named Frank Hamer (who would later go on to gun down the infamous bank robbers Bonnie and Clyde). The situation was so perilous that for a while Canales needed an escort in and around the state capital. One of these escorts was legislator Samuel Ealy Johnson Jr. (father of Lyndon B. Johnson), who sometimes accompanied Canales to the hearings. The apple didn't fall far from the tree in the Johnson family, it seemed.

I began visiting Room 120 regularly, just to spend time with J.T. Canales's portrait. Under his encouraging and kind-eyed gaze, I dove into the Supreme Court decisions that had upheld slavery, Lincoln's Emancipation Proclamation, the Reconstruction Amendments, the history of Jim Crow segregation, *Brown v. Board of Education*, the Civil Rights Act of 1964, and of course, *Bakke*.

During the holiday break at the ranch in Los Rincones, I worried I might get a notice not to return to Michigan. But nothing came. So I went back to Ann Arbor in January 1979 and immediately went to the

Registrar's office to find my grades. There they were—Yale Kamisar had given me a C-plus and I received a B in Torts. The feelings of elation and relief were overwhelming, but more than that, I felt confidence. Frank Sinatra said it about New York City, but for me, it was about Michigan Law: If I could make it there, I could make it anywhere.

When classes reconvened that January, there were fewer students, as predicted. Many of the ones who didn't come back were white students who'd crowed about us "third worlders." The meritocracy seemed not to discriminate—one way or the other.

During spring break, the law school's dean asked if I would be willing to travel to Texas to recruit Mexican American students. He couldn't have known that I'd adopted Canales as my patron saint at Michigan Law, but his instincts were rewarded. I eagerly accepted. I was able to put my studies on the back burner, and I traveled to Houston. From there, I went to Austin, San Antonio, and down to the border along the Rio Grande.

This was my first time in the Texas borderlands, and it felt like a kind of homecoming. At Pan American University in Edinburg—a school that was 95 percent Hispanic—I set up a table with Michigan Law materials and talked to students about opportunity and possibility. Over and over, ambitious young men and women dressed in suits or pencil skirts and blouses would come up to my table and ask, "Why Michigan?"

"Because Michigan supports us. They wanted me, and they want people like you too."

Some bought it; others were skeptical. How could I blame them? They probably had an innate understanding of being promised one thing and then given another entirely. As Mexican Americans along the border, theirs was a legacy of disappointment, and that was putting it mildly, especially in a place like Edinburg, Texas.

The recruiting trip—whether it resulted in a hundred new students or just one—reinforced my sense of purpose. And though I could never have known it at the time, it presaged the long arc of my life. I would be back to these Texas borderlands decades later as US ambassador to Mexico, fighting and advocating for much of the same thing.

My 2L and 3L years passed in a blur. Casebooks. Study groups. Endless hours of thinking and writing and reading. In the end, I kept up my grades, even improving them as the months progressed. As my comfort increased, so did my urge to blow off steam. As per usual, I did this on the basketball court, where we formed a team of misfits that (usually) beat the pants off whoever dared challenge us.

As my final semester wound down, I found myself in the surreal position of fielding job offers from Big Law with salaries as high as $50,000 per year. In 1981, that was a *lot* of money, more than our ranch at Los Rincones could make in three years or more.

But I was torn. I would soon have a law degree—was I meant to use it only to chase money? Studying the law had opened my eyes to its power as an instrument of social change. Constitutional Law had been my favorite subject. There was a direct line between the 14th and 15th Amendments, decisions like *Bakke*, and people like me. All of us sat on a continuum of struggle, and I wanted to be a part of that fight.

In addition to various law firms, I also fielded offers from civil rights organizations, including the Mexican American Legal Defense and Educational Fund (MALDEF), the leading legal civil rights organization for Hispanic Americans. This was exactly the kind of work I wanted to do—but there was a problem. The pay was a pittance compared to my private sector offers, and I had some serious student loans to pay back.

Ultimately, I signed up with Sherman & Howard, a prestigious Denver firm. I was told the work there would focus on natural resources and water law—subjects that connected directly to life in the Valley. I knew Dad would be proud. Furthermore, they were supportive of my intention to do pro bono civil rights work so long as it didn't interfere with my paying clients. It wasn't the pure civil rights path I'd originally envisioned, but it could work. And besides, this was just the first step into my career. Things could change. Things *would* change. There was no other way.

And so, I graduated from Michigan Law. But there was one more thing I wanted to do before returning to the Valley. With the money from my signing bonus, I walked into an Ann Arbor car dealership and bought my first-ever new car—a 1981 Plymouth Reliant. It was a small, beautiful sedan with a gear shift on the console and an impressive dashboard.

Following commencement, I loaded my stuff into the Reliant and began the drive back to Colorado. (My good friend Larry Atencio drove the Chevy LUV back to the Valley a few days later.) This time, I wasn't an uncertain young man heading into the unknown. I was a lawyer. I hadn't passed the Colorado bar yet, but I would. I was confident of that.

When I reached the Valley, I drove straight to our white and green house in Los Rincones and parked out front. Mom rushed to greet me.

After a long round of hugs and kisses, I looked to Mom and held out the keys to the Plymouth. "Mom," I said, "this car is for you."

She looked confused. "But I don't know how to drive, mi hijo."

"I know. I'll teach you," I said.

And I did. Over the next several months, before starting at the law firm, I became my mother's driving instructor. As with everything else in her life, she was a quick study.

Later, when I was working on a complex water rights case on the twenty-ninth floor of the firm's Denver office building, my phone rang. It was Mom, calling from Alamosa.

"Kenny, mi hijito!" she exclaimed. "I just passed my driver's test! I have my license!"

My mother was sixty-one years old, and for the first time in her life she had the freedom to go wherever she wanted, whenever she wanted, without depending on anyone else.

I smiled. "How do you feel?"

"I feel . . . free," she said.

I told her I was proud of her and that I loved her. We hung up, and I looked out at the Denver skyline, thinking about the journey that had brought us to this moment. There was a long way to go, but a circle involving family and aspirations and a lot of hard labor had been closed.

My mother drove that Plymouth Reliant well into her eighties. Every time I saw her behind the wheel, I remembered why I'd chosen the law in the first place. It wasn't just about winning cases or making money—it was about expanding possibilities, fighting for justice, and ensuring that everyone had the chance to feel and be free.

PART IV

EVERYONE MATTERS

13

TWO WORLDS

Not long after the day Mom earned her driver's license, my friend Bill Marsh knocked on my office door on the twenty-ninth floor of Sherman & Howard. Bill was one of the firm's senior partners, an experienced, take-no-prisoners natural resources litigator. Though he wore suits to court, he otherwise looked and acted like a rancher, dressing in jeans, a black leather vest, and black cowboy boots.

"Got a minute, Ken?" Bill asked.

Lawyers, who literally bill in six-minute chunks, don't have many minutes. At that time, my big case involved the Keystone ski area, which was trying to secure local water rights for snowmaking. This wasn't exactly the civil rights work I'd dreamed about at Michigan, but it was important for me to learn all sides of water law for when I returned to the Valley, which was practically defined by disputes over water.

While I was busy, I couldn't say no to Bill. He was one of my bosses, and besides that, I liked him. "Of course," I said.

Bill stepped halfway into my office and leaned casually against the doorjamb, a cup of coffee cradled in his right hand. "I was hoping you could help me on the Saguache Country Club condemnation, down in the Valley," he said. "The federal Bureau of Reclamation is offering a hundred dollars an acre. The ranchers and duck hunters who own it don't have much money and think their land is worth ten times that."

"A country club in the Valley? There's no such thing," I said with amusement.

"It's more of a hunting ranch than a country club. Lots of water. The Russell Springs run right through it. But they fancy themselves a country club. Down in your neck of the woods, actually. The San Luis Valley. You up for that?"

It sounded straightforward, and I was always eager to do something to help locals in the Valley, so we took the case. Since it was a federal case, it was a big deal. Over the next several months, I drove the four hours south whenever I could, passing through the familiar lands of my childhood to meet with neighboring landowners who reminded me of the ranchers I'd grown up around—men who understood that land was often worth more than its appraised value. We'd eventually force the federal government to pay nearly $1,000 an acre, but what mattered more was that I was building a reputation as someone who could navigate both worlds: the twenty-ninth floor of a Denver law firm and the dusty back roads of rural Colorado.

The firm expected 1,800 billable hours a year. I gave them that and more, often working six-day weeks and pulling all-nighters to write briefs to satisfy the partners' exacting standards. But the work that mattered most to me—the work that would eventually set me on my then unforeseen path to public service—happened when I was helping clients who couldn't pay.

One of those cases involved getting the Denver Board of Education to comply with a landmark Supreme Court decision handed down in 1973. The Court had ruled in favor of the plaintiffs, Wilfred Keyes and a group of other parents, holding that Denver's schools had engaged in de facto segregation that ran counter to the precedent set by *Brown v. Board of Education*. This segregation occurred not through explicit laws, as had been the case across the Deep South, but through manipulation of school district boundaries and their locations. For example, in Denver, Manual High in the Whittier neighborhood was essentially all Black, North and West were all Hispanic, and the southeast Denver schools were predominantly white. The courts found that there was no room for segregated Black, brown, and white schools in public education and that the Denver Board of Education had violated the equal protection clause of the 14th Amendment.

By 1982, the heated debate was focused on the proposed remedy, which mainly involved busing kids to integrate the schools. Resistance to busing was fierce and occasionally crossed into violence in the streets and at school board meetings. A former superintendent had even suggested that integrating Black and Hispanic kids into the same schools was all that was needed. The Black kids were Black and the Hispanic kids were "whiter" than them, so that would achieve "desegregation" as far as he was concerned.

My engagement in this case involved the desegregation issue, but focused on the parallel claim the case covered: teaching English as a second language in Denver's public schools.

A group of Hispanic teachers organized the Congress of Hispanic Educators (CHE) to represent the more than ten thousand Hispanic children in the Denver Public Schools. MALDEF agreed to represent CHE, and they intervened to ensure that "limited English proficient" children learned in settings where they could understand the language of instruction and not be left to learn in the silence of their own thoughts. Peter Roos and Norma Cantù, MALDEF's legal counsel, reached out to me for help. I happily agreed.

Over the next few years, I spent over a thousand unpaid hours on this case, working late into the night with Peter, Norma, and the leadership of CHE. Peter often slept at my house as we tried to fashion a remedy. And we did. We first convinced the Board of Education, and the federal district court in Denver approved our settlement. The remedy is still in effect today.

This was precisely the kind of law I wanted to do—using my profession as an instrument of social change, continuing the fight that had taken me to Michigan in the first place. Like Michigan Law itself, this work placed diversity at the center of the table. And thanks to CHE and MALDEF, I was able to do it.

Somehow, in the few waking hours I had left in my life, I found the time to date a young woman named Esperanza Hernandez. I'd actually first met her during a trip to Denver in the summer of 1980, between my second and third years at Michigan. I'd been clerking at Sherman & Howard and was living with my cousin Sisto, who owned a hair salon in the Radisson Hotel on Grant Street. He seemed to know everyone in town.

"Come on, primo. Vamos!" Sisto had called to me one warm June night after work. I was in his living room, where I often slept on the couch, poring over a red leather–bound, gold-embossed law book. "You can't spend every Friday night reading about cases. You need to have some fun!"

I looked up at him. I'd known Sisto since I was a child. He was four years older than me, like my brother Leroy, and the two of them had the same indomitable energy. He had grown up in Cuba, New Mexico, with most of my mother's family, and his Spanish was fluent and rolled off his tongue naturally—the Spanish of the old New Mexicans. Sisto had been on the front lines in Vietnam and had seen the brutality of war, though he didn't talk about it often. Mostly, we just loved hanging out. And that night, as usual, he was right. I deserved to live a little, didn't I? I closed the book with an audible slap and set it aside. "OK, Sisto. Let's go."

We left his house on Corona Street, hopped in his Corvette, and scooted down Colfax Avenue near the Denver Mint. We were headed to the Denver Marina, a popular bar for young Mexican American professionals, although at twenty-five and still in law school, I hardly felt professional.

We entered and wedged into an open spot at the bar. He ordered a Dewar's on the rocks, and I ordered a Budweiser. The Marina was always hopping, especially on Friday and Saturday nights. Rock and Tex-Mex music blared from the sound system as couples, friends, and strangers shuttled to and from the dance floor. Disco lights illuminated the tables as people laughed and chatted. I had never been much of a ladies' man, but Sisto was charming, and he knew how to talk to anyone. I saved his spot by the bar while he worked the room, and after a short while, he brought back two women in their mid-twenties.

"Ken," Sisto said, "this is my friend Margie. And this is Hope. Margie and Hope, this is my cousin Ken. He's from the country and trying to learn about the big city," he laughed.

I asked Hope if she wanted a drink. She said yes, and we ordered a margarita on the rocks and another Budweiser.

Hope was strikingly beautiful, with light brown hair, green eyes, and a big smile, and she radiated a confidence that made me acutely aware of my country-boy awkwardness. She worked for Mexicana Airlines as an executive assistant to the director. She'd grown up in Commerce City, the daughter of a highway construction laborer and a homemaker, but she carried herself like she owned the place.

I was terrified that if I asked her to dance, she'd say no. So I didn't ask.

But for whatever reason, Hope didn't seem to mind my shyness, and at least to start, she did most of the talking. Her given name was Esperanza, but everyone in Denver called her Hope. She told me funny stories about dealing with irate passengers, about the travel benefits that came with her job, about her plans to see the world. She spoke perfect and beautiful Spanish, much better than mine. She was independent and sharp, and I would soon learn that she was unafraid to disagree when someone made a point she thought was wrong.

"So where is this law student from?" She glanced at Sisto. "Where was it again?"

I answered for him. "The San Luis Valley. My family ranch is near Alamosa," I said, since she'd probably never heard of Manassa or Los Rincones.

"OK. What does a law student from a ranch do for fun?"

"Basketball," I said. "And reading."

She laughed. "Reading is usually work."

"Depends on what you're reading."

"What are you reading now?"

"The Colorado water code."

She laughed again. "I love reading. But the water code . . . that is *definitely* work."

By the end of the night, I'd managed to get her phone number.

Our courtship unfolded slowly over the following years, shaped by the rhythms of both our lives—law school in Ann Arbor and work in the Valley for me, jet-setting around Mexico and even the world for Hope. When I first started at Sherman & Howard in 1981, I didn't even live in Denver. Instead, I commuted from Idaho Springs, thirty-plus miles west of downtown. I lived in the same small house we had lived in during my fifth-grade year, which Dad hadn't sold after all those years. Even with all the long hours I spent working, I still drove back and forth, back and forth from Idaho Springs to Denver and to the Valley.

In 1982, I moved into an apartment on Pearl Street in Denver. Hope and I continued to date. When I pulled all-nighters at the firm, Hope would sometimes show up late at night with homemade sandwiches.

"You know you're going to kill yourself working like this," she said one Sunday afternoon in 1984 as I reviewed case law for one of my pro bono jobs.

"Just until I pay off the loans," I said—a bit nonsensically since the work I was doing at that moment was unpaid.

"And then what? You'll find another reason to work yourself to death?"

She was right, of course. By then, she'd been to the Valley, and she'd met the Salazars. She saw the truth plainly: The ranch had taught us that survival meant constant labor. Law school had only reinforced that lesson.

But thank God, Hope saw through all of that. Yes, she was Mexican American like me. She was a city girl, far more cosmopolitan than I could ever hope to be (or wanted to be), and she'd carved out her own space in a world that often tried to make her smaller. She understood ambition and struggle—but she also understood that life was more than work.

She taught me that lesson too. At some point that year, I realized I loved her for it—and for a lot of other reasons. It was then that I started to think, *I want to marry this woman.*

I prayed that she felt the same about me.

In the summer of 1984, I traveled to Indianapolis to take part in a US–Soviet young leaders' program—one of those Cold War exchanges designed to foster understanding between future leaders of both superpowers. I'd been recruited into the program by another senior associate at the firm, Tom Strickland, a man who was a few years older than me and who had become a friend. This was the same year the Baltimore Colts moved to Indianapolis, and as part of the program we got to tour the new stadium, the Hoosier Dome, which left quite an impression on some of the young Soviet men.

Following our tour, we gathered for a reception at the governor's mansion on North Meridian Street, located in one of the nicest-looking neighborhoods I'd ever visited. The governor's residence—then occupied by Robert Orr—looked like something out of an English period drama and, to me at least, felt huge and imposing. Everything was perfect—the furniture, the art, the people working there, the food. It was about as far from Los Rincones as one could get; it made me wistful for my home and my humble Colorado roots.

As I stood in the mansion's study, surrounded by Soviet officials and their American counterparts, I was suddenly overcome with a need to talk to Hope. I still can't fully explain why. Maybe it was because I felt so out of place. I was getting better at functioning in settings like this, but they still felt foreign. Perhaps because of that, I wanted to ground myself; I wanted to reach out and grab something I knew.

I excused myself from the polite conversation and wandered into one of the mansion's hallways. There, on an antique wooden side table, was a white telephone. I picked it up and dialed Hope at her apartment in Denver. It rang a few times before she answered.

"Hello?"

"Hey, it's me," I said.

"Hey, Kenny. Where are you?"

"Indianapolis. At the governor's mansion, actually."

"Oh. Fancy you."

"Yeah," I said. And then: "Listen. I love you." Silence. "And I want to marry you, Esperanza Hernandez." There. I'd said it.

More silence before a sharp gasp. I could almost hear Hope cock her head to the side and give that sidelong squint she did whenever she wasn't sure about something. "Kenneth Salazar, are you seriously proposing to me over the phone from a governor's mansion?"

"Yes?" I said.

She laughed. It was the same laugh I heard the first night I met her. And then, "Sure."

"Sure?"

"Yes, Ken. Yes. But when you get back, you're going to do this again. Properly."

"Great. OK. I will. Thank you." I couldn't believe how awkward I sounded, but total elation does that to a man.

"You're welcome, Kenny. See you in a couple days."

We hung up, a mile-long grin stretched across my face. I stood there alone for a minute or two, unsure of what to do next. I took a deep breath and managed to come down to Earth. Then I went back to the Soviets and the Americans.

When I got back to Denver, Hope and I went out to buy a ring—nothing fancy, but something definitely respectable. We planned the wedding for August 3, 1985, at Our Lady of Guadalupe in Conejos, near Los Rincones, the oldest church in Colorado.

I could not have been happier.

◆◆◆

The wedding was pure Valley. We sent invitations to five hundred people, but close to a thousand showed up. That's how it works in the Valley—you invite one person, and the whole family turns out. The church overflowed, with people standing in the aisles and spilling into the sprawling church grounds.

Father Pat Valdez, a family friend and the parish priest from the nearby town of San Luis, performed the ceremony. Hope wore a beautiful wedding gown bought for the occasion. I wore a rental tuxedo we had picked up in Pueblo.

The reception lasted all afternoon. Mariachis and a local band traded sets, and tables groaned under the weight of the food and dishes served by cousins, aunts, and neighbors. Kids ran between the tables. Old men told stories about my father and grandfather. Hope's Denver friends mingled with my Valley relatives—two worlds coming together under the August sun.

Dancing went until two in the morning, though Hope and I left at midnight as tradition demanded. We drove to Taos for what we generously called a honeymoon. That night, we stayed in a beautiful lodge, and the following night we had dinner in Chimayó, where my ancestors had lived in the 1600s. Hope had won a contest from Trans World Airlines for free tickets to Spain, and we planned to take a real honeymoon later that year. But between the ranch and my caseload, that trip never materialized.

"We'll go eventually," I promised her.

"I know," she said. But there was something in her voice that suggested she was beginning to understand what she'd signed up for. I'd pitched myself as "a lawyer and a rancher," and that was true. But as a practical matter, it meant she was living life with someone who was perpetually caught between two worlds, always rushing from one obligation to the next.

14

REPORTING FOR DUTY

I hit my stride at Sherman & Howard in 1986. The water rights practice was thriving, and I'd become the go-to associate for complex natural resources cases. But it was my pro bono civil rights work that truly made waves beyond the firm.

Along with the case involving the CHE, I worked on other civil rights cases representing limited English proficient children. I also helped organize a diversity pledge for Denver's major law firms committing them to actively recruit minority and female lawyers. I helped my sister Elaine with legal issues in her founding of a radio station, KRZA, in Alamosa, bringing public radio to the Valley for the first time. And I helped Flo Hernandez Ramos and Adrienne Benavidez start KUVO, another new public radio station, to Denver. These weren't court victories, but they were legal and community victories, using the skills and connections I'd developed to build institutions that would stand the test of time.

That fall, State Treasurer Roy Romer, a Democrat from the eastern plains, won Colorado's gubernatorial race with just over 58 percent of the vote. Not long after his victory, Tom Strickland came to my office and said straight-up: "Hey, Ken, you know Roy Romer's transition team is looking for people, right?"

"The governor-elect?"

"One and the same. He wants a diverse senior staff, and you've made a name for yourself. Says he's going to govern for all of Colorado, not just Denver. You would be a hell of a fit."

"That's great," I said. I'd voted for him, and I hoped what Tom said was true.

"Can I give his team your résumé?" Tom asked.

I shrugged. Politics seemed like another world, one I wanted nothing to do with. I had my work, my cases, my causes. Hope and I were getting ready to start a family. The ranch still needed help every summer. My plate was full. "I think I'm good, Tom," I said.

"Come on. It's a good opportunity."

"OK, OK, sure," I said dismissively, turning back to a water case in the western Rockies.

Not long afterward, on a Sunday in November 1986, my bedside phone rang at 5:30 in the morning. It was so early that I thought it was Dad calling about the hay or a water rights question. Hope groaned and pulled a pillow over her head as I fumbled for the receiver.

"Hello?" I asked groggily.

"Ken Salazar?" a woman's voice asked.

"Yes?"

"My name is BJ Thornberry. I'm with Governor Roy Romer."

I sat bolt upright and swung my legs out of bed, planting my feet on the floor. "Good morning, Ms. Thornberry," I said, shaking my head vigorously to expel the cobwebs of sleep.

"The governor would like to speak with you. Do you have a minute?"

"Now?" I asked, briefly wondering if the new governor and his staff slept.

"Yes, Mr. Salazar. Is that all right? I can connect you directly."

"Sure. I mean, yes. Please. Thank you."

"One moment."

The line went quiet before clicking back on. “Ken? Roy Romer.” This was the same confident, uplifting voice I’d heard many times on TV and the radio. It was him, the newest governor of Colorado.

“Good morning, sir,” I said. Hope stirred behind me. I didn’t turn to look, but I could sense she was now paying attention.

“Good morning. Sorry for the early call. Look, let me get right to it. I have your résumé here”—I could hear what sounded like his index finger hammering his desk—“and I want you to work with me in the governor’s office. I want you to be my lawyer.”

“Sir?” I said, not sure I’d heard correctly.

“Chief legal counsel. My lawyer. I’d like you to come on board. You tick all the boxes. Rancher. Rural. Michigan Law. Strong on water and the environment. Hispanic. And people I trust like Tom Strickland, Wellington Webb, Paul Sandoval, Polly Baca, and Ruben Valdez all speak very highly of you.” I smiled. He must have been reading from a checklist of people who had weighed in on my behalf.

“Thank you, sir,” I said.

“So, what do you say?”

I looked at the clock: 5:33 AM. “Can I talk to my wife and call you back?”

“Of course. I’ll put BJ back on, and she can give you some of the details to help you figure it out. I’d really like you to come over. Talk to you soon, Ken.”

“Thank you, sir.”

And just like that, Governor Romer was gone. BJ said I could start immediately, though the salary would be $40,000, about half of what I was currently making at Sherman & Howard. It was a huge pivot, yes, but it was also a great opportunity.

In my heart, I knew I had to take the job. I loved working at the firm, but the dream of practicing law in a way that would make the world a better place for everyone—or at least all Coloradans—remained intact in my heart.

I flopped back into bed and, staring at the ceiling, told Hope about the offer.

After a moment of silence she said, "You're going to take it." This wasn't a question. It wasn't even an admonition. It was an observation.

"But the pay cut—" I argued.

"I'm not happy about that, but we'll manage."

"The hours—"

"Can't be worse than now."

"I told you you were marrying a lawyer and a rancher," I said. "Not a politician."

"That's true, that's true. But life happens, Kenny."

"OK, then. But just for a year or two. I'll learn about government and see what Romer can do. Then go back to the firm—or maybe finally move down to the Valley and hang up that shingle in Alamosa."

I turned to her in the bed. I could just make out her smile in the predawn darkness. "Sure, Ken. Just a year or two," she said.

I called the governor the next morning, although not quite as early as he'd called me. BJ answered and put me through. "Morning, Governor," I said.

"Good morning, Ken. I was wondering if you'd call," Romer laughed. "So what's it going to be?"

"When do I report for duty, sir?"

15

THE POWER OF THE STATE

When I told Mom and Dad about my decision, Henry was characteristically blunt: "Tienes pájaros en la cabeza." *You have birds in your head.* We stood in the kitchen at Los Rincones. It was a Friday, well past dark, and Dad had just come in from changing the oil on our old John Deere 520. Mom was finishing up with the dishes and stretching Saran Wrap over a large bowl of her famous bread dough. I'd just made the drive to the Valley for the weekend and was weary from the road and an intense week of working and grappling with my decision to leave the firm. Henry especially couldn't get past the idea that I was giving up an $80,000 annual salary after seven years at the firm. For him (and, honestly, for me), this was an eye-popping figure, one that he took pride in his son earning.

"It doesn't make sense," he continued. "You've worked hard, and you're about to become a partner. And you have Hope to think about, with the baby coming."

Hope was indeed pregnant with our first daughter, Melinda, whose birth we'd celebrate the following summer. But even though Hope had reservations about me changing jobs, she understood why I wanted to do it, and I'd hoped that Dad and Mom would understand too. Working for the governor might enable me to help people across the state, especially forgotten parts of the state—rural communities, farmers and ranchers out on the plains and in the mountains, Black people in Denver, Native Americans in the southwest, and poor people in the big cities.

"It's only for a year or two," I told them. "I'll get some experience in government and see if Romer can have an impact. If it doesn't work out or if I don't like it, I can always go back to practicing law. The firm isn't going anywhere, and I'll leave on good terms."

"If that is what you want to do," Henry said, settling into a kitchen chair. In that moment, I had gained his support.

"Yes, Dad. It's going to be fine. I promise."

Finally, Mom said, "I think he is right, Henry. Maybe God wants this for Kenny."

"Yes," Dad said after a minute. He turned to look at me. "But don't think you'll get out of helping out down here just because you're with the governor in Denver."

I grinned and gave him a hug. "The thought never crossed my mind, Dad."

I started the following week. At thirty-one, I was the youngest member of Governor Romer's senior staff and the only Hispanic in his inner circle. My office was small, efficient, and unassuming, furnished only with a roll-top desk, two sturdy chairs, and a wooden door I could close for privacy. But it had a window with a priceless view of the Capitol driveway circle, where I often saw the governor coming and going. His office was just down the hall, and I quickly learned that I would be thrown into every crisis, every politically sensitive issue, every problem that needed both a legal eye and a sensitivity to the lives of regular Coloradans from all four corners of the state.

My first test as Governor Romer's chief counsel was a battle between poor, rural school districts and wealthy school districts. I knew the issue well. I'd worked on it pro bono while at the firm, arguing that poor, often rural, kids were getting less than half the per-pupil funding of kids in wealthy districts like Cherry Creek or Aspen. We argued for the plaintiffs that this was not right and that the state had to do better. Sadly, we lost the case, with the Colorado Supreme Court saying that the allocation of funding was a matter for the legislature, not an issue that the court could adjudicate or rectify.

A few weeks after I started work, the governor called me into his office to discuss a bill that could make the state's school finance system fairer. "Ken, you know this issue. Senator Al Meiklejohn and education leaders like Representative Norma Anderson want to work on it. Al and Norma are Republicans from Jefferson County. I want you three to meet and start hashing this thing out."

Senator Meiklejohn arrived in the governor's office the next day. He was a towering, thin man with white hair, and he looked every bit the elder statesman. As he stepped into the office, he and Romer greeted each other warmly, two political pros who knew how the game was played.

"Al, I want us to work together on this school finance issue," the governor said. "Our system is unfair, and fixing it should be a bipartisan undertaking. Ken knows a lot about it; see if you guys can craft a solution."

Meiklejohn turned to me and gave me a hard look. Here I was, the young, mustachioed, Hispanic lawyer everyone had heard about, the one who'd just left the arduous but lucrative world of Big Law to work for the government, of all things. "It'd be my pleasure, Governor," Meiklejohn said. "I'm happy to work with Ken and Representative Anderson on this. We'll see what we can do."

We got to work. Ready to prove the value of our task, I spent the next two weeks writing a legal treatise analyzing and comparing the school finance systems of all fifty states. I delivered it to the governor with all the pride of a first-year associate handing in an airtight brief or devastating complaint.

He received it, scanned it, and slipped it into his brown leather briefcase. "Good work," he said. "Now get back to Meiklejohn and find us a solution." I'm not sure if the governor ever read my legal treatise on school finance.

And so I did as he said. Over the next few months, the senator, his staff, and I hammered out the details: formulas, funding mechanisms, phase-in periods. We brought in rural superintendents and Denver administrators, teachers unions and business groups, PTA presidents and school boards. It all felt very familiar. We had lost this fight in court, but we would win it in legislative hearing rooms.

Governor Romer signed the Public School Finance Act in the spring of 1988. I stood in his office as he put pen to paper, feeling proud to have been a part of something that would lift up the forgotten rural parts of the state and create a more level playing field for all Colorado children and families. As Governor Romer smiled and shook hands, the newly minted law still sitting on his desk, I had a realization that was obvious but still profound.

I of course knew how government was intended to work. I'd taken civics, and I was a lawyer. But it struck me anew: We had accomplished something here that we simply could not have as advocates working in the courts. In that moment, I knew in my soul that my professional life as a lawyer had taken a turn. The state had power. It was not just the law that was an instrument for justice; government itself could be that instrument, if wielded correctly and in good faith.

16

LA SIERRA

Late in the morning on March 6, 1989, two legislators showed up in the governor's executive offices at the Capitol in a state of near panic. Senator Larry Trujillo, a Democrat from Pueblo, and Representative Lewis Entz, a Republican whose district included the Valley, were there to tell us that "all hell has broken loose in San Luis."

Stewart Bliss, the governor's highly effective chief of staff, quickly convened a meeting. Stewart, a Republican who had been a successful business executive with Kaman Corporation, had an impeccable reputation as a problem solver. I had helped the governor convince Stewart to leave the private sector and take the job; fortunately, he had accepted.

We huddled in the conference room as Senator Trujillo and Representative Entz told the governor, Stewart, and me about a massive raid led by federal law enforcement against alleged "illegal poachers" just before dawn in and around San Luis.

I knew San Luis well. Located in the heart of Costilla County, it is the oldest continuously inhabited town in Colorado, having been officially established by a group of hardy Mexican American settlers moving north from Taos in 1851. Father Pat Valdez, the man who'd married Hope and me, was the local priest, and whenever I passed through town on the way to Los Rincones, I'd try to stop and visit him in the small rectory behind his church. The community there was mostly Mexican American, and the town itself was quiet and small—nothing like Alamosa, which felt like a huge metropolis by comparison.

But it hadn't been quiet that morning.

As soon as I heard them say "all hell has broken loose," I assumed the Taylor Ranch was at the center of the raid. My assumption was correct. The Taylor Ranch, a 77,000-acre tract of land, stretched from the valley floor just east of San Luis up into the foothills and peaks of the Sangre de Cristo Mountains—including the towering 14,047-foot Culebra Peak, the only privately owned fourteener in the state. The land was owned by a North Carolina logging magnate named Jack Taylor, but the locals still hunted on it and took small amounts of firewood every year. They didn't call this land "the Taylor Ranch"; for them, it had always been "La Sierra."

They used La Sierra in this way because they believed they had the right to do so. The residents were the heirs of the original grantees of the Sangre de Cristo Land Grant of 1844, issued by the Mexican government back when this area was part of Mexico. After the Mexican-American War, the Treaty of Guadalupe Hidalgo guaranteed these rights. Article VIII of the Treaty stated that "property of every kind now belonging to Mexicans now established there shall be inviolably protected." Besides, hunting and gathering in these lands wasn't just their way of life, it was a necessity: Costilla County was then and is now the poorest county in Colorado. At the time, around 36 percent of residents lived below the poverty line. For locals, the food and fuel gracing the Sangre de Cristo foothills were there for the taking. Just as they always had been.

According to Trujillo, however, these subsistence hunters were now being labeled as illegal poachers, and the action against them involved hundreds of state and federal law enforcement agents. There'd been Black Hawk helicopters, men in SWAT gear, and a lot of guns.

"These men were arrested at gunpoint in their pajamas, Governor," Trujillo exclaimed, "right in front of their wives and kids, and taken from their homes in handcuffs. The community is up in arms."

"We're both concerned there might be violence," added Entz, who seemed more sympathetic to the raids. Nevertheless, he was genuinely concerned for what might happen. "People could be killed. We think you need to send someone down there with authority to quiet things down."

Governor Romer leaned back in his chair, his fingers laced in front of him. "Ken can go with both of you to evaluate the situation and report back to me. You can take my plane, right away." He didn't have to tell any of us twice.

Senator Trujillo, Representative Entz, and I left for the airport immediately. We quickly boarded the governor's small King Air turboprop for the one-hour flight to Alamosa. I peered out the window as we crossed over the jagged snow-packed peaks surrounding Medano Pass, where it seemed as if the tops of the mountains could nearly touch our wingtips.

En route, I learned a bit more about what had happened from Trujillo and Entz, though their details were still spotty. It seemed that the raid had come as the result of a two-and-a-half-year undercover operation undertaken by the US Fish and Wildlife Service, the FBI, and the Colorado Division of Wildlife. Federal agents had posed as buyers of hunting trophies—antlers, elk heads, and eagles, which were endangered and illegal to kill or possess—in order to build a case against these suspected poachers. Using these trophies as evidence, along with statements allegedly made by the men who'd killed the animals, the feds had secured warrants and, that very morning, executed the raids.

All three of us, as well as the governor, knew that tensions between the locals and the Taylor Ranch had been at a low simmer for some time. And the situation had already boiled over at least once. A few years earlier, Jack Taylor was sleeping in his bedroom at the ranch's lodge when shots rang out. It is not uncommon to hear the crackling patter of gunshots in the Valley at any time of day or night, but it is rare in the extreme for those shots to be directed at a house. Glass shattered, wood splintered—and Taylor was hit in the leg. The presumed reason for the attack? Taylor had recently fenced off part of his land, thereby restricting access to grounds the locals regarded as public use.

That night, Joe Espinoza, then the mayor of San Luis, personally drove the wounded Taylor two hours north to Pueblo for medical treatment. Taylor recovered. But after he got back on his feet, he never returned to the Valley.

The ranch sat in a kind of limbo after that, its future uncertain, its fences still standing but its owner gone. This is usually the goal when people shoot up a house: to scare people off. And so the locals went back to their old ways—hunting elk in the fall, gathering firewood before winter, running a few cattle up the mountain slopes in summer. It was an uneasy peace. The boiling pot returned to a simmer.

Until these raids, of course. Our King Air touched down at the Alamosa airport—a small rural airport with just a couple of hangars and an office building. We taxied, stopping next to one of the Black Hawk helicopters that had been used in the operation. It looked totally out of place, an instrument of war in this remote mountain town. We deplaned and were met by a state trooper and other officials. We'd planned to visit the jail straight away, but one of the officials told me that Chips Barry, the director of Colorado's Department of Natural Resources, urgently needed to speak with me. A local official led me to a small room inside the main building and closed the door. A minute or two later, the phone rang. I picked up.

"Hello, this is Ken," I said.

"Ken. Chips Barry here. You in the Valley?"

"Yes, we just landed. Still at the airport."

"Are you alone?"

I wasn't sure why that mattered, but I responded, "Yes."

"Look, this operation is highly sensitive. Be careful what you say."

Was Chips threatening me in some way? He had left me in the dark, in my view, doing a disservice to the governor. "You should have told me about this," I said pointedly.

Chips responded, "All confidentiality needed to be maintained. After I was brought into the loop, I only told the governor—me and the US attorney went and briefed him a few days ago."

My heart skipped a beat. "I should have been in that room, Chips."

"Yeah, but the feds told us they'd be going house to house throughout San Luis as well as some other towns in Colorado and New Mexico, and we needed total confidentiality." I didn't like the implication: that as someone from the San Luis Valley I might have jeopardized the operation if I'd known about it.

"Thank you, Chips. I understand the ethical demands of my office. You should have briefed me. Instead, you kept me in the dark. Now you've put the governor in the middle of this mess."

I could picture Chips's face turning red as he said, "Ken, I wanted to protect you. I know some of your family live in the area, and I didn't want you to be in a compromising position."

"Protect me? Bullshit." I don't curse often, and Chips knew that. "Don't patronize me. And for what it's worth, my family doesn't live in San Luis or Costilla County. They live thirty miles west of there, on the other side of the Rio Grande." I took a deep breath. "I'll see you when I get back to Denver."

I ended the call and rejoined the others. Soon enough, the State Patrol drove us to the Alamosa County Jail, the only facility in the Valley large enough to accommodate the number of arrestees. Tempers were running high in San Luis and it was safer for everyone if these men were held elsewhere. No one wanted a riot.

The Alamosa Jail was a low brick building that held maybe a dozen people on any given day for things like disorderly conduct or DUI. But that day was different. Even the parking lot was chaos—crowded with federal vehicles, State Patrol cars, and unmarked sedans with government plates.

One hundred and ten men had been arrested. Inside the jail, men were being processed, fingerprinted, and photographed. They sat on benches, most in their own clothes, a couple in jumpsuits. Almost to a man, they looked equal measures angry and bewildered. These were not hardened criminals; they were regular local people. I'd later learn that several of these men and their neighbors, some elderly and afraid, couldn't understand why their yards and fields were suddenly crawling with bands of men with tactical gear and automatic weapons—or why these men were breaking down the doors of their trailers and family homes while the sun rose over the Sangre de Cristo Mountains. One man later told a reporter from the *LA Times*, "I woke up and thought it was an invasion, maybe of aliens, or Russians," he said. "Then I found out it was our government."

We were directed into a small conference room in the jail and given a briefing by some of the officials in charge. They covered the staging, the equipment used, the number of people arrested, and the general evidence supporting the raid. I listened and asked questions, as did Trujillo and Entz. I was in fact-finding mode, but I also questioned whether this massive law enforcement action had been necessary. Had they considered a less intrusive way to get these guys? Had they thought of involving the local sheriffs in some way? Could they have acted differently to protect the well-being of the innocent women, children, and elders who'd witnessed their family members being cuffed and taken away at gunpoint?

We got some answers. It seemed that, no, they had not considered less intrusive methods. Furthermore, it seemed that the buyer—one of the undercover agents—had made a point of purchasing eagles, among other things. Eagles are protected, and any killing or selling of them is strictly forbidden. He'd purchased ninety-five. Here was a government employee, a member of the US Fish and Wildlife Service, essentially creating a market for contraband, the procurement of which involved murdering one of the very species his agency was tasked with protecting. To make matters worse, the officials involved appeared to have preyed not only on these majestic creatures but on the poverty of the men they were targeting. In a community where average household incomes were around $7,500 per year, the $200 or $300 these alleged poachers received for delivering an eagle was real money.

And of course, there was at least the stench, if not actual evidence, of racial bias, since the accused were Mexican American.

As one local put it, the problem lay in "the way they handled the situation, the tactics they used—the guerrilla tactics. We're not bad people here."

The San Luis Town Council would later state in a resolution that the federal agents had "creat[ed] a market for the purchase of wildlife from unsuspecting victims of entrapment." In no way did I condone or support the killing of any of this wildlife, but as the defendants would argue, the government had manufactured crimes that wouldn't have existed without their intervention. Nevertheless, some defendants would be prosecuted and subjected to various fines and other penalties.

The community's trust in government, already fragile, had been shattered.

I spent nearly four years as Governor Romer's legal counsel. In 1990, he appointed me to be director of the Department of Natural Resources (DNR)—ironically, to take over Chips Barry's job. One of my first tasks, at the governor's direction, was to diversify the executive ranks of this agency, which when I came in consisted almost exclusively of white men.

There were eighty executive members of the various commissions in charge of wildlife, water, parks, oil and gas, and other natural resources across the state. None were Black, or Hispanic, or Native American. There was only one woman, Rebecca Frank from Grand Junction.

At the governor's direction, I'd already spent years pushing to diversify Colorado's state workforce, including at the DNR. But the general response was always the same: "Ken, we agree that it's exactly what we ought to be doing. The problem is we can't find qualified women or minorities." In my view, this was the same ignorant response put up by anyone who didn't want to make a real effort to diversify. In this case, I told them exactly what they needed to do: Meet with organizations, reach out to communities, and advertise—literally, in newspapers and on the radio—that the DNR wanted diversity. But the boards remained captive to the patronage of the good old boys' network.

So I put the word out. I organized a recruitment summit with nearly a thousand people, attended by environmental groups, hunting and angling groups, and minority and women's organizations. The summit was a success. The next day, the headline in Colorado's *Rocky Mountain News* declared, "Minorities Wanted."

I put up Jesse Boyd, a Black pastor from Denver who loved to get out on the streams and fish whenever he could. I put up Arnold Salazar (no relation) from the Valley, who—like most people from the Valley—had been hunting since he was a kid. I picked Vicki Cowart, a respected geologist, to lead the Colorado Geological Survey, and Laurie Mathews to head up State Parks. Laurie would go on to lead the creation of Colorado's premier conservation program, known around the nation as Great Outdoors Colorado, and she and Vicki would signal to women that the natural resources and environmental world was for them too.

But the Senate Agriculture, Natural Resources, and Energy Committee chair, Republican Senator Tillie Bishop from Grand Junction, decided to oppose the nominations of Jesse Boyd and Arnold Salazar, the only Black and Hispanic nominees to the Wildlife Commission. I met with Senator Bishop, but he wouldn't budge. I then wrote him a letter, explaining that the DNR was trying to overcome the exclusion of women and minorities and to include all communities in the use and protection of our natural resources. I got no response.

I finally called him. I said, "Senator Bishop—Tillie—you are my friend, but what you're doing is wrong. You aren't even giving Jesse and Arnold a chance to prove themselves! At the very least, they deserve a hearing to make their case."

Senator Bishop responded, "Well, Ken, I've spoken to the director of the Division of Wildlife, and he believes there are more qualified people than Jesse Boyd and Arnold Salazar. What's the use deliberating over them if they're not going to pass muster anyway?"

"How can you say that if you haven't even given them a hearing?" I asked forcefully. "Tillie, if this is going to be your position, I'm going to have to publicize a letter I have written holding you responsible for the lack of diversity in the Department."

Tillie responded, "I'm sorry, Ken. Your director of the Division of Wildlife simply doesn't think they're qualified. That's just how it is."

"Well, Tillie," I responded, "in that case, I'll do what I have to do." With that, the call ended.

Despite Tillie's stubbornness on our phone call, it didn't take long for him to buckle. That Monday, he scheduled the hearing first thing—before I got the letter out. Both were eventually confirmed.

To the surprise of many, but not to me or the governor, our candidates were great successes. Arnold Salazar would go on to serve eight years on the Wildlife Commission, and his work was impressive enough that even the hunters and anglers who'd opposed him eventually nominated him for chairman—a position he held for four years. As for Jesse Boyd, a park on Colorado Boulevard in Denver bears his name to this day, honoring his impact in his community and government, demonstrating to Black kids that Colorado's lands and rivers also belong to them, and always will. I was gratified when Tillie pulled me aside a few years later and said, "Ken, you were right. These guys are good. And they changed the Department for the better. Thank you for pushing us to include more people like them." I smiled, shook his hand, and hugged him.

Appointment by appointment, meeting by meeting, we changed the face of Colorado's natural resources management. By the time I left in 1994, those commissions still had room for improvement, but they were no longer the exclusive clubs they'd been before. We'd proved that diversity wasn't about lowering standards—it was about finally recognizing that major talent had been locked out of the room for far too long.

Meanwhile, down in the Valley, the Taylor Ranch remained. Jack Taylor had died in 1988, and his estate was managed by his son, Zach, who wasn't quite sure what to do with his father's big tract of Colorado land.

To me, this was an opportunity.

I called Zach Taylor and asked if he would be interested in selling the ranch to the state. He said, "Yes, if we can get the right price."

In 1993, I went to Governor Romer with a proposal. "I think you should create a commission," I said. "Bring everyone to the table—ranchers, environmental groups, county commissioners, the local community, economic development people. Let's solve this once and for all."

Governor Romer agreed, and the Sangre de Cristo Land Grant Commission was born. It came together even faster than I hoped, garnering twenty-three members representing every conceivable interest. There was Father Pat Valdez; the mayor of San Luis, Joe Espinoza; Charlie Jaquez from the Land Rights Council; the Costilla County commissioners; and state legislators like my friends Representative Lewis Entz and Senator Tillie Bishop, both Republicans. There were environmental groups worried about watershed protection and endangered species. And there were San Luis Valley economic development representatives looking for opportunities to help Colorado's poorest and least built-up county.

We met throughout the summer and into the fall. I drove back and forth from Denver, sometimes twice a week, building trust and working to find common ground. By September, we had a plan: The state would purchase the ranch for $30 million and manage it jointly with local communities. Historic subsistence rights would be recognized and allowed—hunting, fishing, gathering firewood for personal use, and building small corrals and buildings for non-commercial activity. Conservation management would protect the watersheds and sensitive wildlife. Any logging would be carefully managed. Recreation opportunities would be created to help people access the mountains and climb Culebra Peak, bringing tourist dollars to a place that desperately needed money. We would also create a nationally recognized visitor center that explained the history of the Sangre de Cristo Land Grant. It was everything I'd hoped for.

The final public review meeting was set for September 27, 1993, in the San Luis Parish Hall. It was packed when I arrived. I recognized many faces: people whose families had been in the Valley as long as mine. But there were others I didn't know.

Father Pat opened with a prayer for wisdom and peace. I began my presentation, explaining how the plan would work, how it honored both history and practical needs. For the first few minutes, it seemed to go well. People were listening, nodding.

Then someone shouted from the back: "Vendido!"

Sellout.

More shouts followed. "The government stole this land!"

"They should give it back for free!"

"Why should we compromise? It's ours!"

I tried to explain that neither the Taylor estate nor Colorado would simply hand over $30 million worth of land and that this plan was good for everyone. But the protesters, though few in number, just got louder and louder. Most of the local residents were silent and seemed embarrassed. Father Pat was red-faced. The commission members and stakeholders were in disbelief after all the community outreach.

I suddenly noticed one of the standing agitators holding a rifle. It was pointed at the ground, but it seemed to be in a ready position. The sheriff's deputies moved closer to me.

"You don't belong here!" someone screamed, even though I'd grown up just thirty miles away and my family had been in the Valley for generations. "Get out!"

I tried to bring order, telling the protesters they were free to express their opposition directly to me during the public comment period and also to sit and talk with me after the meeting. But neither the sheriff's deputies, Father Pat, nor I could calm or appease them, and the shouting continued. Ultimately, I recessed the meeting and huddled with the other commissioners, telling them we would reconvene and deliver the report to the governor as planned. They agreed and I adjourned the gathering, informing the crowd that Father Pat and I would work with the local community to attempt to resolve the issues raised in the room.

Over the next month, I traveled to San Luis every weekend to present the commission report to church gatherings at all the local villages. Without the agitators, these presentations went smoothly, and the community once again expressed its support.

But then, one Saturday before the evening mass, the agitators from the public review meeting showed up again, sitting in the front pew. As I began to speak, they shouted that Father Pat was out of line for letting me be there. I asked for calm, and this time I was able to finish my presentation.

Afterward, as I walked out of the church with Father Pat, we were confronted by the protesters. There was a lot more shouting, and I tried again to make my case. Finally, Father Pat took me by the arm and led me into the rectory. He told me to come back the next morning after the 11:00 AM mass to address the congregation once again. I agreed and left to drive the thirty miles back to Los Rincones, where Hope and our two girls, Melinda and Andrea, who'd been born in 1988, slept. The whole time, as I drove across the desert landscape, I scanned the rearview mirror to make sure I wasn't being followed. This was customary nighttime situational alertness for me, having driven endless miles throughout the Valley. But this night, I had a heightened concern given what had just happened in front of the church.

Early the next morning, Father Pat called me at my parents' home in Los Rincones. He sounded concerned. "Ken, don't come back to San Luis today. It's not safe for you here."

We went about our morning and, after mass at our church in Conejos, started the five-hour drive back to Denver. I decided I wanted to see Father Pat in person, so when we passed through San Luis, I drove to the rectory and parked outside. All was quiet. I went up to the unassuming building and rang the doorbell for Father Pat. But he didn't answer. I thought I caught a glimpse of someone moving a curtain in the upstairs window. I rang again, but still no one answered. It was like San Luis had become a ghost town. I walked back to our Jeep, hopped in, and left.

A little while later, I delivered the final report to the governor, who accepted the recommendations. But after the contentious public review meeting, the legislators on the commission decided that community support was insufficient for the project to proceed. Senator Bishop and Representative Entz withdrew their support. That was the effective end of the Sangre de Cristo Land Grant Commission, and the sale never went through. Thirty million dollars, meaningful development, land use rights, an official recognition of the history of San Luis, the land grants, and the Valley—all gone. The community never benefited.

The ranch was eventually sold to another wealthy out-of-state buyer. Then another. And another. Today, it's owned by a Texas man who is building a sixteen-foot-high fence around it and buying as much adjacent land as he can. With Governor Jared Polis's support, the Colorado legislature passed a bill in 2025 requiring county approval for such fences, which was a small victory in a war that began over a century ago, when the original Mexican land grants were in dispute. And in 2026, the unending and bitter litigation continues, with a legion of Colorado's best lawyers representing the residents of the community pro bono against the Texas landowner.

I've often thought and even dreamed about that night in the parish hall—and about Father Pat's warning. About how I couldn't return to a place that was, by all reasonable accounts, one of *my* places. I also thought about the role of government in community affairs. Sometimes being right isn't enough. Sometimes building consensus isn't enough. Sometimes the old wounds run too deep, and the mistrust is too strong. But you keep trying, because democratic government—for all its flaws—is still the only tool big enough to address historical injustices. It's the only way to build a community that serves the greatest possible number of people, even if it is rarely, if ever, perfect.

17

FIRST RUN

Governor Romer leaned back in his chair, studying me with his sharp, bespectacled eyes. It was late spring 1997, and I'd asked to meet with him in his office on East Colfax Avenue to discuss something that had been gnawing at me for months. I'd been out of government since early 1995, working in the private sector on natural resources and environmental issues, but I wanted to return to public service. I'd learned the power of the state under Governor Romer—who was term-limited and would be out of office after 1998—and I felt like I could do more good for more people as an elected official.

We sat at the same table where Romer and I had met countless times. Afternoon light slanted through the tall windows, illuminating the dust motes dancing between us.

After catching up, Governor Romer asked, "So Ken, to what do I owe the pleasure?"

"Well . . . I'd like to run for office."

"You want my job?" he asked with a smile.

"No. I mean, maybe, but I'm a long way from that. I want to run for attorney general, Governor."

"Ah," he said, smiling. Standing from his chair, he walked to the window, his hands clasped behind his back. "You would be a fantastic AG, Ken. I have some thoughts about it."

"Thank you, sir."

He turned and faced me. "So what's your platform? I know how you like to keep notes. Surely, you've written this all out."

I smiled. "You're right. The platform is simple: I want to make communities safe. Fight crime and gang violence. Protect the elderly and the vulnerable. And stand up for rural Colorado. I want to protect the environment and serve as a steward for land and water as well as agricultural communities like the one I come from. These appear to be at odds sometimes—conservation and agriculture—but if my family has learned anything, it's that they actually go hand in hand."

He nodded thoughtfully. "That'll play across the state. You have my support, Ken. You would have had it no matter what, but this is a good platform. It can win. But . . ." The governor paused.

"Yes?" I prompted.

"You know I speak my mind. I have to tell you candidly, you have rocks in your knapsack that I never had in mine. This state is conservative and has never elected a Hispanic to any statewide office. You're from a place very few people have heard of, you are a Democrat, and you are Hispanic."

"Governor, those rocks are useful. They've made me stronger. I can lean on my background in farming and ranching and as a water expert. I can appeal to rural Colorado and also to folks here in Denver. As a Mexican American, I can organize the Hispanic community to vote in record numbers. I want to put together a unity platform. And what's more, I think this state is ready for that. To be honest, I think it's been *waiting* for that, whether people know it or not. But there's only one way to find out."

The governor said, "I will help you in every way I can, but it won't be easy. So let's get to work. What do you want me to do?"

I had been hoping he'd say that. I quickly responded, "Will you send a letter to your supporters asking them to help me and my campaign?"

He agreed immediately. "Of course. Write it for me, and we will get it out!"

And with that, I was on my way.

I got to work. My friend Joan Padilla and her sister Angela recruited an army of volunteers. Along with my secretary and trusted aide, Velina Wallick, I mapped out the state, developed databases, and came up with a plan to establish grassroots operations in each of Colorado's sixty-three counties. And we landed on a slogan: "Fighting for Colorado's Land, Water, and People."

Almost as soon as I started campaigning, I was asked about my slogan: "Why don't the 'people' come first?" Often, it was folks in Denver, Boulder, or the suburbs who asked this, which made sense. City people hardly give a second thought to the land their house or apartment building sits on, and they take water, which flows from the tap, entirely for granted. They don't have to think about reservoirs or well pumps or irrigation ditches or headgates, and that's fine. It's one of the benefits of city living.

So I would respectfully remind them of what I regarded as an eternal truth: "Because without land or water, you don't have any people." That usually got a smile.

Of course, I practically never had to explain my slogan to people out in the plains or mountains, especially where it concerned water. As the saying goes, "Whiskey is for drinking and water is for fighting." That's the West in a nutshell for you.

Beyond that, the slogan reflected who I was and where I came from, which I was all too happy to discuss as I crisscrossed the state.

Not long after my meeting with Governor Romer, I headed down to the Valley in my green 1994 Ford Ranger pickup to have it serviced before hitting the road for the next eighteen months. In Manassa, I pulled into my cousin Harold's repair shop, where he had been caring for our family's vehicles for years. (Harold and his sister, Dora, were my godparents and had baptized me in 1955. It was Dora who gave me the name Kenneth—for reasons I still do not understand.) We did a lot of our own repair work, and the truck was in excellent shape, but with all I was undertaking, I didn't want to miss anything.

I handed Harold the keys and asked him to give it a full inspection: belts, filters, tires, brakes, oil, fluids—everything. "I'm going to put thirty or forty thousand miles on this thing, easy," I said in Spanish.

"This for that political thing you're doing?" Harold asked.

"Yessir," I said.

"You got my vote, Ken Salazar!"

One down, many more to go.

Aside from a campaign vehicle, I also needed one more critical component for my run at attorney general: a campaign manager.

My friend Tom Strickland had someone in mind. He called me one morning and said, "Ken, you need to meet Ken Lane."

"Two Kens?"

He laughed. "Yes. He was a campaign manager for Ben Nighthorse Campbell and was his chief of staff in the House and Senate. Before, you know . . ."

I did know. Ben Nighthorse Campbell had been a Democrat and, at that moment, was the only Native American in the US Senate, as well as only the fifth Native US senator of all time. But during his first term in the Senate, he became increasingly disillusioned with what he perceived to be the Democratic Party's dismissal of rural and Native issues. He officially became a Republican on March 3, 1995.

"Where is Ken Lane now?" I asked.

"He works at the Pentagon. But he's in Pueblo all the time—his family is there. I'll put you in touch. Maybe he'll be interested."

Over the 1997 Christmas holiday, Hope, Melinda, Andrea, and I stopped at a restaurant in the Holiday Inn in Pueblo while on our way to the Valley. There we sat with Ken Lane, a white man with brown wavy hair and erudite-looking glasses. Over breakfast, Hope and I sized him up while the girls colored on placemats.

After we got through the pleasantries, Ken Lane said, "So you're going to run for AG?"

"That's the plan."

"Against the Republican tide that's coming?" He wasn't being pessimistic, just realistic. "Campbell's going to cruise to reelection now that he's switched parties. Bill Owens is probably going to be our next governor. Republicans might win everything in the state."

"Except attorney general," I said.

He studied me for a moment, then laughed. "I like the confidence." He leaned forward. "Look, I left Campbell's office because I believe in what the Democratic Party stands for—opportunity for working people, environmental protection, and equal justice under the law. But you're going to need more than principles to win this thing."

"What do I need?"

"You need to be everywhere. You need to outwork, outhustle, and outlast your opponent."

"That's what I do best, Ken Lane."

"You need to transcend or circumvent party politics." He paused. "And you need someone like me managing the campaign while you're out there being the candidate."

"So you're interested?"

"You bet."

I looked at Hope. She nodded. "Then Ken Lane, you're hired." I stuck my hand across the table, and we shook. We would work out the specifics later, but I had my campaign manager.

We put together detailed plans on criminal justice and increasing safety in communities, protecting businesses and consumers, and protecting Colorado's land and water. I presented those plans to skeptical advocacy groups, voters, and members of the media who were unsure what to make of an underdog Mexican American running against a typical "strong on crime" Republican, former District Attorney John Suthers.

On the campaign trail throughout Colorado, I encountered the reality Governor Romer had warned about. At a luncheon in Fort Collins in Larimer County, the home of Colorado State University, I asked a group of about ten people—all Democrats—for their advice.

Sue Furniss, a local party leader, expressed her support for me but also cautioned, "Larimer County will be difficult. When I moved here from the East Coast in the 1950s, I saw signs on restaurants that read, 'Whites Only.' I was confused since I didn't see any Black people anywhere. I was later told that the signs were intended to keep Mexicans out, that these Mexicans belonged north of the railroad on the other side of town, where all the laborers lived. I'm telling you, Ken, it's hard to win here as a Democrat. Mexican or not."

The room went quiet. This blatant prejudice was not ancient history, but within living memory. Undeterred, I asked this group if they would help. I recounted my family's connection to Colorado State University in Fort Collins—Leroy, John, Margaret, and June were all alums—and highlighted the lead role CSU played in Colorado agriculture. I promised I would come to Larimer County as many times as it took to turn the tide. In the end, the group agreed to become my local organizing committee.

In the spring of 1998, during the Democratic Party's local assembly in a rock-ribbed Republican county on the eastern plains, I asked a local organizer if he would be one of my coordinators. He agreed, but like Sue Furniss, told me flat-out that I had a tough row to hoe.

At the county assembly, he addressed the small crowd, saying, "I know you're wondering whether Ken Salazar is qualified to be attorney general. The office requires one to be a lawyer in good standing. He is Mexican, and so I too wondered whether he was qualified, but I went to Denver and checked with the Supreme Court, and he is a lawyer in good standing. I've met with him several times. He's a rancher himself and is committed to helping us in these rural areas. Nobody from Denver really cares to listen to us—but Ken Salazar does."

This white man from the prairies had initially met me with suspicion, but once he got to know me, he embraced me with everything he had. He worked relentlessly, organizing the county, putting up billboards, and ultimately getting me more Republican votes in that county than anyone ever expected.

That year, my green Ford Ranger ended up logging more than fifty thousand miles and traversing every county in the state. Cheyenne County, where I talked to wheat farmers about water rights. Mineral County, where old-time miners worried about environmental regulations killing their livelihood. Summit County, where ski resort workers couldn't afford to live in the towns in which they worked. Pueblo County, where some of my family members still worked in what was left of the steel industry. Mesa County, where conservative Republicans wondered if I'd protect their gun rights. Boulder County, where liberals wondered if I was progressive enough. Every single county, multiple times. Local fairs, Rotary Clubs, chambers of commerce, high school gymnasiums, VFW halls, church basements. Wherever two or more Coloradans were gathered, I was there, usually arriving in my green pickup, always ready to talk about Colorado's land, water, and people.

November 3, 1998, was my first real election day. Yes, I'd been involved in elections for other people, principally Governor Romer, but this was the first one where I was on the ballot. I did not sleep.

Whether you expect to win or lose, every election night is exhilarating. In this case, I didn't know what to expect. All the other races—for governor, the state legislature, and Congress—looked like certain Republican wins. And later in the evening, when a local TV station, Channel 9, started calling races, Ken Lane's prediction was borne out.

In 1998, at least, Colorado was a red state. Bill Owens won the governorship, Campbell won the Senate, and all statewide elected offices seemed like they would be held by Republicans.

The clock ticked past midnight, and November 3 turned to November 4. The outcome of the attorney general race was still up in the air. Within the campaign, there had been wild speculation that I had won, then that I'd lost, then that I'd won again. At one point, my friend Floyd Ciruli, a pollster and commentator on Channel 9, called the election for my opponent. Floyd seemed sad as he made the announcement. But other outlets left it open. The main holdout was Larimer County, where I'd spent so much time and effort with my friends Al Yates, Sue Furniss, Pat Stryker, and Crissie Snow. The suspense was unbearable, and even though I still had a shot, I was prepared to lose. If I did, I knew in my heart that it wouldn't be for lack of effort or grit. I had given it my best shot.

An air of melancholy descended over me in the middle of that night. The whole thing had been a roller coaster, and I wanted off, at least for a few hours. I left Joan Padilla, my campaign volunteers, and the rest of my staff at around 2:00 AM and drove home. Hope and the girls had gone to bed. Most of the rest of my family was in town for the big day, and Leroy and Elaine were up, so I sat with them for a while before trying to get an hour or two of sleep on the couch. It was impossible.

After what felt like a lifetime, the sky outside began to brighten, turning a drab gray before hinting at blue as the sun crested the horizon. Hope woke up and brewed a pot of coffee, whose pleasant smell filled the kitchen and dining room. She made me a cup—one sugar, a little half-and-half—and set it in front of me. "Any news?" she asked.

"Not yet," I said.

"Well, that's better than 'Ken Salazar lost,' right?"

"Yes. Yes, it is."

A short while later, the phone rang in the kitchen. It was still before 7:00 AM. I grabbed my coffee, went to the kitchen, and picked up.

"Hello?" I answered.

"Ken?" a familiar voice said.

"Yes."

"John Suthers," the voice said. I'd heard it many times before on the radio, on TV, and across the debate stage. Butterflies suddenly fluttered in my stomach. "I want to congratulate you. The results from Larimer County are in, and it seems as though you've pulled ahead. I am conceding the race."

Hiding my elation, I replied sincerely, "Thank you. You ran a good campaign, and I look forward to working with you after things settle down."

I hung up and pumped my fist. Then I whooped to Hope—a little too loudly, considering the girls were still asleep. "We did it! We got this!" I exclaimed.

In the end, I prevailed by eleven thousand votes. Not a landslide, but decisive enough to avoid a recount. I was the only Democrat elected to statewide office that year, and the first Hispanic elected to statewide office in Colorado history. As it turned out, my 1998 election for attorney general was a bellwether for Colorado. Things were changing, and within only ten years, Colorado would go from an almost-red state to a reliably blue one.

Inauguration day was January 12, 1999. The air was crisp and cold. The ceremony was held on the west steps of the Capitol, the same building where I'd worked for Governor Romer, where I'd first learned that good leadership in government could achieve faster, more effective results than litigation alone.

Mom and Dad drove up from the Valley in their good clothes—Dad wearing the same dark suit he'd worn to every important event since my high school graduation, Mom in a blue dress. My brothers and sisters came from California, from Texas, from the Valley. Hope stood beside me with Andrea and Melinda, our daughters now old enough to understand that something important was happening.

The oath was administered by Supreme Court Chief Justice Mary Mullarkey, who'd given me my first paid internship years earlier when she served as the state's solicitor general. It was a historic moment: the state's first female chief justice swearing in the state's first Hispanic attorney general. We smiled at each other, fully aware that we were breaking barriers together. And though we didn't say it—we didn't need to—we knew there were many more barriers ahead.

As I laid my hand on the Bible and repeated the oath, I couldn't help but think of so many people who'd helped me reach this moment. J.T. Canales, the Hispanic trailblazer at Michigan Law. Dad and Mom, living examples of tireless hard work and a refusal to give up. Leandro and his work with the United Farm Workers. And Coach White, my booster in high school who'd argued for me and against his racist peers as they nominated students for the National Honor Society. He'd said, "Ken, this is why you need to come back here. So you can help change these things." I realized proudly that I was making good on the promise I had made to Coach White.

After the oath, I wrapped an arm around Hope and raised my fist to the crowd. I smiled so hard it hurt. It was a good gathering, full of people from all over Colorado: Hispanic and white and Black, rural and urban, Republican and Democrat. My entire staff was there, including my volunteers, Governor Romer, and the hundreds of people who had worked on the campaign and who'd believed I could win. They had given me a shot at the basket, and I had delivered.

The newly inaugurated Governor Owens shook my hand. "Congratulations, Attorney General Salazar. I look forward to working with you."

"Thank you, Governor. I look forward to working with you too."

I was sincere. Being the only Democrat in statewide office meant I'd have to work across the aisle every single day. It meant finding common ground and rejecting division. It meant demonstrating that I was there to serve all of Colorado—its land, its water, and its people.

18

THE FIGHT FOR DIVERSITY

Immediately following my victory but before I was sworn in, I took a "thank you" tour of Colorado, driving thousands of miles across the plains and mountains, through towns and cities and the largely uninhabited parts of the state. In the Valley, I returned to Centauri High to attend a school-wide celebration for my victory that had been organized by school counselor—and dear friend—Celina Espinoza. As I celebrated with the people who had supported me, I remembered the joy my mother took in the freedom of driving when she finally obtained her license, and my spirits rose even further.

Mile after mile, I listened to Bruce Springsteen's rendition of "This Land Is Your Land," to Willie Nelson, Kris Kristofferson, and Dolly Parton, to Mexican American music like Los Huracanes del Norte and Little Joe y la Familia, as well as to the famous civil rights songs of the 1960s. I memorized "No Nos Moverán," Joan Baez's rendition of the farmworkers' anthem "We Shall Not Be Moved," often thinking about the laborers stooped over in the summer in Weld and Mesa Counties, picking crops that fed the nation. I sang along with Pete Seeger's "We

Shall Overcome" as he insisted, "We are not afraid!" The breadth of music and the variety of people I met reminded me of why I'd run in the first place. I believed wholeheartedly that walking the talk on diversity was imperative. Everyone had to be in the room.

Which is why I assembled the most diverse team in Colorado history in the Department of Law at 1525 Sherman Street. Women and men, Black, brown, and white, all in leadership positions and as practicing line attorneys.

We faced many challenges. When the Columbine High School shooting occurred in April 1999, I spent most of my time working with law enforcement, victims' families, and schools to strengthen crisis response and safety protocols. Our office established a fugitive prosecution unit that worked with the Mexican government under Article IV of their Federal Penal Code to apprehend and prosecute murderers who had fled Colorado to Mexico. Some of the murders in question were decades old, but we believed no one was above the law and that the victims' families still deserved justice. We fought consumer fraud, protected water rights for rural communities against raids like those of billionaire-funded American Water Development, Inc., and stood up to predatory lenders targeting vulnerable Coloradans. Through it all, we transformed the office into one that fought actively for justice. It was everything I'd hoped for as a law student.

I cruised to reelection in 2002, claiming over 57 percent of the vote, with support from both rural and urban voters and both Democrats and Republicans. I felt like I had succeeded in uniting Colorado.

Then, in early 2003, a call came that would crystallize everything my office and I had been working for. It was from Dean Jeff Lehman of Michigan Law. I'd had some cursory contact with Dean Lehman, so we knew each other, but we weren't in the habit of making social calls. After he introduced himself, I asked, "What can I do for you?"

"I need something important, Attorney General Salazar."

"Please, call me Ken."

"Well, to be frank, our school is in the bull's eye, Ken. I assume you've heard of Barbara Grutter?"

Of course I had. She was a white Michigander who'd sued the university in 1997, claiming reverse discrimination after being denied admission to the law school. She claimed she would have gotten in if Michigan didn't have an affirmative action program that gave "her" slot to a minority. The case, *Grutter v. Bollinger*, had been going on for years and would be heard by the US Supreme Court in the spring of 2003.

I told Dean Lehman I'd been following the case. He said, "I know this is a big request, Ken, but I was hoping you might file an amicus brief with the Court for us. Would you consider that?"

I leaned back in my chair and looked out at the Denver skyline. Twenty-three years earlier, I'd driven to Ann Arbor as a young Mexican American student that Michigan had actively recruited. Now, I was being asked to help defend the very programs that had opened doors for students like me.

"Dean Lehman," I said, "I'm honored you called. I'm happy to do it. Let me think about how to go about it and get back to you."

"Thank you, Ken."

"You'll hear from me soon." I hung up.

Supporting Michigan in this case came with significant political risk. By then, I had a plan for my future. In the back of my friend Paul Sandoval's tamale shop, we'd sketched it out on a napkin. I would run for governor in 2006, and if I won that and it went well, then I would consider running for president in 2012. But filing an amicus on behalf of Michigan meant I would be attacked by Colorado conservatives opposed to affirmative action, as well as some Democrats who were leery of racial issues and diversity. Those attacks had the potential to derail my future ambitions.

I called Hope to make sure I wasn't making a mistake—and also to gauge her willingness to see me attacked by my opponents. Fortunately, she understood and gave me her full support.

Then I gathered my leadership team and asked them what they thought. There was Deputy Attorney General Don Quick, Solicitor General Alan Gilbert, Chief of Policy Ken Lane—all white men; Deputy

AG Felicity Hannay and Chief Deputy AG Barbara McDonnell, white women; Deputy AG Christy Arguello, Assistant AG Joan Padilla, and Special Assistant Velina Wallick, all Hispanic; and Deputy AG Karen Howard, a Black woman.

After I relayed Dean Lehman's request, Christy responded, "Like always, you'll do what's right based on the truth and let the politics take care of themselves."

Alan, a nonpracticing Jew and a fellow Michigan Law alum, observed, "Being a silent bystander led to some of the most painful eras in history. Look at what happened during World War II. People can't be erased. There will be others who feel the same—I bet we could easily get the New York attorney general to help us."

"Great," I said. "Maybe we just ask all the state AGs to come on board and see what happens. Most Coloradans will understand why we're doing this, I think. Diversity is our strength. Let's explain it. Let's get to work."

I called Dean Lehman and told him that I was going to try to get other states to sign on too.

"That would be wonderful. Thank you, Mr. Attorney General!"

I'd have to figure out the best way to approach my peers across the country, but before that I had to tell the most senior Republican in Colorado my intentions. I didn't want the governor to hear about my efforts through the press; I wanted him to hear it from me directly. So I picked up the phone and called Governor Bill Owens. We did not always see eye to eye, but we had a good working relationship, and I could lean on that.

It's important to remember that in Colorado, as in most states, the attorney general and the governor are two separate and wholly independent executive officers. My job was to represent the people in court and defend the interests of Coloradans in legal matters. The governor's job was to enforce the law and see that the administration was well-run. The upshot was that I did not need the governor's permission to support Michigan Law.

When I told Governor Owens I would be taking a vocal and very public position defending affirmative action in the Michigan case, there was a long pause on the line. "You know I disagree, Ken," he said calmly. "I'm against quotas."

"This isn't about quotas, Governor. This is about fairness and how you measure merit. It's about opportunity for everyone, not just the privileged." I paused. "I will file the amicus on behalf of the people of Colorado. It won't have your name on it."

"I can't stop you. You are the attorney general."

"I appreciate that, Governor. Thank you."

After that, I began strategizing about how best to reach out to my peers across the country and to blunt the criticism that was sure to come. Because I was Mexican American and because Colorado was small (its population was only around 4.5 million—roughly half that of New York City), I knew I'd need to strategize to gain the support of non-minority attorneys general, especially Republicans. How might I convince some of them to join me?

That's when I remembered an op-ed President Gerald Ford had published in *The New York Times* in August 1999. It had been titled "Inclusive America, Under Attack." President Ford was a revered Michigan Wolverine alum. I asked an aide to dig up the article.

Gerald Ford was a Republican who'd served as president after the Watergate scandal forced Richard Nixon to resign in disgrace. If I could get him to officially endorse my effort to enlist other attorneys general in my amicus brief, then maybe I would be able to land some like-minded Republican supporters.

So I reached out to President Ford to ask if I could use his op-ed.

I didn't think a former president would take a call from a state AG, but to my surprise, he eagerly agreed to chat.

"Mr. President," I began, "thank you for your service to the nation. I'm calling about your op-ed supporting Michigan Law's affirmative action program. As you must know, the *Grutter* case will soon be heard before the Supreme Court."

"Yes, I've heard."

"Dean Lehman has asked me to submit an amicus brief, and I was wondering if I could use your piece to help convince other states to sign on."

"Ken," President Ford responded, his voice warm but gravelly from his eighty-nine years, "I know our country has changed, but we must still do more to ensure that everyone has an equal chance in life. That is what Michigan is doing. I would be proud to support you in any way I can. Please use the article in whatever way you want, and I am always available to help."

"Thank you, Mr. President. Your voice will make a real difference." I was elated, reassured, and inspired by his support.

"I hope it does. This is too important to let politics get in the way."

It's worth including Ford's eloquent and timeless piece in its entirety, since, unfortunately, it is as relevant as I write in 2026 as it was when President Ford published it nearly thirty years prior:

> Of all the triumphs that have marked this as America's century—breathtaking advances in science and technology, the democratization of wealth and dispersal of political power in ways hardly imaginable in 1899—none is more inspiring, if incomplete, than our pursuit of racial justice. The milestones include Theodore Roosevelt's inviting Booker T. Washington to dine at the White House, Harry Truman's desegregating the armed forces, Dwight Eisenhower's using Federal troops to integrate Little Rock's Central High School and Lyndon Johnson's electrifying the nation by standing before Congress in 1965 and declaring, "We shall overcome."
>
> I came by my support of that year's Voting Rights Act naturally. Thirty years before Selma, I was a University of Michigan senior, preparing with my Wolverine teammates for a football game against visiting Georgia Tech. Among the best players on that year's Michigan squad was Willis Ward, a close friend of mine whom the Southern school reputedly wanted dropped from our roster because he was black. My classmates were just as adamant that he should take the field. In the end, Willis decided on his own not to play.

His sacrifice led me to question how educational administrators could capitulate to raw prejudice. A university, after all, is both a preserver of tradition and a hotbed of innovation. So long as books are kept open, we tell ourselves, minds can never be closed.

But doors, too, must be kept open. Tolerance, breadth of mind and appreciation for the world beyond our neighborhoods: these can be learned on the football field and in the science lab as well as in the lecture hall. But only if students are exposed to America in all her variety.

For the class of '35, such educational opportunities were diminished by the relative scarcity of African-Americans, women and various ethnic groups on campus. I have often wondered how different the world might have been in the 1940's, 50's and 60's—how much more humane and just—if my generation had experienced a more representative sampling of the American family. That the indignities visited on Willis Ward would be unimaginable in today's Ann Arbor is a measure of how far we have come toward realizing, however belatedly, the promises we made to each other in declaring our nationhood and professing our love of liberty.

And yet. In the last speech of his life, Lyndon Johnson reminded us of how much unfinished work remained. "To be black in a white society is not to stand on level and equal ground," he said. "While the races may stand side by side, whites stand on history's mountain and blacks stand in history's hollow. Until we overcome unequal history, we cannot overcome unequal opportunity."

Like so many phrases that have become political buzzwords, affirmative action means different things to different people. Practically speaking, it runs the gamut from mandatory quotas, which the Supreme Court has ruled are clearly unconstitutional, to mere lip service, which is just as clearly unacceptable.

At its core, affirmative action should try to offset past injustices by fashioning a campus population more truly reflective of modern America and our hopes for the future. Unfortunately, a pair of lawsuits brought against my alma mater pose a threat to such diversity. Not content to oppose formal quotas, plaintiffs suing the University of Michigan would prohibit that and other universities from even considering race as one of many factors weighed by admission counselors.

So drastic a ban would scuttle Michigan's current system, one that takes into account nearly a dozen elements—race, economic standing, geographic origin, athletic and artistic achievement among them—to create the finest educational environment for all students.

This eminently reasonable approach, as thoughtful as it is fair, has produced a student body with a significant minority component whose record of academic success is outstanding.

Times of change are times of challenge. It is estimated that by 2030, 40 percent of all Americans will belong to various racial minorities. Already the global economy requires unprecedented grasp of diverse viewpoints and cultural traditions. I don't want future college students to suffer the cultural and social impoverishment that afflicted my generation. If history has taught us anything in this remarkable century, it is the notion of America as a work in progress. Do we really want to risk turning back the clock to an era when the Willis Wards were isolated and penalized for the color of their skin, their economic standing or national ancestry?

To eliminate a constitutional affirmative action policy would mock the inclusive vision Carl Sandburg had in mind when he wrote: "The Republic is a dream. Nothing happens unless first a dream." Lest we forget: America remains a nation with have-nots as well as haves. Its government is obligated to provide for hope no less than for the common defense.

With President Ford's blessing, I took this op-ed and attached it to a letter I addressed to all forty-nine other state attorneys general, advocating for the merits of affirmative action in college admissions. In the end, twenty-two states signed the amicus brief: Arizona, California, Colorado, Connecticut, Illinois, Iowa, Maine, Maryland, Massachusetts, Minnesota, Montana, New Jersey, New Mexico, New York, North Carolina, Oklahoma, Oregon, Rhode Island, Vermont, Washington, West Virginia, and Wisconsin. While all the AGs who joined were Democrats, their states represented nearly 47 percent of all Americans. It was more than I could ever have hoped for.

Our amicus brief clearly stated our position: "The University of Michigan is doing exactly what was recommended in *Bakke* twenty-five years ago. This is a merit-based admissions system, founded upon individualized consideration by the school of all the qualities an individual applicant can bring to the campus. There are no quotas, as indeed there cannot be."

On June 23, 2003, the Supreme Court released its majority opinion, written by Justice Sandra Day O'Connor. I was in my office when the call came. "We won," Dean Lehman said simply. "Five to four. Justice O'Connor wrote that diversity is a compelling state interest."

It was one of the proudest days of my life.

That year, I had given the commencement address at Michigan Law. Standing before thousands of people—graduates, families, and faculty—I delivered a speech titled "Diversity—An Imperative for America for the Twenty-First Century."

"The students in our great colleges and universities will soon become the leaders in our state and nation," I told them. "They must learn to understand and respect every person, regardless of background or appearance. These are interests vital to Colorado and to our country."

In 2023, the Roberts Supreme Court overturned the *Grutter* decision, effectively declaring affirmative action to be unconstitutional since, in their view, it gave "preferences to students on the basis of race alone" and violated the 14th Amendment's equal protection clause. I felt that the majority opinion, written by Chief Justice John Roberts, was unconvincing, evasive, and wrong. And then there was Justice Thomas, who stated in a concurring opinion that "affirmative action programs . . . cast doubt on whether the achievements of minority students are really based on merit." This was the height of hypocrisy. Clarence Thomas may be the most famous beneficiary of affirmative action, and now he was pulling up the ladder for all who might follow him, helping reverse our march toward a more perfect union.

Everyone needs a chance at success—lower-income white Americans, rural Americans from poorer school districts, women, Native Americans, Asian Americans. Not every person begins at the same starting line, but every person does deserve the same chance, just like Gerald Ford and Sandra Day O'Connor so eloquently and courageously argued.

I've said it throughout these pages, and I'll repeat it here: Diversity is America's superpower. And I don't just mean racial diversity—this is about all Americans who might be considered "out of the mainstream" for any reason. There is no one type of American. That's what "E pluribus unum"—out of many, one—means.

When we denigrate diversity, we do so at our own risk. Rejecting diversity—which can only properly be understood as embracing exclusion—will weaken every facet of our nation and its people.

To continue to work toward a more perfect union, to continue to nurture and protect freedom, we must fight for and defend diversity not just in our universities, but across our entire country. We must resist the existential attacks against diversity led by President Trump and those who follow him blindly. If we don't, America's future is at great risk.

That's a fight worth having, no matter the cost.

PART V

THE PINNACLES OF POWER

The United States Senate

Eighth in Line to the Presidency

THE UNITED STATES SENATE

19

THE UNLIKELY CAMPAIGN

When I won my second term as attorney general, I planned to see it through to the end and run for governor in 2006—but that's not how things turned out.

On March 3, 2004, I got a call from US Senator Ben Nighthorse Campbell, informing me he would not seek reelection. He was seen as a shoo-in for a third term, so his decision was a national surprise. I too was surprised. We were friends and had worked closely on creating the Great Sand Dunes National Park in the Valley and addressing water rights issues with the Animas–La Plata Project in southwestern Colorado.

When I told him I was sorry he wasn't running for reelection and that he'd done a great job for Colorado, he countered with something I wasn't expecting: "You should run for Senate, Ken. Washington needs rural voices from out West. And Colorado needs politicians who understand that the world doesn't begin and end in Denver. I hope you consider it." I knew rural issues were important to him; as you may recall, one of the reasons he'd switched to the GOP was because of his frustration with the Democratic Party's lack of understanding of rural America.

"I really appreciate the vote of confidence and your friendship, Ben, but I'm happy where I am," I told him.

"Just think about it. You would be a great senator."

Initially, I didn't think much about it. The US Senate was not on my radar. It was far away from Hope and the girls, and even farther away from the Valley. I wanted to stay in Colorado. Besides, my brother John was already running to represent Colorado's third district in the House of Representatives, and I didn't want to complicate that for him by also running for Senate.

Even so, I needed the sage advice of Democratic political veterans and organizers like Polly Baca, Federico Peña, Ruben Valdez, Rosemary Rodriguez, Ramona Martinez, Mike Stratton, and Paul Sandoval. Each had made history. Polly was the first Hispanic elected to the Colorado Senate. Federico was Denver's first Hispanic mayor, energizing the city and state under the banner of "Imagine a Great City." Denver International Airport was built under his administration, and he went on to be President Clinton's Transportation secretary and later Energy secretary. Ruben, who hailed from the coal country of southern Colorado, was the first Hispanic Speaker of the Colorado House of Representatives. Rosemary was a founder of the Hispanic League and the Cafecito Group and would become president of the Denver City Council. Ramona also became president of the Denver City Council, and led national efforts with the Democratic National Committee, pushing for the inclusion of Mexican Americans in the Democrats' platform. Mike was from Durango, and he had been the political organizer for Governor Romer and for Senator Gary Hart's moonshot presidential campaigns in 1980 and 1984.

Paul Sandoval was my political godfather, a Chicano tamale maker on Denver's north side. He had been elected to the Colorado Senate at age twenty-five, had never lost an election, and had been an advisor to every Colorado Democrat who wanted to run for office. Even on the bad days, Paul exuded confidence that we could always win.

In 2000, he and I had sat down in his tamale restaurant, La Casita, and sketched out my political game plan on the back of a napkin. I would run for reelection as AG in 2002, governor in 2006, then run for president of the United States in either 2008 or 2012. Now we were discussing changing what seemed like a sure path to the governorship to run for the US Senate. "It won't be easy," Paul said. "Bush is popular and will win Colorado. But you are well known in the Valley and the rural parts of the state as well as here in Denver. With the right message and organization, you can do it. You would be one of only a handful of Chicanos ever elected to the US Senate. You would make us all very proud. But it is up to you." He paused while I took all this in. "Would you like another breakfast burrito?" he asked with a twinkle in his eye. I declined. Laughing, he said, "You should go for it. What do you have to lose? You're attorney general and can still run for governor."

Over the following days, I received a barrage of calls from prominent leaders like Tom Daschle, then the Senate Democratic leader, asking me to throw my hat in the ring. Other Democratic senators, mostly from the West, delivered the same message. I told them each the same thing: "Thank you, I appreciate your support, but I would prefer to stay in Colorado rather than go to Washington."

The situation took a turn on Saturday, March 6. I'd been trying to broker a peace between two prominent Democrats: Rutt Bridges, a successful businessman who'd announced his Senate candidacy long before Ben's decision, and US Representative Mark Udall. Both were allies and close friends, and I feared a drawn-out primary would open a path for a right-wing Republican to win the seat, which, in my view, would be a setback for Colorado. Neither budged—but each separately signaled they would drop out if I decided to run. I was unsure of what to do, so like with all of my major decisions, I went to the Valley for guidance.

I arrived at Los Rincones the next day. My family shared none of my doubts: They wholeheartedly encouraged me to run. John quipped, "Washington won't know what to do with *two* Salazars."

Leroy added, with his characteristic precision, "It is a clear choice. You have already accomplished everything you wanted to do as attorney general; now you can take the same agenda to Washington."

And my sister Elaine, who was always clear-eyed and forceful, said, "You need to go for it. Just be who you are. I've already written your campaign message." She then surprised me with a two-page memo.

I turned to Hope and our girls. Melinda, then sixteen, said, "Just do it, Dad. You can win, and I'll take care of things back here."

Andrea, age fifteen, piped in, "It'll be fun to campaign with you all over the state and go to Washington and celebrate."

But the last word came from Hope. She gave me a long look. "Washington is so far away. I'm worried. But I also think you won't be happy if you pass up the opportunity. You shouldn't live a life with any regrets. So I'll support you all I can."

That was it. I would change course and run for the US Senate.

At my announcement ceremony on the west steps of the Colorado Capitol, standing before what seemed to be a thousand people, I realized this was bigger than my desire to stay in Colorado. This was about being a voice for rural communities, all working families and minority groups who'd been forgotten by Washington. My reluctance to go to the nation's capital hadn't disappeared, but I felt my duty was clear.

I ended up running against Pete Coors of Silver Bullet beer fame. Pete was a household name, Coors ads broadcasting his face on television airwaves across the nation. The Coors family was complicated. They'd funded conservative causes for decades, with Pete's dad, Joe, helping establish the Heritage Foundation. Yet they'd also known tragedy. Pete's uncle Adolph had been murdered during a kidnapping attempt in 1960, a crime that haunted the family.

Early in the campaign, I reached out to Pete directly and met him at his house. "Let's keep this civil," I suggested. "We can disagree on issues without tearing each other down." He agreed, and for the most part, we kept that promise.

What surprised me most was that Pete's uncle Bill Coors quietly supported me. Despite his conservative reputation, Bill was an independent voter, and he respected my work on water rights and rural issues. At one point during the campaign, I visited Bill at his residence. "You understand this state, Ken," he said. "Pete's a good man, but you've got the experience Colorado needs. And to be honest with you, I have never understood how some members of my family have joined the very same conservative forces that tried to kill our brewery during Prohibition." Back then, the Coors family had kept their brewery alive by selling malted milk and so-called near beer. "You'll do a good job for Colorado," he concluded. It was support he never made public, but it still meant the world to me.

The campaign was not that dissimilar to my earlier campaigns for attorney general, except this was a campaign for *United States Senator*, not a state-level official. Those words "United States" said it all. I traveled the country, to Philadelphia, Phoenix, Los Angeles, Miami, New York, and many places in between, raising money, speaking about Colorado, and delivering a national unity message alongside my fellow Senate candidates. I had fundraisers in Denver and the Valley and Pueblo and Grand Junction and on the eastern plains. On many occasions, John and I campaigned together, bringing back memories of the old days when we played cowboys and farmers in Los Rincones.

On election night, Hope and I, along with our girls and several other family members, descended through elevators and back stairways at the Marriott Hotel in Denver to reach the ballroom, filled to the brim with supporters of my candidacy. As soon as I took the stage, the crowd erupted. I stepped up to the mic and addressed them: "I see an America that makes securing our homeland a greater priority, one where every American has the opportunity for a good job, a good education, and affordable healthcare, and where we act as good stewards of our land and water!"

I ended up winning by a little over a hundred thousand votes, good for a nearly 5 percent margin of victory—roughly the same margin by which President Bush won the state in his reelection campaign. We had split the ticket.

After midnight, the press declared John the victor in his race too. He had pulled out a squeaker. When we spoke in the middle of the night, I told him I loved him. "We've come a long way from those fields and potato cellars," John laughed. "I'll see you in Washington, brother!" We would be one of only a couple dozen sibling pairs ever to serve in Congress at the same time. And what's more, we were both Mexican American Democrats who hailed from what was still a Republican-leaning state.

20

THE ONE HUNDREDTH SENATOR

Hope and I went home well after midnight. Sleeping family members were scattered all around the house on couches and in sleeping bags, and I knew I needed to get a couple hours of rest. The next day would be long.

I tried to sleep, tossing and turning in bed, but it was no use. I was too full of adrenaline and joy. After a few hours, as the sun began to rise, the phone rang. Hope answered it. A few seconds later, she called excitedly, "Ken! Pick up the phone. The president wants to speak with you!"

I jogged into the kitchen and picked up the line. "Hello, Mr. President?" I asked.

A woman's voice said, "Good morning, Senator. The president will be on in just a minute." I thought, *I'm not a senator yet, but it sounds good!* I sat at the counter and waited a few minutes.

And then there he was. "Senator, congratulations! You ran a good campaign. I'm looking forward to working with you when you get to Washington."

"Thank you, Mr. President. I look forward to working with you as well."

"I'd like to invite you to the White House for breakfast as soon as possible. The other new senators will be there too. We can all meet in person and discuss the agenda for the next four years. What do you think?"

"Sir, it would be an honor."

Things moved fast. Orientation for the nine newest US senators began on Sunday, November 14, and would culminate with this breakfast meeting at the White House. Hope and I flew to Washington and checked into the Mandarin Oriental hotel, where the other new senators and their spouses were also staying. It was one of the nicest hotels I'd ever been in: sleek, modern, understated—in a word, luxurious. As we settled into our spacious room, I said to Hope, "This is a long way from the roadside hotels in Dove Creek or Lamar."

She agreed. Then she sat at the desk and went through that week's agenda with me. We would both be busy, and she wanted to make sure we were prepared.

The next morning, I woke before the sun rose and went out for a jog along the National Mall. In the crimson glow of dawn, I stopped and gazed in awe at the Jefferson Memorial, the Lincoln Memorial, the Washington Monument, and the grandeur of the United States Capitol with its majestic dome. I marveled that I would now take some part, however big or small, in the future of our nation.

The nine freshman senators, along with our spouses, were welcomed at the Capitol by leaders from both parties. Republicans had cruised in the 2004 election, and Democrats had taken a drubbing: There were seven new Republicans among that year's freshman class, six of whom had wrested control of their seats from Democrats. The only two Democrats who managed to prevail that year were myself and a young Black lawyer, community organizer, and Illinois state senator from Chicago named Barack Obama. Our respective elections were historic: I was only the fourth Mexican American ever elected to the US Senate—the other three had all come from New Mexico—and

Barack was only the fifth Black American to rise to the US Senate in our country's history. Two of his predecessors had come to Washington from Mississippi during Reconstruction; since the passage of the Civil Rights and Voting Rights Acts in the mid-1960s, only two other Black Americans had been senators.

Our new colleagues on the Hill showed us around the Senate floor, speaking aspirationally about working together for the good of all Americans. We were then given an opportunity to say something about ourselves. I introduced myself as Colorado's attorney general and a lawyer and farmer from the San Luis Valley, and Hope introduced herself as a mother of two daughters and the owner of a Denver Dairy Queen.

After learning about Senate procedures and the history of the US Capitol, we gathered for dinner in the Lyndon Baines Johnson Room. The government leaders who'd been there for years told stories about working together—as well as about being in DC on 9/11. In the painful aftermath of that day, the parties put their differences aside to rally around the flag and act for the common good. Many wanted to continue in that tradition, or at least, that was what they said. This was music to my ears.

On Thursday morning, the incoming senators climbed onto a bus and, accompanied by a heavy police presence, drove to the north entrance of the White House. Inside, we were welcomed by Vice President Dick Cheney, Chief of Staff Andy Card, and several others. I was wide-eyed as we were led through the first floor of the White House, past the portraits of the nation's presidents, and into the stately Diplomatic Reception Room. At exactly 7:00 AM, President Bush—always punctual—strolled in from the upstairs residence, greeting us with a smile. "Welcome to the White House! Thank you for coming over." I realized we'd been lined up according to protocol. Senators in the president's party were first, followed by Democrats. Barack and I were at the end of the line.

The president went from senator to senator, giving each a personal comment. When he reached me, his face showed bemused respect. He placed his left hand on my shoulder, shook my hand, and said with a disarming smile, "Congratulations, Senator. You were the one who got away. You ran an impressive campaign and beat a tough opponent."

I smiled. "Thank you, Mr. President."

We then adjourned for breakfast in a small dining room. The president and his team sat at one side of the table while the rest of us congregated on the other. As the staff poured coffee and orange juice, the president said, "I want to work with all of you to do good things for the American people. I can't run again, and Dick won't run, so I hope we can get a lot done over the next four years. To that end, I'd like to hear what each of your priorities are."

The Republicans, who controlled the Senate with fifty-five seats, went first. Since they had campaigned with the president, they echoed messages from his campaign. Though I don't exactly recall what Barack told the president that morning, I do recall my comments.

I told him I wanted to work for Colorado, to make the nation safer, and to create solutions and economic opportunity for rural Americans. Then I added, "Mr. President, you were a border governor; you understand the issues there. You can lead the nation in a new relationship with Mexico and the Americas. I would like to work with you to make this happen."

President Bush smiled and nodded in agreement. "We can work on the border and immigration together. It's a challenge that needs to be solved. I believe we can get it right."

Every new member of Congress was sworn in on January 4, 2005—the same day I vacated the office of Colorado attorney general. It was a watershed moment for John and me, the whole Salazar family, and the country itself.

Not long after our swearing in, we were given our Senate seniority ranks: Barack was number ninety-nine, and I was one hundred. We were both equally new to the chamber and in the minority party, but Barack clocked in ahead of me since Illinois was more populous than Colorado. We joked that we made up the Senate's minority caucus in more ways than one—and we did. We were surrounded by a sea of white faces, though we appreciated that many of those faces were friendly, good-natured, and dedicated to working together for the overall benefit of the country.

You might think that, as a congressman and a senator, John and I would have had an easy time finding an apartment in Washington—but you'd be wrong. The rents were eye-popping to the two of us, coming from out West where space was abundant. We struggled to find any two-bedroom apartment for less than $3,000 a month. In the meantime, we stayed in the least expensive hotels we could find.

One day, I ran into Barack in our Senate offices, and I mentioned that John and I were having trouble finding a place. "You should check out this new building at Third and Massachusetts," he said. "Michelle and I just got a place there. Lots of young people, but it's close and new."

Hope and John's wife, Luz, went to check it out. They liked it. We took apartment 1432 on the fourteenth floor. Barack had a one-bedroom just down the hall.

During those early months, I'd see him from time to time in the elevator late at night, exhausted from working on the Hill as well as writing his book *The Audacity of Hope*. Occasionally, he would step outside for a smoke—he still smoked then—and sometimes, if I bumped into him, we'd ride up together in silence, two junior senators from flyover states, wondering what we'd gotten ourselves into.

I met with many senators from both parties, intent to learn how I could be most effective. I also began to hire staff. Just like when I was attorney general, I wanted my office to be the most qualified and diverse in the Senate. Pete Rouse, who'd recently served as Senator Daschle's chief of staff, and Ken Lane were the primary candidates to run my office. Pete was experienced and wise in a way that eluded most Washington hands. I knew that either Pete or Ken would be a champion of diversity. In the end, Pete became Barack's chief of staff, and Ken became mine. I also hired Cody Wertz, an avid outdoorsman, as my communications director during the campaign; Stephanie Valencia, who hailed from New Mexico, as my press secretary—one of the first

Latinas to serve in the role of press secretary to a US senator; and Felicia Escobar, a Mexican American from San Antonio, Texas, to lead our efforts on immigration reform.

I gave my maiden speech on the Senate floor on March 2, celebrating my forty-ninth birthday, by focusing on what I called "the forgotten America." I spoke about the rural communities and middle-class families struggling to be heard in the corridors of power. I spoke about my upbringing in the San Luis Valley; about how Crowley County east of Pueblo had only one nurse practitioner for over six thousand people; about how a sheriff in Dolores County had to decide if he could hire more officers based not on need but on whether his department could afford to provide new hires with health insurance; about how many sick farmers and ranchers didn't go to the doctor simply because they couldn't afford it. I touched on the scourge of methamphetamine, the urgent need for more broadband access across rural America, and the fact that, in many corners of our country, to be rural often meant to be poor.

I insisted that "rural America needs our help" and that as "the most powerful, prosperous, [and] idealistic country [in] the world, we can do better."

21

THE BORDER AND IMMIGRATION

The months and years that followed were full of victories and defeats, neither of which always fell along strict party lines. The work went beyond Colorado's borders to cover national and global challenges, and in general, I found it to be rewarding, difficult, and collaborative. I made many friends, true friends, on both sides of the aisle. We traveled to the war zones of Iraq and Afghanistan to support our military and to understand the mistakes of those wars. We also traveled to South America to better understand our neighbors in the Western Hemisphere. We came together for legislation on national security and a new framework for America's energy independence. We passed a transportation bill as well as a major farm and agriculture bill. When the 2008 financial crisis shook the fiscal foundations of the country—a time that I and many others in Washington feared would tip into a full-scale depression—we worked to shore up and stabilize the markets, lenders, and insurers at the heart of the meltdown.

Probably because I was the only Mexican American in the Senate, Senator Ted Kennedy asked me to work with him and Senator John McCain on comprehensive immigration reform. I eagerly accepted the invitation, devoting long hours to the task.

The last major reform law had passed in 1986 under President Ronald Reagan. Most immigration legislation since then had dealt with controlling the border—building fences and walls, and providing additional law enforcement resources—rather than properly modernizing it. Nor did any of these bills address the fate of undocumented migrants or their children, a group known collectively as Dreamers. Many of them were young people who had been brought to the country illegally as small children, but who were now adults with no real legal status, despite being American in almost every sense: They spoke English, went to universities across the United States, served in the US Armed Forces, and paid taxes. I knew that President Bush cared and wanted to solve the problems with our immigration system, and so I believed we had an opportunity—and duty—to finally get comprehensive immigration reform done.

On a cold Colorado morning in February 2005, I left my home in Denver and drove down I-25 to meet President Bush, who was in Colorado to visit the National Renewable Energy Laboratory (NREL) in Golden. The president was visiting my home state, so he invited me to breakfast before going to Golden. Over bacon and eggs, we spoke at length about energy and immigration with his team, including Deputy Chief of Staff Karl Rove. We seemed to agree on an initial strategy to fix the border and immigration.

I then joined the president and his team on his tour of the NREL, which had been established by President Carter. Here was a Republican president from the oil-rich state of Texas visiting a renewable energy lab as part of America's "all of the above" energy future. It was an exciting moment. I had been working on proposed energy legislation that included solar, wind, and other renewable and clean energy strategies as part of the national energy framework, and so I was happy to be there.

At one point, the president leaned over to tell me, "We are going to get the energy bill done."

"I hope we can, Mr. President. Imagine if we can get the energy legislation *and* immigration reform done this year."

The president smiled and said, "We'll give it all we got, Ken."

Back in Washington, with the leadership of two Western senators, Senators Bingaman and Domenici from New Mexico, we would achieve the improbable on energy, beginning to free the United States from the traps of Middle Eastern oil and addressing the warming of the planet with clean energy technologies. President Bush signed into law both the Energy Policy Act of 2005 and, later, the Energy Independence and Security Act of 2007. It wasn't that hard. With the wind in our sails, we now just had to do the same on immigration and the border.

Senators Ted Kennedy and John McCain were determined to get this done. We met weekly, and sometimes daily. We discussed not only what we wanted to include in the bill, but also how we could prevent lawmakers who were opposed to the bill from gutting our comprehensive approach. With the leadership of Senators Kennedy and McCain, and the support of President Bush, it seemed like we could get it done.

In April 2006, the president called fifteen senators, as well as the Senate majority and minority leaders, to the White House to discuss immigration reform. Everyone knew that time was running short. In November of that year, there would be a slate of midterm elections, and this time Democrats looked poised to prevail. President Bush's popularity had waned considerably: He had tried to privatize Social Security, and the wars in Iraq and Afghanistan were dragging on for too long and at great cost in national blood and treasure.

We assembled in the Cabinet Room, where President Bush welcomed us with his customary courtesy. Then he bluntly stated, "Senators, I would like to get this done by May 1."

For the next hour, senators took turns briefing the president. While there was nothing disagreeable about what they said, they didn't address one of the main problems: Majority Leader Bill Frist had thus far refused to bring up the legislation for consideration. According to Senate rules, nothing could move forward until Frist acted. As I saw it, he was stonewalling to prevent the president from achieving one of his priorities, perhaps because Frist was contemplating his own presidential campaign.

I was the most junior senator there, but I couldn't help but interject. I raised my hand and said, "Mr. President, with all due respect, we need your direct involvement with the Republican leadership on immigration." Of course, I was talking about Frist, who was sitting right next to President Bush. Frist remained silent.

Senator McCain was less reserved. He glanced at Frist and spun to me before the president could respond, blurting, "My God, Ken! We can sort this out. The president should not be burdened by us!"

I held my ground and asked the president to help move the Senate forward on the bill. Later, Senator McCain pulled me aside and said quietly, "Don't worry. We'll get this done. I promise. Frist just has to work the caucus."

The bill we crafted *was* comprehensive: It strengthened borders and enforced existing laws while also helping Dreamers and creating a path for twelve million undocumented people to potentially earn legal status in the United States. It didn't offer amnesty, and it guaranteed nothing more than the opportunity to become a citizen, for which it also required background checks, payment of back taxes, learning English, and starting the naturalization process at the "back of the line," as it were.

We fought for this bill on the Senate floor, many of us giving speeches until we could barely speak, beating back amendment after amendment designed to kill it. Finally, on May 25, it went up for a vote. Sixty-two senators voted yes—thirty-eight Democrats, twenty-three Republicans, and one Independent. A filibuster-proof majority. When the final vote was counted, I was in the air on my way to Denver to see Andrea graduate from North High School, where I would deliver the commencement speech. As my plane landed, I was informed of the vote results. I was elated. If I could have high-fived everyone in the terminal, I would have. During the commencement speech, I announced the results of the vote on immigration reform to loud applause. Our nation was on its way to a new beginning for immigration and border security.

The legislation was now on its way to the House of Representatives, and we were confident that, with the president's support and the bipartisan success of the bill in the Senate, we would succeed there too.

Instead, things began to go sideways. Dennis Hastert, the Speaker of the House, made it clear that the Republican caucus was only willing to consider a "fence-only" bill, one that would address the needs of law enforcement and the construction of border walls and nothing else. Hastert and other Republicans dragged their feet, intent on not bringing it up for a vote until after Congress's August recess.

That August brought a heated wave of organized opposition. Hundreds of bricks arrived at my Senate office and at my house in Colorado, each hand-etched with the same message: "BUILD THE WALL." At town halls across Colorado, protesters shouted me down. The same thing happened to senators and House members across the country.

Once Congress reconvened in September, the House was in full election mode, and our bill had no chance. The House didn't even agree to go to conference with the Senate to negotiate on it. To them, the bill was dead on arrival. And that's exactly what happened: It died.

But Congress wasn't finished with immigration legislation. Almost as an insult, they voted on the Secure Fence Act on September 14, which called for the construction of a seven-hundred-mile two-layer fence between Mexico and the United States. It passed with overwhelming support. The bill was promptly shuttled over to the Senate, and, despite vocal opposition from senators who sought a comprehensive solution to the problems at the border, it passed with a vote of eighty-one to nineteen. If a senator was up for reelection that year or had presidential aspirations, voting against it was simply too risky. I too knew it could scuttle my political career, but I still voted to kill it.

I knew a fence-only bill would not address the national security and humanitarian issues at stake.

That night, I wrote in my journal: "The so-called Secure Fence Act is now as good as law. I'm offended by the politics that produced it and dismayed by Republican colleagues who conspired in this political game. The fence will do nothing to deal with our immigration challenges, and it sends the wrong signal for the United States' relationships with Latin America." Bitterly, I realized that the border and immigration had become a third rail in American politics. Touch it at your own risk—it could kill your political career.

Our failed efforts at immigration reform were among the lowest points of my time in the Senate. I hoped that maybe, if the Democrats took control of Capitol Hill, we would still be able to get it done with President Bush.

After the 2006 elections, the Democrats did take control of Capitol Hill. When the 110th Congress was brought to session in January 2007, my best friend in Washington, Senator Harry Reid from Nevada, would take the helm as majority leader, and Nancy Pelosi would be named the nation's first female Speaker of the House.

With these majorities came power, and since President Bush remained supportive of immigration reform, I hoped we would finally be able to do what was right for our country, our law enforcement officers on the border, the migrants in our midst, and the Dreamers. It was time to resurrect immigration reform.

So we tried again. But if anything, there was even more opposition in Congress this time around. The situation was infuriating. President Bush twisted arms in Congress, making trips to Capitol Hill to jawbone Republican senators on this issue. While Senator McCain was still a "yea," he was already busy preparing for his presidential campaign in 2008. So at the suggestion of the White House, we formed a new working group, which included two cabinet members: Michael Chertoff from Homeland Security and Carlos Gutierrez from Commerce. Throughout that spring, we met regularly at the White House and at the Senate to map out the substance and strategy of a legislative solution to the problem we faced.

After we'd been at work for some time, I learned that the president would be visiting the Capitol to address the Republican caucus and try to get them behind our latest immigration reform bill. I talked to President Bush and asked him if he would also meet with the Democratic Senate caucus while he was there. He replied, "I will if I'm invited to, Ken."

I immediately found Harry Reid in his office and told him about my conversation with the president. "Harry, I think this is what we need to get this legislation past the finish line."

Harry, who was always to the point, responded with uncharacteristic anger, "Hell no. I will not have that man, that evil man, come and address our caucus."

I was deeply dismayed, but I could not move him. President Bush never did address the Democrats, and despite his efforts with Republicans, the bill came up short: On June 28, twelve Republicans voted for it, and sixteen Democrats voted against it, and it failed by a tally of forty-six to fifty-three.

The next day, I got a call from Air Force One. It was President Bush. "Thank you, Senator, for all your work on immigration. We've done everything we can. There is nothing more we could have done."

"But Mr. President," I said, my voice breaking, "we can't give up, not after all of this work. We have to keep fighting."

"I'm sorry, Ken," he said, clearly hurt that we had failed. "It won't happen on my watch. It'll have to wait for the next president."

It was impossible to deny: The border and immigration was still the third rail of American politics.

This haunted me then and it haunts me now. Not just politically, but personally. Every time I pass through the farmlands in Weld County, Colorado, or the Central Valley in California, or attend mass at Our Lady of Guadalupe in Denver, I think about the families living in the shadows; the children who are citizens by birth but whose parents could be deported at any moment; the workers who pick our crops and build our homes but can't emerge from the darkness of being undocumented—all because a handful of Washington politicians continually lack the courage to do what is right as well as what is urgently needed.

It was a tough lesson I learned: Sometimes the politics of fear beats the politics of hope.

My Family and Our Homes, Then and Now

op left: My great-grandparents Amada Garcia Salazar and Eusebio Salazar, who lived at the)hkay Ranch. *Top right:* My great-grandparents Refugio Salazar and Felipe Cantu, in a photo ıken at Los Rincones.

ıttom left: My grandparents Isidora Montoya Garcia and Jesus Montoya at Cañon de Jemez, ɛw Mexico. *Bottom right:* My grandparents Juan Salazar and Antonia Cantu Salazar (Grandma ta) at the original family home in Los Rincones. (All photos courtesy of the Salazar family)

Top left: My mom, Emma Montoya. This photo was taken while she was working at the War Department in Washington, DC, circa 1941. *Top right:* My dad, Henry Salazar, who arrived in Washington, DC, December 6, 1941, the day before the bombing of Pearl Harbor. The United States declared war on Japan two days later. My dad then was stationed in Hawaii as an army staff sergeant after the bombing.

My parents' wedding day, Cuba, New Mexico, November 25, 1948. Left to right: Juan and Antonia, Henry, Emma, Jesus and Isidora. (All photos courtesy of the Salazar family)

he Salazar family—and our dog Chico—at La Florida on the family ranch on a windy day, ly 3, 1977. Top row, left to right: Elaine, Ken, Leroy, Mom, Dad, Leandro, and John; bottom ow: the triplets, Margaret, Elliott, and June.

Two photos with Mom and Dad. *Left:* At graduation from Michigan Law. I was torn between returning to the ranch, law practice in Denver, or joining a civil rights organization. In the end, I decided I could do all three. *Bottom:* At Los Rincones after feeding the cows, winter 1998. (All photos courtesy of the Salazar family)

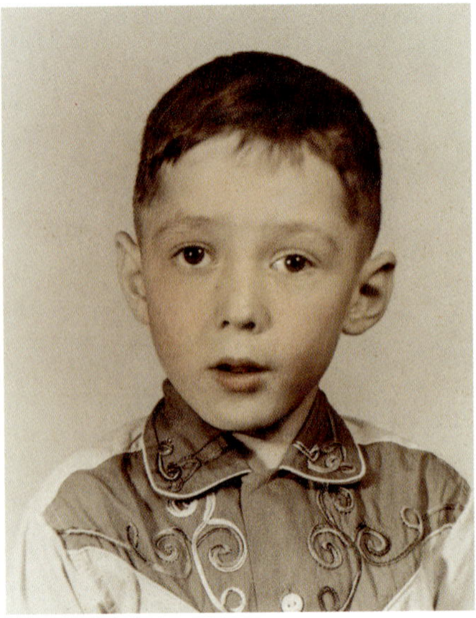

A photo from my kindergarten days—when I trie
to run away from school in Manassa to get back t
the ranch.

Mom and Dad on horseback at the ranch, around 1995. Elliott took this photo, which was the last time they rode.

The work is never really done on a ranc
though here you see the hay has been bale
the fences still need to be mended. (All ph
tos courtesy of the Salazar family)

Vith Hope, my daughters, and my granddaughters on a grand occasion: This day marked
Iireya's quinceañera and Amelia's baptism celebration at the embassy residence in Mexico
ity. Left to right: Blake, Melinda, Amelia, Ken, Mireya, Andrea, Selena, and Hope.

hkay Ranch and the view of the Los Rincones hills at sunrise. In the photo on the right, you
n see the granero, or granary, built by great grandfather Eusebio—a beautiful reminder that
e Salazars have stewarded this land for centuries. (All photos courtesy of the Salazar family)

Top left: Posing for a photo for a newspaper article on our family with John, Mom, and Lero at Los Rincones. John and Mom are holding all of our grade school portraits. (Photo from *Th Denver Post* via Getty Images) *Top right:* After announcing my candidacy for US Senate, wit Mom at the kitchen table at Los Rincones, seeking her guidance, March 29, 2004. (Photo b AP Photo/Nathan Bilow)

John, our mom, then 82, and me, during a reception celebrating our swearing-in as Unit States Representative and United States Senator. (Photo by Glenn Asakawa/*The Denver P* via Getty Images)

My grandfather Juan Salazar and his cousins at El Arco de la Independencia, Monterrey, Nuevo León, Mexico, in the 1930s . . . and me and my siblings in the same spot nearly one hundred years later.

alazar family reunion, July 18, 2025. This gathering was the result of a two-year genealogy roject in our family. My mom and dad's family and relatives joined us at the Ohkay Ranch. All photos courtesy of the Salazar family)

On the Campaign Trail

Top left: I joined then-Senator Barack Obama at his 2008 presidential campaign rally at th rodeo grandstand of the Colorado State Fair. As with everywhere Obama went, the ground were packed and full of optimism. (Photo by Emmanuel Dunand/AFP via Getty Images *Top right:* On the campaign trail running for United States Senate (2004). (Photo by Cava Images/Alamy)

"When a dog runs at you, whistle for him." – Henry David Thoreau

U.S. Senator-elect Ken Salazar and Congressman-elect John Salazar stand outside their boyhood home as they talk to the media about the importance of their San Luis Valley roots. The two brothers grew up in a family of eight children and learned early about the value of hard work, family, community and fait

Salazar brothers prove you can go home again

Bottom left: A backyard celebration with Governor Roy Romer and family (1994). When h contacted me at 5:30 AM one Sunday morning in 1986, I never anticipated that he woul become my political mentor for decades to come. Left to right: Bea Romer, Melinda Salaza Governor Roy Romer, Andrea Salazar, Ken Salazar, Hope Hernandez-Salazar. (Photo courtes of the Salazar family) *Bottom right:* An article in *The Colorado Statesman* showing John and m at Los Rincones celebrating our elections to the US House of Representatives and the US Sen ate (2004). We were among the few siblings ever to serve in Congress at the same time. (Pho from *The Colorado Statesman*)

Colorado Attorney General

Top left: My swearing-in as Colorado attorney general on January 12, 1999—the first time a Mexican American had been elected to statewide office in Colorado. (Photo by Cyrus McCrimmon/*The Denver Post* via Getty Images) *Top right:* At a press conference with Governor Bill Owens and Denver Mayor Wellington Webb on gun safety measures following the tragic Columbine High School shootings. (Photo courtesy of Colorado Attorney General office)

Bottom left: A group photo with me and the deputy attorneys general, reflecting the high caliber and the diversity of our team. (Photo courtesy of Colorado Attorney General office) *Bottom right:* In the San Luis Valley with Representative Scott McInnis, Interior Secretary Bruce Babbitt, Senator Wayne Allard, and Senator Ben Nighthorse Campbell discussing the establishment of the Great Sand Dunes National Park. The dream became true. We created the national park, protected the precious water of the Valley, and created economic opportunity in rural America. (Photo by Fred Bunch/National Park Service)

Ambassador to Mexico

I held regular press conferences at the residence in Mexico City to demonstrate the need for a transformative and durable relationship between the United States and Mexico, and in support of the Mexican free press. (Photo by Raj Valley/Alamy)

Bottom left: Walking with President Andrés Manuel López Obrador at the new Aeropuerto Internacional Felipe Ángeles, or AIFA. *Bottom right:* Welcoming President Biden to Mexico City, January 8, 2023; it would be his only visit to Mexico. Presidential visits to Mexico City are a tradition that dates back to Harry S. Truman's 1947 visit when he came to honor our nations' alliance after WWII. Truman became the first president to visit Mexico City, ninety-nine years after the end of the Mexican-American War. (Photos courtesy of Ken Salazar)

At the border with US and Mexican officers, inspecting human smuggling tunnels under the binational border.

·omewhere over
·he Arizona–
onora Border,
·hich I saw
·rsthand many
·mes by car and
·elicopter.

Throughout Mexico, I would meet with the bishops about security for the Mexican people and their priests. Here I am with Monseñor Ramón Castro Castro in Cuernavaca.

As part of my visits to cities on both sides of the border, I met with Henry Muñoz III to celebrate making the Missions of San Antonio a World Heritage Site. (Photos courtesy of Ken Salazar)

US Special Presidential Envoy for Climate John Kerry visited Mexico eight times for meetings with President López Obrador to advance the US–Mexico climate agenda. Here we are at Palenque in the Selva Maya, one of the largest rainforests in the Western Hemisphere.

Death from the Guatemalan border: Here a this site, at Tuxtla Gutiérrez, a tractor-trailer fu of human beings crashed. Fifty-six people die and many were injured. They had paid $15,00 each to the human smugglers to get them to th United States.

I promoted the Transoceanic Corridor across the 180-mile narrow Isthmus of Tehuantepec in an effort to create a beltway of security and prosperity in southeast Mexico. Here I am on the train at the inauguration of the project with President López Obrador, his cabinet, governors from the southeast, and business leaders in Mexico, including Carlos Slim. (See the map of the project on the last page of this insert.)

I worked closely with the US Chamber Commerce and the Mexican Chamber Commerce to integrate the supply chai between the United States and Mexico. V became the number one trading relatio ship in the world. Here I am with Francis Cervantes and Carlos Slim working or visit to Washington to promote the Unit States-Mexico-Canada Trade Agreeme (Photos courtesy of Ken Salazar)

Working together with Claudia Sheinbaum, then-mayor of Mexico City, to complete the new JS embassy complex. The US embassy in Mexico is one of the most important embassies for he US in the world. The new complex underscored the critical relationship between our two ations.

t the Guelaguetza festival in Oaxaca with Governor Jara and Indigenous tribes. Guelaguetza is one ' Mexico's most spectacular cultural celebrations, in which Oaxaca's Indigenous and Afro-Mexan communities showcase their ancient traditions through parades, dancing, food, and music. I as happy to celebrate along with the crowd, but President Biden's imminent decision to end his esidential campaign hung over the day for me. (Photos courtesy of Ken Salazar)

From 2021 to 2025, many of our wonderful family and best friends visited the ambassador’s residence in Mexico City to inspire and support my work. (Photos courtesy of the Salazar family)

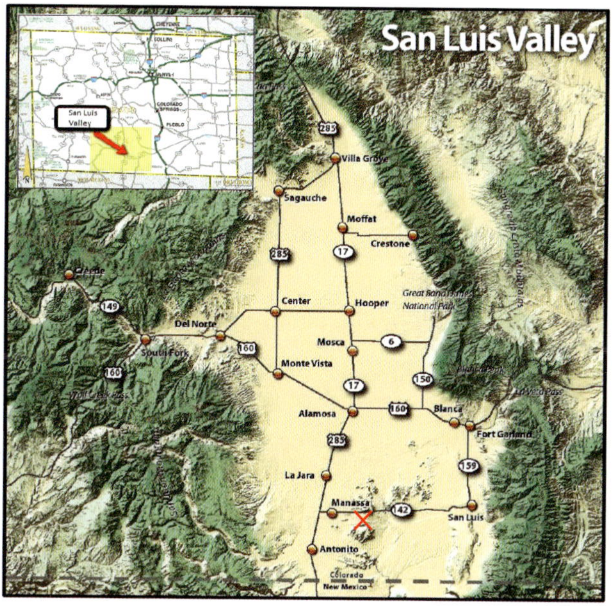

The San Luis Valley is my home. This map of the Valley shows its unique geography: It is not a narrow strip but rather a long, uneven oval surrounded by towering mountains. At over eight thousand square miles, it is the largest alpine valley in the world. The red *X* east of Manassa marks Los Rincones. (Map courtesy of History Colorado)

Three crucial treaties established and then changed the border between the United States an Mexico. The red line on this map shows the boundary lines between the US and New Spai established by the Adams-Onis Treaty of 1819. The second treaty reaffirmed the same bounc ary between the United States and Mexico in 1828 following Mexican independence fro Spain. Twenty years later, all of what is now the western United States below the red line– more than half of Mexico—was then lost by Mexico as a result of the Mexican-American W and the Treaty of Guadalupe Hidalgo of 1848. Mexican Americans in this part of the cou try, including my family, remained on their lands and were given the right to their propert their language, their religion, and citizenship in the United States. (Map by Bill Rankin, Ya University)

The map depicts Mexico, Central America, and the top of South America showing the land bridge from the Darién Gap in Panama all the way to the US–Mexico border. Migrants fleeing poverty in South America traverse the dangerous gap that connects South America to North America, proceed through Panama, Costa Rica, Nicaragua, Honduras, Guatemala, and Mexico, paying human smugglers as much as $15,000 to lure them to the United States. (Map by Peter Hermes Furian, Adobe Stock)

Just as I traveled to all fifty US states as secretary of the Interior, as ambassador, I traveled many times to each of Mexico's thirty-two states—from the deserts of Sonora in the north to the rainforests of Campeche in the Selva Maya—to get to know their diverse people, their greatness, their history, and their everyday challenges. (Map by pop jop/iStock)

This map of the Isthmus of Tehuantepec shows (in red) the 180-mile-long transoceani corridor—a railroad and roadway—from the Pacific to the Gulf of Mexico. I joined Presider López Obrador in strongly supporting the development of the transoceanic corridor becaus it created a beltway of security checkpoints, shown by the dots along that red line. I urge President Biden and Democratic and Republican senators and representatives for the US to g fully behind this project to advance our national security. (Map by the Government of Mexic

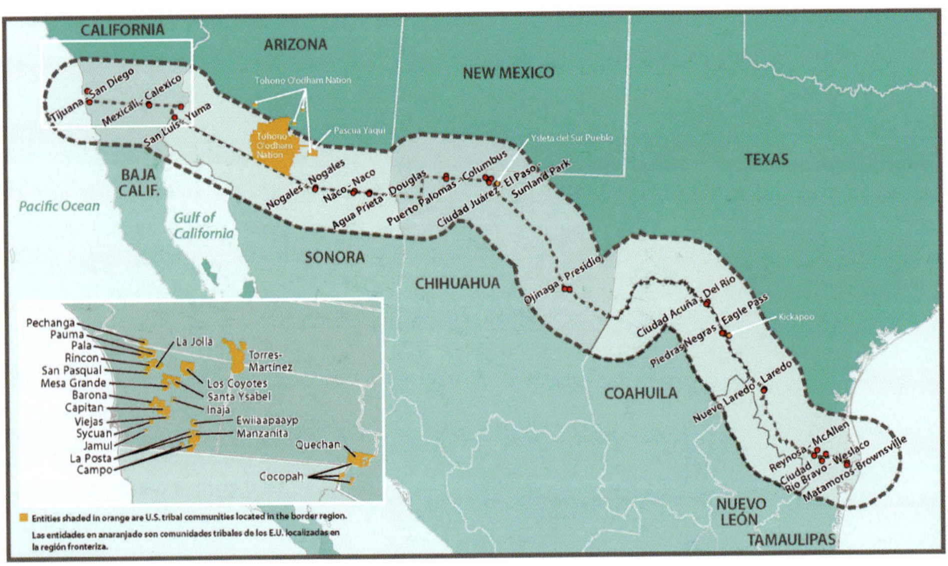

The US–Mexico border, showing official crossings between the cities on either side of the bc der. The area indicated by the dotted line is a binational border zone extending about six miles on either side of the border. (The inset shows US tribal communities at the Western pa of the zone.) (Map by the U.S. Environmental Protection Agency)

EIGHTH IN LINE TO THE PRESIDENCY

22

CUSTODIAN OF AMERICA'S HERITAGE

What is the opposite of diversity? Exclusion. Or more diabolically, erasure.

As I write, diversity is under siege across the United States. The inclusive America that Gerald Ford and Sandra Day O'Connor stood for is under relentless attack everywhere—in the military, in corporate America, in higher education, and in the courts.

I am especially pained by this because it seems like just yesterday that we were truly on the cusp of a more inclusive America, steadfast in our continued march toward a more perfect union. Ideas and actions that seemed to enjoy broad support—such as celebrating our diverse cultural heritage—would nowadays be bitterly debated in Washington. There are many reasons for this profound reversal in the nation's view toward diversity and inclusion, but whatever the cause, the result is the same: The United States under Trump has embarked on a full-throated project of erasure.

But in 2008, it seemed the United States was turning the page on its long and complicated past with race and finally expanding who got to be considered an American in the fullest sense of the word. That year, the United States elected its first Black American to the nation's highest office. The euphoria of that presidential run and its previously unimaginable result remains one of the brightest, most hopeful moments in our nation's history.

Even Republicans seemed to rejoice in Obama's victory—not because they favored him for president, but because of the change his victory symbolized. President Bush himself put it eloquently when, on November 5, 2008, he said from the White House Rose Garden: "No matter how they cast their ballots, all Americans can be proud of the history that was made yesterday . . . They showed a watching world the vitality of America's democracy and the strides we have made toward a more perfect union. They chose a president whose journey represents a triumph of the American story." He continued, "Many of our citizens thought they would never live to see [this] day. This moment is especially uplifting for a generation of Americans who witnessed the struggle for civil rights with their own eyes—and four decades later [we] see a dream fulfilled."

I couldn't have said it better myself.

Adding to my own euphoria was the fact that the 2008 election was historic for another reason: The Democratic Party had won not just the presidency, but also the House and a filibuster-proof sixty-seat majority in the Senate. All of us—President Obama, Vice President Biden, Majority Leader Reid, Speaker Pelosi, myself, and many others—had a rare opportunity to show the American people what we could achieve.

Not long after the election, Barack vacated his Senate seat and set up his transition office in Chicago's Kluczynski Federal Building on South Dearborn Street. I'm sure he was happy to have the chance to live at home in Chicago before he, Michelle, and their two young daughters relocated to the White House in January 2009.

I was of course sad to see Barack leave the Senate, but I was beyond elated to have him in the White House. The Great Recession was still in full swing, and the country continued to reel from its effects, but I knew that he could tackle that and much more over the next four years.

Since senators have six-year terms, I was not up for reelection that year but instead would be on the ballot in the 2010 midterms. Hoping to get an early start on that campaign, I decided to announce my intention to run in early December 2008, less than a month after Election Day.

President-elect Obama had other plans for me.

Just as I was about to take the stage in Denver to announce my reelection campaign at one of the largest political fundraisers in Colorado history, my phone rang. It was the president. I picked up. "Hey, Ken! This is Barack Obama," he declared, practically beaming that bright smile of his through the phone. "Thanks for answering. You got a minute?"

I was about to step in front of a crowd of a thousand people, but when the president-elect asks if you have a minute, you don't say no. "Always, Mr. President," I said, enjoying his new title.

"I'd like you to come over and join the team, Ken."

"Excuse me, what do you mean?"

"Given your history with land and water rights in the West, I'd like you to lead the Department of the Interior. It would be a great opportunity, and I know Interior issues are important to you. You deserve to finally have a say in them."

"I-I . . ." I stammered. Finally, I found my voice. "I'm actually about to announce my campaign for Senate reelection, Mr. President."

"I understand. Think about it. Go ahead and make your announcement. But when you get a day or two, please come to Chicago. I hope to talk with you soon, Ken."

"Thank you, Mr. President. I will do that. Again, I'm sending a big hug and my warmest congratulations. I am so excited for you and the country."

I did announce my reelection campaign that night, but I also got to Chicago as soon as I could. I touched down at O'Hare on December 16, caught a cab, and gave the cabbie the address downtown. His eyes widened, but he didn't say anything other than "Yes, sir." A short while later, he turned off the meter, looked at me in the rearview mirror, and said, "You going to see the president?"

I handed him $40 and said, "Keep the change. I'm excited for America's new president too." I left it at that.

I checked into the building, which was crawling with Secret Service officers, and was led to Barack's office. He had a basketball on his desk and was just finishing a call. Moments after I walked in, he hung up and stood. We high-fived and gave each other a big hug.

We spoke about the election victory and his desire to have me join his cabinet. It was an incredibly high honor, but I remained ambivalent. Barack's pitch was to the point: "Ken, we can help change the world together. We can do more in four years with you at Interior than you could do in forty years in the Senate." We talked about how I could help lead the effort on energy independence, which had been one of my focuses in the Senate. We talked about being stewards of America's treasured national parks and monuments, as well as of other magnificent landscapes that had not yet been protected. We talked about our country's troubled relationship with Native Americans and how we had a rare opportunity to right past wrongs.

He made a compelling case, but I couldn't say yes or no on the spot. Before he had to move onto his next appointment, I said, "Barack, you will be a great president, I have no doubt, and I'm humbled that you've asked me to serve in this capacity. But I need to go home and talk to Hope and to a few other people. I may be of more help to you as a US senator."

He laughed and told me not to take too long to decide. I assured him I wouldn't.

Over the next several days, I remained undecided, though pressure to agree came from all sides. Hope was on board and thought it was a chance to do big things for the country and replicate some of the work

I'd done in Colorado on a national scale. My family in the Valley was on board as well.

In Washington, I consulted with Harry Reid and my staff. Harry told me bluntly, "You should do it. Senators and governors would die for the chance to serve on the president's cabinet. Especially Obama's cabinet. And people from out East don't understand the West or public lands or water. You can also serve as a link between the Senate and the White House."

My special assistant Joan Padilla said, "You work so hard in the Senate. This will be just as hard. But if that is what your heart tells you to do, I know you can do it."

I also needed to seek the advice of my close friend Senator Daniel K. Inouye, a Hawaii Democrat who'd been in the Senate since 1963 and who was soon to be the chairman of the Senate Appropriations Committee. Senator Inouye was eighty-four years old and at the pinnacle of a long and storied career in public service. He was a Japanese American World War II war hero who'd been part of the 442nd Infantry Regiment, which—along with the 100th Infantry Battalion—was almost exclusively Japanese American. These two units only existed because a group of Japanese American men petitioned the US government for the right to serve and fight, even while the same government was incarcerating their family members in internment camps across the American West (including one in Granada, Colorado).

The 442nd landed in Italy in 1943, and from the beginning, they proved their mettle, winning battle after battle. But their valor came at great cost.

On a spring day in 1945, then-Lieutenant Inouye was part of a group of soldiers storming a German position on the Colle Musatello ridge. During their attack, he suffered a gunshot wound to the stomach but kept fighting. As he neared a German gunner's position, Inouye pulled the pin from a grenade and rose to throw it—but as soon as he came up from cover, a German soldier opened fire with his 30mm "rifle grenade," a gun that fired a kind of explosive shell commonly used to assault tanks.

It struck Inouye's arm and nearly blew it off. Inouye hit the ground and looked at his wound. What was left of his lower arm was barely attached to the rest of him—but his right hand still clung to the live grenade. Thinking quickly, he pried the grenade free with his good hand and threw it into the German bunker. Almost as soon as it entered the bunker, it exploded, killing many enemy combatants. Inouye was evacuated by his fellow soldiers, and at a field hospital nearby what was left of his arm was amputated without anesthesia. It took nearly two years for him to recover from his wounds, and he was honorably discharged in 1947 with the rank of captain. For this action, he received a Purple Heart, a Bronze Star, a Distinguished Service Cross, and, finally, fifty-three years later, the Medal of Honor from President Clinton.

While Captain Inouye's valor was truly extraordinary, it was almost pedestrian for the 442nd. Combined with the 100th, these units of Japanese American soldiers are the most decorated in all of US military history. For their actions between 1943 and 1945, the men who served in them received over 18,000 citations, including 9,486 Purple Hearts, twenty-one Medals of Honor, and eight Presidential Unit Citations. No two fighting units have come close to this level of recognized courage and commitment—not during WWII, and not at any other time since.

And on top of all that, Senator Inouye was also the second most senior senator in the Capitol. So when he gave me advice, I always took it seriously.

Quietly, but with conviction, he said, "Ken, it is good that the president has offered you this position. The Department of the Interior is the most important department in the United States, you know. You will be the custodian of America's natural resources. Even more importantly, you will be the custodian of America's cultural heritage. These are the twin pillars of the Department."

He continued, "When you walk around departments like Defense or State—or any other department, for that matter—the corridors are mostly adorned with portraits of wealthy white men. Many of them are good people. But where are the rest of us? Where do you see Blacks,

Hispanics, Native Americans, women, poor whites, Chinese Americans, and, yes, Japanese Americans in these buildings? All of those Americans have been left out of the so-called mainstream. They have fought for and built America and have been treated as if they do not belong in our story. This is what I mean. This is why it is the most important cabinet position in the United States. At Interior, under this president, you can get our history and heritage right."

I called President Obama soon after my meeting with Senator Inouye and said, "I accept."

"Ken, thank you," President Obama said. "I'm glad to have you on the team."

I was unanimously confirmed by the Senate and sworn in as the fiftieth secretary of the Interior on Inauguration Day, January 20, 2009. That day—the excitement, the pageantry, the visual of a young Black couple walking down Pennsylvania Avenue to take up residence in the White House—will always be one of the most emotional, meaningful, and just downright fun days of my life. And while I knew I had a lot of work to do in my new job, I was excited to take on such an important role.

As I knew from visiting it as a senator, the Interior secretary's office is one of the largest and most beautiful in all of DC. As the story goes, Harold Ickes, FDR's Interior secretary, oversaw construction of the building. Before the plans were finalized, he went over to the postmaster general's office, which was known to be the largest in Washington, and measured it. Ickes then spoke with his architect to ensure that his new office, completed in 1936, would be just a little bit bigger.

It was large, and it was beautiful. It had a desk, a marble-faced wood-burning fireplace, dark mahogany paneling on the walls, and original bronze fixtures. There were three large area rugs, a conference table that sat a dozen people, a coffee table, two couches, and four or five lounge chairs.

On my first day, I was greeted at Interior by a jubilant crowd, a small number of the seventy-two thousand Department employees whom I soon came to know as the real custodians of our national heritage and natural bounty. As I walked through the halls to my new office, someone in the crowd came forward and tugged at my arm. "Mr. Secretary," he said, "I'm Kirk Dietz, curator here. I'm in charge of the art."

"Nice to meet you," I said.

"There was a painting that used to hang in the secretary's office, and I think you might want to put it back. Can I bring it by later so you can have a look?"

"Of course, Kirk. I'd be happy to take a look at it," I said, before a staffer pulled me further into the building.

Later that day, Joan knocked on the door and showed the curator inside. He was pushing a four-wheel dolly that held a large, framed painting covered in Bubble Wrap. I helped him wheel it inside and set the painting on the conference table. "Secretary Norton had this removed a few years ago," Kirk said, "even though it had hung behind the secretary's desk since Harold Ickes put it there in the 1930s." He carefully cut the Bubble Wrap away and uncovered the painting. It showed a small band of Native Americans in camp, somewhere in the desert Southwest. It was simple but quite beautiful.

"It's called *Navajos Breaking Camp*," Kirk said. "Norton took it down because she didn't want a depiction of Native Americans in this room. Rumor holds that she had it removed out of spite following a dustup in the *Cobell* litigation, not long after the judge in the case found her in contempt of court."

The *Cobell* case was a class action suit brought by a large group of Native Americans against the US government, with a Blackfeet woman named Elouise Cobell as lead plaintiff. I knew a lot about the case from my days in the Senate, since it had been going on since the mid-1990s.

"Thank you for bringing this here," I said to Kirk. "Please put it back where it belongs." A few hours later, it was professionally hung on the wall over the secretary's desk, right in between two windows that looked out onto the street. As Kirk departed, I looked at the painting and mused out loud, "I hope it stays there for a long, long time."

One Saturday morning a few weeks later, President Obama came to play basketball in the Interior Department's gymnasium. After we'd played together for a while, I asked if he would like to see my office. "I'd love to, Ken," he said, and we went upstairs.

As we toured the room, I pointed to the painting. "That painting was placed there by Harold Ickes. It was meant to remind everyone who comes into the office that the Department has a special responsibility to empower Native Americans across our nation."

"It's a beautiful painting," the president said, "and an important message. I'd consider bringing it to the White House, but this really is the perfect place for it. It should stay here as a symbol of our commitment to Indian country."

I agreed. Still in our basketball gear, we walked out to his waiting car. I waved goodbye as it drove away, closely guarded by its accompanying motorcade.

As in the Senate, I experienced many triumphs and crises at Interior. I also had my share of crises that our team managed to turn into triumphs. The most difficult ordeal by far involved the 2010 Deepwater Horizon accident on a drilling rig in the Gulf of Mexico, an environmental and industrial disaster that killed eleven rig workers and sent oil spewing into the Gulf for eighty-seven days. During that time, millions of gallons of crude oil erupted from the wellhead on the seafloor, nearly one mile deep in ink-black waters, creating a 43,000-square-mile oil slick. It took all of my resolve and that of countless others to cap the well, address the needs of the people who lived along the Gulf, and manage the environmental impact—not to mention survive the political fallout. My staff and I did not take a day off for over three months, nor did many others at the Coast Guard, the Army Corps of Engineers, the Environmental Protection Agency, and the National Security Council.

I knew the accident had the power to take down the president, and it was only through dedication, belief, and countless hours of people power that we were able to both stop the spill and save enough of Obama's reputation that he wouldn't pay for it in 2012. If anything, our collective disaster response—especially in contrast to the government's response to Hurricane Katrina in 2005—might have helped his prospects that year.

Fortunately, my time at Interior was not dominated by any other disaster on the scale of Deepwater Horizon. For the most part, I was free to implement the president's agenda. And I admit that he was right about how much we could do: We accomplished more in four years than I thought possible.

From the get-go, we set to work diversifying the ranks at Interior. I hired Hilary Tompkins, a Navajo lawyer with degrees from Dartmouth and Stanford, to be Interior's lead solicitor. I hired former Idaho Attorney General Larry Echo Hawk, a member of the Pawnee Nation, to serve as assistant secretary for Indian Affairs. Larry was the first Native American ever to be in charge of Indian Affairs, and Hilary was the first Native American to be solicitor.

Over the first few months, as we brought over a hundred new people onto the "Obama-Salazar Dream Team," we made sure that they were not just highly qualified, but broadly representative of the nation we were charged with protecting and serving. There were white Americans, women, Native Americans, Black Americans, Hispanic Americans, Asian Americans—the full panoply of America's people, right there at our headquarters in Washington.

Joining me from the Senate was Matt Lee-Ashley, one of my staffers, who hailed from Colorado Springs. Along with Kate Kelly from Cherry Creek, Colorado, we would work to protect our nation's treasured landscapes and tell America's story throughout the fifty states.

I brought in my old friend Tom Strickland, a prominent lawyer and political veteran, to serve as both my chief of staff and as the assistant secretary for Fish and Wildlife. Together, we interviewed finalists to serve as the director of the National Park Service (NPS). This was an especially important position because the Park Service would be celebrating its centennial in 2016. When I interviewed Jon Jarvis, a career park ranger, to lead NPS, he commented that we were "in the business of telling America's story in perpetuity"—and I agreed. But I told him bluntly that Interior and the Park Service had failed to fully tell America's story, sharing with him my conversation with Senator Inouye. I pointed to the National Mall, America's front yard, and said that it "did not celebrate a single woman, Japanese American, Black American, Mexican American, or member of so many other American communities who had contributed so much to the nation's story." I asked him to describe in writing his own commitment to diversity. Shortly after that, he delivered to me a long memo on recognizing and remembering the contributions of these forgotten and ignored Americans through NPS. I liked what I read, and I decided to hire him.

We initiated a new conservation program, which the president branded as "America's Great Outdoors," to protect and preserve our land and water throughout all fifty states. We aimed for President Obama's conservation legacy to rival that of both Teddy and Franklin Roosevelt.

We started with a bang. In March, I introduced President Obama in the East Room of the White House for the signing of the thousand-page Omnibus Public Land Management Act of 2009. The president signed the bill to thunderous applause. It set aside two million acres of wilderness and protected rivers and established new wildlife refuges, parks, and heritage areas across the country.

But this first law was only the beginning. With the help of governors, ranchers, hunters and anglers, environmentalists, and communities across the nation, we identified and protected some of the most important conservation areas in all fifty states.

We worked with President Obama and his team to fulfill the vision of Interior as custodian of all of America's heritage and protect our treasured landscapes. Pete Rouse, Jim Messina, and Valerie Jarrett led the effort from the White House with a dedicated staff. Pete and Jim had followed President Obama from the Senate in 2008. Jim hailed from Montana's Big Sky Country and loved the outdoors; he knew about the importance of conservation. He would go on to run Obama's successful 2012 reelection campaign. Valerie made sure the president delivered on all of his commitments. She had graduated from Michigan Law in 1981 and was a champion of the president's diversity efforts. And Pete Rouse was the calm leader who was wicked smart and would simply get things done. Pete's mom was a first generation Japanese American. His grandmother and aunt had been placed in internment camps during WWII. Pete instinctively shared the president's diversity agenda and would be the perfect partner.

Beyond conservation, we also helped achieve energy independence for the United States by implementing the national framework we had established when I was in the Senate. We developed renewable energy projects as well as responsible oil and gas development projects on public lands and oceans, with the goal of making the United States less dependent on oil produced in global hot spots like the Middle East. We also created opportunities for young people and veterans to work outdoors through the 21st Century Conservation Service Corps. And we launched a new era of respect for Native Americans—the first Americans—enacting an agenda aimed at righting past wrongs and injustices. The damage done to the Native American and Alaska Native tribes was profound and, in many instances, unspeakable. At the president's direction, Interior initiated the first White House Tribal Nations conference. For the next eight years, the president and his cabinet would lead an annual summit at the White House and Interior to implement a shared agenda with Indian country.

As part of this new beginning, we immediately took on the complex and bellicose litigation between the United States and tribal nations that had continued for far too long: *Cobell.*

23

YELLOW BIRD WOMAN

The *Cobell* case was a class action lawsuit first brought against the United States in 1996. That year, Elouise Cobell, a member of the Blackfeet Nation from Montana, filed it on behalf of hundreds of thousands of Native Americans. The complaint alleged decades of mismanagement of Individual Indian Money accounts—government-managed trust funds that held royalties from oil, gas, timber, and grazing leases on reservations and other Native American lands. These weren't tribal funds, but money owed to individual Native Americans, money the federal government had been legally obligated to protect since the Dawes Act of 1887—and which Cobell and her fellow plaintiffs alleged the US government had done a negligent job of "protecting."

The Dawes Act had divided tribal lands into individual parcels of 40 to 160 acres, supposedly to help Native Americans become farmers and ranchers like white settlers. But almost immediately, the government deemed Native Americans "incompetent" to manage their own affairs, so the Interior Department held these lands in trust, leasing them out and collecting the revenues. As the original landowners died, their parcels were divided among heirs, then divided again and again down through the generations. Some parcels now had hundreds of owners, each owed tiny fractions of lease payments that our department had lost track of decades ago.

A few weeks into my tenure, a career lawyer from our Salt Lake City office came to brief me on the case. Tom Strickland, Deputy Secretary David Hayes, and Hilary Tompkins joined me in the briefing. The lawyer laid out the case's history with the detached precision of someone who'd been through it many times before.

"When the lawsuit was filed," he explained, "it was against the Clinton administration, with Secretary Bruce Babbitt as the named defendant. During the Bush administration, the defendant's name was changed to each of his secretaries—Gale Norton and then Dirk Kempthorne. Now it's your turn, Mr. Secretary. The case will be known as *Cobell v. Salazar.* You'll be the defendant." He paused, then added with what sounded like reassurance: "But you don't have anything to worry about."

I leaned forward. "I know a little about this case, so let me get this straight. Hundreds of thousands of Native Americans have sued Interior for billions of dollars. Since the case was filed, seven trials have been held. The courts have ruled that the United States has broken its fiduciary duties to Native Americans. And I don't have anything to worry about?"

"Yes, Mr. Secretary," he replied. "While we lose some of these cases in the lower courts, when we get this to the Supreme Court, we always win."

"How long will that take?"

"We have to get ready for trial, complete discovery, and file motions. The trial will take several weeks. The court will issue its decision, and then the appeals will begin."

I put my hands on the table and looked directly at him. "With all due respect, is our job to do the right thing or to win the litigation? If doing the right thing requires us to recognize wrongs committed against Native Americans and correct the injustices of the past, will that be a win? I know there have been efforts to resolve this litigation, and the president and I believe that we need to continue them. This case has been going on for too long."

"Well, sir, that has never been our instruction. There have been informal settlement discussions, but to no avail."

I thought about what this lawyer *wasn't* saying. I knew from my Senate days that previous administrations had at times discussed settlements as high as $30 billion, but those talks always collapsed. The first judge on the case, Royce Lamberth, a Reagan appointee, had become so fed up with the government's obstruction that he'd held two cabinet secretaries in contempt. In a 2005 ruling, he wrote that the Interior Department was "the morally and culturally oblivious hand-me-down of a disgracefully racist and imperialist government that should have been buried a century ago, the last pathetic outpost of the indifference and anglocentrism we thought we had left behind." Harsh words—so harsh that they served part of the basis for an appeals court removing him from the case in 2006 for the stated reason that he had lost his impartiality. His replacement, the venerable Judge James Robertson, inherited a toxic mess.

"I respect your tenacity as an advocate," I said to the lawyer from Salt Lake City. "But one of my jobs as secretary is to serve as trustee for Native Americans and to manage the relationship between the US government and all the tribal governments. You just said, 'That has never been our instruction.' Well, here is my instruction: I want this case resolved. I have the president's support. We are beginning a new era in our relationship with Indian country. This case stands as a significant barrier to this new beginning. Please see if we can get this done."

He was clearly surprised by my directness, and likely also by this reversal from my predecessors' positions, but he took the admonition in stride. And to his credit, he began to work diligently toward resolving this unfortunate affair.

A few weeks later, I informed the court that I would personally appear as the named defendant before Judge Robertson for a "status conference." Secretaries rarely appear in court—as Interior secretary, I was the named defendant in thousands of cases—but I saw this as a defining moment for the litigation and chose to put aside the legal and political risks raised by Department lawyers. Surrounded by my team, I sat at one side of a large table, while Elouise Cobell and her legal team sat on the other side. When the clerk announced Judge Robertson's entrance, we all rose.

Robertson looked every bit the distinguished jurist: tall and white-haired, with scholarly glasses and piercing eyes. "Welcome, everyone," he began. "Secretary Salazar, thank you for attending today."

I began, "May it please the court." I then explained that the Department would like to try to resolve this long-running case. I informed Judge Robertson that President Obama and I were committed to a new relationship with Indian country, and the case hung over this relationship as a painful reminder of the lack of trust between the United States and Native Americans. We had approached the plaintiffs, and we knew they were willing to engage in good faith negotiations. I also knew that even if we did get to a settlement, it would have to be approved by Congress, which might be an uphill battle.

Judge Robertson turned to the plaintiffs, who nodded their agreement. "As with all cases, if it can be resolved, that would be preferred," Judge Robertson said. "I look forward to being updated about this. Let me know if the court can help in any way."

As we adjourned, I approached Elouise Cobell in the hallway outside the courtroom. This was our first meeting, and I was struck by her quiet dignity. She was in her early sixties, dressed professionally and wearing a turquoise necklace that spoke to her Blackfeet heritage. She was the great-granddaughter of Mountain Chief, a celebrated leader of the Blackfeet Nation, and had grown up without electricity or running water on her family's cattle ranch. Despite—or perhaps because of—these humble beginnings, she'd become the treasurer of the Blackfeet Nation and founded the first Native American–owned national bank. In 1997, she'd won a MacArthur "genius grant" Fellowship and donated much of the $310,000 award to support the *Cobell* lawsuit.

As I approached her, I could see wariness in her eyes. How many government officials had made promises to her over the years?

"Ms. Cobell," I said, extending my hand. "I'm optimistic we can get something done."

She took my hand, studying me. "I hope so, Mr. Secretary."

"If things get stuck, I might have to call you directly."

The beginnings of a smile crossed her face. It was the start of what would become one of the most meaningful relationships of my tenure at Interior.

The negotiations over the following months were intense and complex. We were trying to put a price on the government's mismanagement, to quantify damages for lands lost, royalties stolen, accounts mishandled. The plaintiffs alleged losses exceeding $150 billion—an astronomical amount. We had to find a number that acknowledged the wrong, but that Congress would actually approve.

By the fall of 2009, we had the framework of an agreement. But there was one sticking point: attorney's fees. The plaintiffs' lawyers were asking for over a hundred million dollars for their many years of litigation.

This was a poison pill. Congress, which is full of lawyers, would never approve a settlement with such massive legal fees, no matter how justified they might have been.

So I asked Elouise Cobell, whose tribal name was Yellow Bird Woman, to visit my office in Washington. She accepted.

She came to my office a short while later, and as she stepped in, tears formed in her eyes. "I'm sorry," she said, her voice catching slightly. "I never thought I would see the day that I would be walking into this office. I'm a pariah here, Mr. Secretary. I've been going after the people who've sat in this room for so, so long . . ." she trailed off.

We were alone. I guided her to a couch and gestured that we sit. Yes, this litigation had been going on for over twelve years, but the betrayal had been going on for well over a century. As the treasurer of the Blackfeet Nation, she knew that the US government had mismanaged massive sums of money from reservation land while her people still lived in poverty. And they'd added insult to betrayal: When she'd asked federal officials about the discrepancies in the Indian Money accounts, they told her she didn't know how to read a financial statement—this to a person with a business degree who'd founded a successful bank!

I leaned forward and clasped her hand. "Ms. Cobell," I began, "the United States government bears responsibility for a very painful past with Native Americans. Yet, through all the Trails of Tears, broken treaties, massacres, and relentless efforts to destroy Native languages and peoples, you have survived. Now, with President Obama, we hope to right some of those wrongs—to make sure you have a partner in the United States that respects you and your sovereignty. We will work with you to achieve your dreams. Because your dreams are part of the American dream."

I indicated the painting behind my desk, the same one Gale Norton had supposedly removed in a tiff after Judge Lamberth found her in contempt of court.

"This painting behind me is called *Navajos Breaking Camp.* Except for a few short years, it has hung over that desk since the 1930s. Some Interior secretaries probably thought highly of that painting, others probably disliked it, and still others might have been totally indifferent to it. But for me, it is a reminder that you and your people cannot be erased. I believe, and the president believes, that Native Americans must be recognized and respected as our equals in their lands, history, and culture."

"Thank you, Mr. Secretary."

Then I turned to the matter at hand. "We are close to the finish line. We have a settlement. But to get over the line, we need to talk about your legal fees. What your lawyers are asking for is exorbitant. I can't get this settlement approved by Congress with fees that high; they won't feel that it's a worthwhile use of funds. So here's what I propose: Ask your lawyers to reduce their fees—ask them to think of this as a civil rights litigation, not a class action lawsuit—and let's ask Congress instead to use that money to create a college scholarship fund for Native Americans. What do you think? Will you help us get this done?"

She looked at me for a long moment. I knew what I was asking. But I think she also understood the political challenge.

"Yes, Mr. Secretary. I will do all I can."

A few days later, we had an agreement. The settlement totaled $3.4 billion—far less than the $150 billion in damages the plaintiffs had alleged, but still the largest settlement ever paid in a class action suit brought against the United States. It included $1.5 billion for direct payments to individual Native American class members, $1.9 billion to help tribes repurchase and consolidate those impossibly fractionated lands, and $60 million for scholarships to provide financial assistance to Native American and Alaska Native students—now called the Cobell Education Scholarship Fund. As of writing, it has helped thousands of Native American students get their educations.

When I presented the settlement to the Senate Indian Affairs Committee, senators like Byron Dorgan from North Dakota, John McCain from Arizona, and Lisa Murkowski from Alaska each congratulated me. We were all elated that we had finally achieved what many thought was impossible.

Late one night in December 2010—a year after my meeting with Elouise Cobell—I was working at my desk when my phone rang. It was my friend Harry Reid.

"Harry, you're up late."

"Good news, Ken. Your settlement has been approved." It had passed the Senate by unanimous consent a few weeks earlier, and now the House had voted it through by a wide margin: 256 to 152.

I breathed a sigh of relief.

President Obama signed the legislation on December 8, 2010. In the years that followed, over two million acres of land were restored to tribes, and hundreds of thousands of Native Americans received compensation for the harm caused by over a century of mismanagement. Did these individuals receive a lot of money? No. But I hoped that it nonetheless signaled a new beginning for the US government's relationship with Native Americans.

Elouise Cobell died on October 16, 2011, less than a year after achieving what she'd fought so long for. The Blackfeet Nation had honored her with warrior status in 2000, a fitting tribute to a woman who'd taken on the United States government—and won.

In 2016, President Obama posthumously awarded her the Presidential Medal of Freedom.

24

OVERLOOKED NO MORE

When I assumed my post at Interior in 2009, I requested a comprehensive review of national landmarks, cultural sites, and monuments. What we discovered was alarming. You could walk the entire National Mall and not find a single memorial to a woman or person of color or anyone out of the so-called mainstream. The same was true throughout the country.

We went to work rectifying many of these oversights. We worked on landmarks and monuments of all kinds across the United States: the Martin Luther King Jr. Memorial right next to the Lincoln Memorial in Washington; Fort Monroe National Monument in Hampton, Virginia, a refuge for formerly enslaved people during the Civil War; the Charles Young Buffalo Soldiers National Monument in Wilberforce, Ohio; the Harriet Tubman Underground Railroad National Historical Park in Church Creek, Maryland; monuments for Japanese internment camps during WWII; and the Belmont-Paul Women's Equality National Monument in Washington in recognition of suffragists like Alice Paul, Susan B. Anthony, and Elizabeth Cady Stanton.

I also directed the National Park Service to launch initiatives on Women's history, Asian Americans and Pacific Islanders, and American Latino heritage to help tell a more complete story about our nation's history.

Throughout these efforts, I was acutely aware of the National Park Service's failure to recognize the heritage and contributions of Hispanic Americans. Among 2,400 landmarks and cultural sites across the country, only a handful were dedicated to Mexican or Hispanic Americans.

Leaders in Washington had been aware of this shortcoming for many years. In 1993, Smithsonian Secretary Robert McCormick Adam, Jr. appointed a fifteen-member task force to investigate where his institution had failed Hispanic Americans. The task force report, titled *Willful Neglect*, concluded that the Smithsonian had ignored the contributions of Hispanics and Latinos in its exhibits. It concluded that a new national museum could help fix this. It took fifteen years, but in May 2008, President Bush signed a law creating a commission to study the creation of a National Museum of the American Latino. Now, as secretary of the Interior, it was my job to implement this law.

Working with a team at the White House, President Obama appointed this commission, which we officially launched in my office at Interior. Members included San Antonio architect Henry Munoz, III, who sat as chairman; actress Eva Longoria; musician Emilio Estefan of the Miami Sound Machine; and Denver television executive Cindy Peña. Together with their colleagues, they planned a new museum in the nation's capital to portray the art, history, and culture of Hispanic Americans. Their report, *To illuminate the American Story for All*, was delivered to President Obama on May 5, 2011. Nine years later, with large bipartisan support, Congress authorized the creation of the National Museum of the American Latino. As of this writing, fundraising for the museum continues across the country.

Alongside this initiative, we launched a National Park Service scholarly review on American Latino heritage. I announced its creation at the headquarters of the United Farm Workers at La Paz in Keene, California, along with National Park Service Director Jon Jarvis and National

Park Foundation President and CEO Neil Mulholland. I framed the challenge plainly, directing the National Park Service to investigate, preserve, and interpret the stories, places, and people of Hispanic heritage across the country. The Park Service had done meaningful work protecting early Spanish colonial sites, from the Castillo de San Marcos in St. Augustine, Florida to the Juan Bautista de Anza National Historic Trail in California. But that wasn't the whole story. "There are many more contemporary stories," I said to the assembled forum, "that deserve to be preserved and told so that all Americans can understand, appreciate, and honor the contributions of Latinos in this country."

The National Park Service produced a report titled, *American Latinos and the Making of the United States*. It was broken into four main sections—Making the Nation, Making a Life, Making a Living, and Making a Democracy—which included sixteen chapters on topics like education, religion, the arts, food, sports, the military, immigration, and the Latino struggle for inclusion.

In October 2011, the White House held an event called the American Latino Heritage Forum that we hosted at the Department of the Interior. In the press release for the event, President Obama wrote, "Diversity has always been America's strength. We are richer because of the men and women and children who've come to our shores and joined our union. And we are better off because of the ideas that they've brought, and the difference that they've made, and the impact they've had on our lives."

Later that day, I meandered down to the National Mall with my security detail in tow. I did this frequently both for exercise and to see how we were progressing on the projects on the Mall I oversaw as Interior secretary. In the crisp evening, I stopped at the World War II memorial, pausing first by the plaque honoring Senator Bob Dole, which Senator Inouye and I had ordered to be placed there commemorating Senator Dole's role in creating the Memorial. I then walked over to the New Mexico statue—each US state and territory (as well as Washington, DC) has its own statue here—and stood before it. There, I reflected on my mom and her work at the War Department when she was only 19 years old. And I remembered my dad's service as a staff sergeant stationed in Hawaii picking up the pieces after the attack on Pearl Harbor.

Only a few months earlier, I'd been with Mom at the Santa Fe National Cemetery to visit her older brother's grave, which sat among thousands of white marble stones. As we stood at the foot of his gravesite, she told me about how she'd been working at the War Department when the cable came through that her brother Leandro had been killed fighting in the battlefields of Northern Italy.

I quietly asked, "How did you feel when you got the news?"

She took a deep breath and spoke softly, "I cried for what felt like weeks. I was so close to my brother. He and I grew up together riding horses and taking care of the cows. Everybody thought I was a tomboy because I could ride a horse as well as him, and we would race around the hills of San Miguel to see who could ride faster. He was more than my brother. He was my soulmate. I still miss him."

"Do you remember the funeral?" I asked.

Tears welled in her eyes. "I couldn't go. We weren't allowed to return home because they needed us in Washington. The war was raging. But I heard from my dad many times about how painful it had been to receive the coffin of his son. They were told they could not open it, and they didn't. I imagine it would have been too hard to see what was inside."

We walked slowly to the car, my arm wrapped around her slender shoulders, and then drove the 120 miles north to Los Rincones. We traveled mostly in silence but we also talked about my mom's family in New Mexico and Leandro. I told Mom how as secretary I'd learned how stories like ours had been painfully omitted from the national story. And I recounted that unlike my Uncle Leandro, who was buried at the National Cemetery in Santa Fe, many Mexican American soldiers had not been allowed to be buried in some National Cemeteries in Texas. That was why the American GI Forum was created in Corpus Christi in 1948—to fight this type of discrimination, even in death.

We entered the San Luis Valley and crossed the prairie at the state line between New Mexico and Colorado and were soon in the town of

Antonito. Right on Main St. is a prominent white adobe building with large lettering adorning its entrance: SPMDTU. Sociedad Protección Mutua de Trabajadores Unidos. The SPMDTU had been founded in 1900 to fight for the rights of Mexican American workers and against discrimination in Colorado. Grandpa Juan and Dad were members. I remarked to Mom that the history of the SPMDTU was also a story that needed to be told as part of America's heritage.

As we approached Los Rincones, Mom and I stopped at Los Cerritos to visit the small Catholic cemetery near our home. We pushed through the squeaky metal turnstile and wandered to Dad's grave. As we prayed solemnly together, I remembered the sacrifices he had made for his family and the pride he had taken in being a United States citizen and Army soldier. In 2001, we fulfilled his instructions that he be buried in his World War II uniform.

We then got back in the car and I drove Mom home to Los Rincones. Five years later, we would bury her, right next to Dad.

25

AMERICAN PATRIOTS

American patriots are not only famous heroes like Abraham Lincoln, Susan B. Anthony, or Harriet Tubman. American patriots are everyday people doing extraordinary things. That was the case with the forty passengers and crew of United Airlines Flight 93, who died on September 11, 2001, in the rural fields of Shanksville, Pennsylvania.

It must have seemed like an ordinary, uneventful day when those forty people first boarded that plane. But once the passengers figured out they were being hijacked, they showed their mettle and rushed into action. The plane was bound for Washington, probably to destroy the Capitol. But these heroes broke into the cockpit and forced Flight 93 to crash. None survived.

In early 2009, representatives of the families of Flight 93 passengers and crew came to see me at the Interior Department. Led by Gordon Felt, brother of passenger Edward Felt, they took turns sharing their pain and telling stories about these heroes who were no longer with us. After a little while, one of them brought up the purpose of their visit.

"Mr. Secretary, nearly ten years after that day, no monument exists. President Bush was a strong supporter, but still the monument has been delayed and delayed. And now landowners and their lawyers have practically halted the project. We need your help, Mr. Secretary."

"I'm here for you," I said, committing to their cause. "It would be my honor to help." I knew from earlier briefings that there was a group of Shanksville landowners who'd held out on selling their property to the government, and I suggested that maybe I could talk with them directly to negotiate a solution. I said this knowing full well that the lawyers at Interior would tell me it was too risky—but I wasn't interested in the bureaucracy. As the meeting ended, I hugged each family member in turn, promising to be in touch.

Over the next several months, I traveled to Shanksville a half dozen times, meeting with landowners and members of the local community. With my colleagues Jon Jarvis, Kendra Barkoff, and Kate Kelly at my side, we began negotiating with the landowners, trying to find a way forward.

The landowners were split. Some were ready to make a deal, but others gruffly complained that the federal government had offered only peanuts for their valuable land. They felt like they had also been harmed. Terrorists had made their property a burial site, a place of national agony. And now the powerful federal government wanted to pay bargain prices. No matter the worthiness of this noble cause, I could see how it stung. I understood the importance of people's personal ties to their land, and I felt I knew what it was like to be in their shoes. I suggested independent appraisals and promised to help raise the necessary money to ensure that they would at least be compensated justly.

Speaker John Boehner and former Presidents Bill Clinton and George W. Bush helped with this effort, raising millions of dollars to purchase the land and design and build the memorial. The groundbreaking took place on November 7, 2009. The family members who'd visited my office at the Interior Department were present, along with Pennsylvania Governor Ed Rendell, my good friend Senator Bob Casey Jr., several members of the National Park Service, my staff, and me.

The first phase was completed and dedicated less than two years later, on September 10 and 11, 2011. Over those two days, a spirit of unity engulfed the field in Shanksville. The events were attended by President Obama and Michelle Obama, Vice President Biden and Dr. Jill Biden, former President Bush and Laura Bush, leaders from across the country, and many of the people of Shanksville. There were no partisan divides that day. The monument—gray and austere in the midst of Pennsylvania's green fields—was a testament to America's citizen heroes, men and women from many backgrounds who saved our nation's capital that late summer day in 2001.

When I returned to Washington, I took another one of my frequent walks on the National Mall, stopping at the Vietnam Veterans Memorial. I passed the names of thousands of American heroes, finally stopping at Panel 41E. My eyes scrolled down to Line 21, searching for the name Manuelito Herrera, who had been killed in action on February 25, 1968. I can still vividly recall his military funeral at Los Cerritos cemetery, which my entire family attended. Manuelito had picked potatoes in the fields alongside us before enlisting in the Army. I remembered standing among the tombstones with his family members, hearing the twenty-one-gun salute and the wailing of the bugle as it played "Taps." Throughout, his family softly cried. We resolved never to forget Manuelito.

I thought about Manuelito, and Mom, and Dad, and my uncle Leandro. Their stories—ones about sacrifice, about service, about belief in the United States—stood as examples of Senator Inouye's plea that we never forget our past. He insisted that we pay tribute to heroes of all stripes: war heroes in addition to civil rights heroes; regular people in addition to luminaries; people who had suffered in addition to people who had fought to end that suffering. This is what American diversity really means. It is not about valuing this type of person or that type of person—it is about valuing *every* person, no matter who they are, what they look like, or where they come from.

In the United States, we must celebrate people from all walks of life to best preserve the ideals of our nation. Ideals that are being torn down today by a president who knows the meaning of neither sacrifice nor service.

26

HONOULIULI

With his dying word, a simple "aloha," Senator Daniel K. Inouye passed away on December 17, 2012, at the Walter Reed National Military Medical Center, succumbing to a respiratory illness. He was eighty-eight years old.

In his fifty-eight years of public service, he never lost an election—first as a territorial representative and senator, then, after Hawaii attained statehood in 1959, as a US congressman and senator. He had witnessed the Japanese attack on Pearl Harbor, been a fearless warrior for freedom in WWII, and had become the nation's highest-ranking Asian American official in US history as president pro tempore of the Senate, the person third in line of presidential succession. To me, he was a man whose life defined the word "legacy."

A small part of his legacy was what he did for me: guiding me to the Interior Department to serve as a custodian of America's heritage. During my tenure as secretary, I tried to serve as custodian for all of the nation's people. I would travel to all fifty states to recognize and celebrate the history, struggles, and heritage of each state. However, by the end of 2012, my self-created pilgrimage was incomplete. I had traveled to *forty-nine* states. The one I had yet to visit was Senator Inouye's home state of Hawaii.

President Obama had won reelection a little over a month before Inouye's passing and, while I hadn't made a formal announcement, I knew that my time at Interior was coming to an end. I would have stayed longer, but financial and family demands required me to step down, which I would do in the spring of 2013.

On December 23, 2012, Senator Inouye's body was transferred from the Capitol Rotunda, where he had lain in state, to Honolulu. I traveled to Hawaii to honor him and attend his state funeral. And so, in the end, I would accompany my friend to complete my tour of all fifty states as secretary of the Interior.

As I flew those many miles west from Washington to Hawaii, I thought about the conversations I'd had with Senator Inouye. He'd told me that the proudest day of his life was when President Franklin Roosevelt signed the order in March 1943 that created the Army's 442nd Infantry Regiment. But while Senator Inouye didn't talk much about what happened on the battlefields of Europe, he did talk about what it was like for the Japanese Americans who had been forced into internment camps across the American West.

I had often recounted to Senator Inouye a point of Colorado pride that Ralph Carr, our governor during WWII, was alone among Western state governors in standing against the internment of Japanese Americans. Carr, who was white, took a great political risk when he publicly advocated for the rights of Japanese Americans under the Constitution, saying they were "as loyal to American institutions as you and I." It wasn't just talk: He actively opposed statewide bills that would have restricted their rights, and he opened Colorado's doors to Japanese Americans who faced incarceration in places like Washington, Oregon, and California, saying they could move to Colorado to avoid internment.

Even after the federal government set up an internment camp in Granada, Colorado, Governor Carr insisted that the people held there be treated humanely and given opportunities to work outside the camp on nearby farms and ranches. Throughout this dark moment in US history, Governor Carr publicly condemned anti-Japanese hate speech and any form of violence against Japanese Americans.

Of course, this stance cost him his political career. But I imagine he was at peace. Ralph Carr was truly a profile in courage, an example that people in any era, including ours, would do well to remember and replicate.

Whenever Senator Inouye and I discussed the internment of Japanese Americans, he spoke about a place I'd never visited: the Honouliuli Internment Camp. We had placed the site on the National Register of Historic Places in early 2012, a necessary first step to Honouliuli possibly becoming a national monument. Inouye told me, "Ken, this is a special site that deserves recognition. When people like me and my family disappeared in Hawaii during the war, they often ended up in Honouliuli. One day, a person could be going about their business, spending time with their family, or attending church, and the next day they were gone without any notice. Just gone. Someday, we must go there together."

We never did get to go there together, at least not physically. After the celebration of life for this most beloved Hawaiian son—complete with people from across the nation and the Pacific Islands, Native Hawaiians in colorful clothes, and a twenty-one-gun military salute—I took a car to Honouliuli. It was now owned by the giant agricultural firm Monsanto and formed part of one of their research centers. Before flying to Hawaii, I'd reached out to Monsanto's president to see if I could access the site. He'd told me that he'd see if it could be arranged, but that it was surrounded by private land. I told him, "It is important to me, and it was important to Senator Inouye, that I be able to visit it. Please see what you can do."

He came through. The car ride to Monsanto's compound took about forty minutes, and when I got there, I was greeted by a company supervisor. He got in my car and told the driver where to go, driving over rough dirt roads surrounded by weeds and tropical flora. We dropped down into a wide depression, an area the Japanese internees called "jigoku dani"—"hell valley"—due to its unrelenting heat and the fact that they were imprisoned there against their will. There were a few low buildings scattered here and there, but mostly the site was overgrown and dilapidated. It looked like a forgotten place—probably a place that had been intentionally forgotten. I spent more than an hour among the ruins. Words that Senator Inouye had spoken many times rang in my mind: "We must remember our history so that we don't repeat the mistakes of the past. That's the only way that America will continue to become stronger."

As I left the site to return to the bustle of Honolulu, I kept thinking over and over of two World War II veterans: A young Daniel Inouye, stationed far from home in Italy among hundreds of heroic Japanese soldiers, and another young man named Henry Salazar, who had been sent to Hawaii as an Army sergeant in the aftermath of Pearl Harbor. Two patriots—one a Mexican American rancher and farmer from the San Luis Valley, the other a Japanese American son of a jeweler and housewife—fighting for their country and doing their part to protect the American dream.

PART VI

THE AMBASSADOR

A New Beginning

The Borders

The Presidents

The Warning Bells

Heartbreak

A NEW BEGINNING

27

THE APPOINTMENT

I left the Interior Department and government work entirely in April 2013. After more than two decades of public service, I needed to take care of my family. It was time to return to Colorado, practice law, and help on the ranch.

I ended up founding the Denver office of an internationally renowned law firm, WilmerHale. The firm had led efforts to end apartheid in South Africa and had worked on the *Grutter* affirmative action case for Michigan Law. For me, it was a perfect fit. From 2013 to 2021, I worked in their offices at 1225 17th Street, took care of Hope, our girls, and our granddaughters, and helped expand our ranch in the Valley. In addition to buying a hay ranch along the Conejos River, we built a new adobe house, right next to where my great-grandparents' home once stood, just up the road from Manassa.

By then, Leroy, John, Elliott, Margaret, and June had returned to the Valley. All lived close to our family homestead in Los Rincones, and some of their grown children also lived close by. June and her husband, Ted, had left their jobs in Albuquerque and moved to Los Rincones with their young son Eric. They were there to care for our then-ninety-year-old mother, who was in the final years of her long and remarkable life. The Valley was exerting its gravity on all of us Salazars. It was wonderful to be near each other again.

After the 2016 election, I watched the first Trump administration from the sidelines, working on cases in Colorado and across the country. I was dismayed by many things Trump did, including his reckless abandonment of rural America and public lands, as well as his mistreatment of migrants and his racist politicization of the border. His unbelievable attacks on non-white immigrants as coming from what he called "shithole" countries said it all.

I did what I could to aid the opposition to Trump, including helping to elect a Colorado congressional delegation that included Representatives Joe Neguse, a Black lawyer born to Eritrean immigrants, and Jason Crow, a white retired Army Ranger. Both would ultimately take lead roles in the impeachments of Donald Trump.

During the 2020 election, I campaigned for Joe Biden and was overjoyed when he prevailed. Even with all the baseless claims of a stolen election—claims made more sinister by the horror of January 6 and Trump's incitement of the mob that stormed the Capitol that day—I knew we were once again in good hands. President Biden was a decent man, and after all the upheaval of the first Trump term, decency was what the country needed. I think that is primarily what Americans had voted for.

During the last months of Trump's presidency, I began to think of once again returning to government. My family and the ranch were doing well, and while we still had the trials and tribulations of any family, I yearned to return to public service. I was intent on helping fix our broken borderlands and, especially after Trump, to help foster a new era of understanding between the United States and Mexico.

I didn't want to serve in the cabinet; I wanted to go to Mexico as US ambassador. I reached out to Biden's transition team not long after the election to express my interest in this role. They said they would convey this to President Biden and that I'd hear back soon one way or the other.

One day in March, as I was driving my thirteen-year-old granddaughter Mireya to the doctor to get her allergy shots, my phone rang, displaying an unknown Washington, DC, area code. I didn't usually answer calls like this, but some intuition told me that it might be important. I answered. "Hello. Who is this?"

"Ken?" a familiar voice said.

"Yes."

"Joe Biden here."

"Mr. President!" I exclaimed. "How are you doing, sir?" I pulled out of traffic and guided my truck to the curb to make sure I didn't get too distracted.

"Great. Just great. Listen, Ken, got a question for you. I want you to be my ambassador in Mexico. What do you say?"

"Sir, I would be honored. I hope with your leadership we can transform the relationship between the United States and Mexico forever."

"Ken, that is *exactly* what we need to do."

"Mr. President, in that case, we'll need to act with urgency. It will be hard, but we can do it."

"I agree," the president responded. "And is that your granddaughter I hear in the background? I remember meeting her. How is she doing?"

"She's doing great, Mr. President." I turned to Mireya, who sat next to me in the passenger seat. "Mireya, say hi to the president!"

Speech had come late to Mireya, and when she was two years old, we learned that she was on the autism spectrum. By this time, she had come a long way with her communication skills beyond sign language. In almost perfect words, she said, "Hello, Joe Biden. How you doing?"

"Good," he said. "Take care of your grandfather. He is going to go to Mexico."

Mireya giggled and responded, "OK. Papo can do this."

I thanked the president again and told him I'd see him soon.

Even for a former senator and cabinet official, the vetting process to become an ambassador was interminable and onerous. I had my Senate hearing in May, was confirmed unanimously in June, and was officially sworn in on August 11. Exactly one month later, on September 11, 2021, I finally landed at Benito Juárez International Airport in Mexico City to officially assume my post.

28

FIRST IMPRESSIONS

As soon as I landed in Mexico City, my family and I were escorted by armed bodyguards from the airplane into a waiting bulletproof Chevy Suburban and driven to the ambassador's residence. Our vehicle was trailed by another SUV containing heavily armed guards, while yet more guards had headed out before us to secure the route to our new home. In all, thirty or forty men and women were tasked with protecting us.

As the motorcade weaved through traffic, I asked the chief bodyguard in the front seat, "¿Cómo ves tu trabajo?" How do you see your job?

In Spanish, he answered, "Our job is to keep the ambassador safe and protected from attacks. We are always prepared, and members of the unit will always be with you."

We pulled onto the beautiful Paseo de la Reforma, where thousands of people strolled happily along the boulevard in a scene that seemed peaceful and full of life. The disconnect was obvious: Was this a safe country with happy people, or a dangerous one where anything could happen, anywhere, at any time?

Of course, the answer was that it was both.

Still, I had some trouble accepting this—the only other places I'd traveled that prompted this level of personal security were in the war zones of Iraq and Afghanistan—and so I asked the bodyguard, "Is it really that dangerous?"

"One never knows," he said. "A few months ago, the Mexico City chief of police, Omar García Harfuch, was attacked right here, a few blocks from your house, in the early morning hours on his way to work. His driver and bodyguard were killed, but he survived. The story is that the cartel Jalisco Nueva Generación wanted him dead for the work he was doing here."

It was hard to imagine, given how pristine the Paseo de la Reforma was. I wondered how the million or so US citizens living in this beautiful city felt about the attack.

As we arrived at the residence, we were greeted by even more armed guards. Here I was in a cosmopolitan megacity of twenty-five million people—one of the most visited and livable cities in the world—and yet I would always be surrounded by armed guards.

That night, I remarked to Hope, "This is surreal. I'll never be alone."

"No, but at least you will be safe. Please, Ken, I know how independent you are. Don't venture out on your own."

"I won't," I promised. And I never did.

Two days later, Hope, our granddaughter Mireya, our daughter Melinda and her husband, Blake, and I were officially welcomed at the US embassy. It was a formal but very festive event with mariachis and food. Melinda, who was pregnant with Amelia, beamed and cheered as I introduced her in the courtyard. Melinda and baby Amelia would visit me frequently in Mexico City to support me and learn Spanish. Amelia was actually baptized in Mexico City at the Basilica of Our Lady of Guadalupe.

During my first three months at Mission Mexico, I was in constant motion. I crisscrossed Mexico continuously, meeting officials, priests, business leaders, law enforcement officers, and regular Mexicans. I visited the southern border three times, where the Selva Maya rainforest straddles much of Mexico and Guatemala, an area where migrants continuously streamed into Mexico. I visited the northern border twice, where the United States meets Mexico and where the landscape is dominated by desert and vast open stretches. I went to the Mexican states of Chiapas, Tabasco, Campeche, Yucatán, Quintana Roo, Nuevo León, Coahuila, Chihuahua, Sonora, and Baja California, and I was beginning to learn more about the federal district of Mexico City, a beautiful, complex metropolis. I flew back and forth to DC to meet lawmakers, White House staff, ambassadors, business leaders, agency heads, Vice President Kamala Harris, and the president himself. In my first ninety days, I traveled more than thirty thousand miles—roughly six thousand miles more than the circumference of planet Earth.

I undertook this intense schedule to demonstrate to both the Mexican and US governments that I meant business. I had been given President Biden's blessing to transform the relationship between the United States and Mexico, and that is what I intended to do. From the highest level to the most pedestrian, everyone in Mexico had to know the mission of my work.

THE BORDERS

29

THE US–MEXICO BORDER

In early December 2021, I made my third trip to Mexico's northern border. My earlier trips had been to the eastern end of the border, but now it was time to see the western side in detail, from San Diego and Tijuana to El Paso and Juárez.

I started in the middle of this section in Nogales, Mexico, a medium-sized city of about three hundred thousand people that lies right across the border from its twin city, Nogales, Arizona. My staff and I arrived on a chilly December night and drove through town in our armored SUV, twinkling Christmas lights strewn on houses and hardscrabble desert trees. They had been put up to celebrate the holidays, but for me they felt like small symbols of a new era.

We were hosted that evening by the consul general for Nogales. The area around the residence was full of vehicles and security personnel, and our heavily guarded car was ushered through the main entrance. My staff and I walked through the house to the backyard, where we found about two hundred people eating tacos and socializing. The mayors of

Nogales, Mexico, and Nogales, Arizona, were there, as were the heads of various state agencies, law enforcement officials, and business leaders.

After we arrived, I gave a speech. I spoke about the shared history of our people all across the borderlands and about the vision the United States had for transforming the border: updating the infrastructure on both sides, increasing security, and finding a way to handle the migrant flows reaching the border that, in those days, numbered around six thousand per day.

Most of my conversations that night centered on the ways all of these issues affected the law-abiding people on both sides of the border, people for whom the border was not a hard line but a fluid one that was crossed often for work, school, socializing, and so on. It was not uncommon for extended families to include both Mexican and American citizens. Nearly everyone at the consul's residence that night seemed to feel that there existed a pronounced lack of understanding of the reality of the border. I heard it said multiple times: "Nobody in Washington or Mexico City really knows or cares about what's happening here."

I was there to convince them that those days were over.

That night, my staff and I were driven up to Tucson, about sixty-five miles due north. Early the next morning, we were taken from our hotel to a Customs and Border Protection (CBP) compound where I climbed aboard a waiting Black Hawk helicopter for a tour of the Tucson sector. This 262-mile-long section of the border covers most of Arizona, from the Yuma County line in the west to the New Mexico state line in the east.

I took my seat in the rear of the chopper and put on the headset that would help me hear my fellow passengers over the whomp of the Black Hawk's rotor and engine. Riding in a helicopter is a physical experience—you feel it as much as you hear it—and almost as soon as I strapped in, I felt the chopper come to life, first with a growl and then a roar. Within a few minutes, we were airborne, dust flying everywhere outside as we climbed. Once we reached a high enough altitude, the pilot spun the chopper to the south and pushed the throttle. My stomach briefly lurched as we accelerated to a crushing speed of more than 150 miles per hour, the ground below screaming past in a rust-hued blur.

After twenty-five minutes or so, the pilot slowed down and brought us within what felt like a hundred feet of the ground. We hung over an older section of border wall, one that had been around since before President Trump had promised to erect his "big, beautiful wall" across the entire 2,000-mile-long border. Of course, the wall was never fully built; only around 460 miles were either repaired or constructed.

This section stretched for miles to the east and west, but it was not in great shape. The pilot pointed south across a huge expanse of barren ranch lands on the Mexican side. "Mr. Ambassador, can you see down there?" he asked in a loud baritone over our headsets. "Those little parallel scars in the earth?"

"I see them, yes."

"That's a smuggler track," he said. He explained that the cartels, working with smugglers, had forged these rugged roads for four-wheel vehicles. "They bring the migrants right up to the fence on those tracks," he said. "We find people all the time out here—men, women, children—climbing the wall. Sometimes they make it, sometimes they fall on either side and need medical attention."

"What do you do with them?" I asked.

"Mostly we try to turn them around and send them right back to Mexico."

We didn't see any people that day, but we knew that somewhere out there, people were trying to cross or waiting to do so. Across the length of the borderlands, roughly six thousand people would encounter CBP agents or other law enforcement officers within the next twenty-four hours—and six thousand was surely an undercount. It was impossible to know how many would make it across undetected.

The pilot dropped the chopper even closer to the ground, hovering right at the edge of the cloud of dust produced by our rotor wash. From that short distance, I could see that the wall here was quite shabby. It had many gaps. Some had clearly been carved with blowtorches by the smugglers, while some were open sections that had been reserved for gates that were never installed. Immediately after taking office, President Biden stopped the construction of the wall. But even where the wall was intact, there were obvious signs of activity. Discarded ladders and ropes lay randomly in little arroyos and depressions, and clothing, bags, and other personal items had been abandoned near the base of the wall or were draped on sections of concertina wire to facilitate scaling the razor-sharp barbs.

We spun east, continuing to hug the ground. The US side was also barren ranchland, but instead of four-wheeler tracks there were obvious trails made by humans and wildlife. It was easy to picture a group of twenty or so people, shambling along, exhausted, carrying gallon water jugs given them by the smugglers or recovered from the brush where US religious volunteers and humanitarian organizations sometimes hid them. These folks weren't trying to help the migrants get into the US, but they were trying to help them at least survive. It was not uncommon for CBP officers and local ranchers to find corpses in the barren desert.

All these migrants were hoping to somehow find that illusory freedom the smugglers had sold to them. Called "coyotes," these smugglers would point one hand to the north, indicating the direction of the land of possibility, and hold out the other, demanding payment. That so few of their clients would ever find what they were looking for was not their concern. All they wanted was money in exchange for their peddling of false promises.

We flew back to Tucson and met with that city's vivacious and effective mayor, Regina Romero. It was good to see her and share our vision of the future. That evening, we headed for El Paso, Texas, over three hundred miles to the east. We could have hitched a ride on another chopper, but I wanted to be on the ground. So we grabbed an armored SUV and requested to be driven through the night to Texas.

In the car with me was a driver, a single State Department security detail officer, and Jen Schmidt, one of my most senior staff members. The lights of suburban Tucson soon gave way to desert wilderness. The moon was a day or two from full, but the sky was overcast, so the landscape around us was bathed with a dim, diffuse blue light. As we barreled along I-10, the fastest route from Tucson to El Paso, I leaned forward and said to the driver, "I'd like to be as close to the border as possible. Can we get off the interstate at some point and take back roads?"

"It'll add an hour at least, sir," the driver said, with no hint of annoyance.

"If it's all right with you, it's all right with me. I would like to see the border as close-up as we can. Jen, that OK?"

"Of course, Ambassador."

"I'm good with it," the driver said.

"Thank you," I said, leaning back.

We kept going for a while and got off the interstate in Benson, Arizona. Jen and I chatted as we drove. I had only known Jen for a couple of months, but she had already become a trusted colleague. In her late thirties, she was an Oregonian with a degree in environmental policy, and she and her husband, Chad, had two small kids, both under five years old. All four lived in State Department housing in Mexico City, which was her first foreign soil posting. She had joined the foreign service after stints in the nonprofit world—she was answering the call to serve our country as well as her and Chad's personal desire for adventure.

We spoke about her children, especially her older one, who was already more fluent in Spanish than she, and the challenges of encouraging the Mexican leadership to move forward with various environmental projects—a process with which Mission Mexico would become increasingly entwined. Though junior foreign service officers have no say in where they are sent, Jen told me that she counted herself lucky to have been posted to Mexico City, which she called "one of the most amazing places I've ever been."

Eventually, the drive gave way to silence. Jen buried herself in her phone and iPad, updating calendars and returning emails, while I stared out the window. South and east of Benson, we passed through what appeared in the nighttime to be an expanse of nothingness. For mile after mile there was little to no sign of human activity—no lights, no towns, no industry. This was a bit of an illusion, of course. For all of the ruggedness of the American Southwest, this is land that has been touched by countless human hands, land that has been lived on for thousands of years. Hiding out there in the darkness were mineral mines, national parks and monuments, transfer depots, gas stations, diners, ranches, and homes, some of them completely off-grid.

I felt a kinship for what was out there, for what I could and could not see in the moonstruck night. I understood what the people out there struggled with—the land, the weather, the harshness. It was another forgotten place, one taken for granted in Washington, DC.

Our driver knew the whole sector like the back of his hand. He would call out little hamlets and one-gas-station towns on both sides of the border as we passed them. Agua Prieta, Rodeo, Animas, Windmill. By around 11:00 PM, we had crossed into New Mexico, and soon the road came right along the US–Mexico border. About seventy miles from El Paso, Jen said, "Mr. Ambassador, I'm starving."

"Me too," I said. I turned to the driver. "Do you know anywhere around here we can eat?"

"Nothing on this side," he said. We were in Columbus, New Mexico, and everything was closed. "But we're close to Palomas, in Mexico. Could try there."

"Is it safe?" I asked.

"We'll stop at the border and ask the officers," the driver said.

A short while later, we pulled up to the Palomas border crossing and chatted with the the CBP officers. They said that yes, it was safe—there was little to no cartel activity here—and there were a few all-night restaurants. We showed them and their Mexican counterparts our diplomatic passports and very quickly found ourselves in a bustling Chinese restaurant on the main street in town. We had Hunan beef, fried rice, and scallion pancakes and sipped cold beer, all of which tasted just as delicious in Mexico as it would have at any decent Chinese restaurant in the States.

After dinner, we crossed back to the United States, and a little over an hour later, we arrived at the Hotel Paso del Norte, a historic landmark less than a mile from the border in downtown El Paso. As we entered, we passed an eight-foot-tall statue depicting Pancho Villa, the famous Mexican revolutionary, and US General John Pershing, a memorialization of the two men's brief period of friendship in 1914. A few years later, the men would be mortal enemies, with Pershing given ten thousand soldiers to capture Villa and stop his cross-border raids. Despite being outnumbered, Villa escaped, though he would later be assassinated by political enemies within Mexico.

The next day was another whirlwind, full of visits and meetings. I began with the mayor of El Paso, Oscar Leeser. We connected with a contingent of CBP agents, who gave us a tour of the border crossing facility at Bridge of the Americas. It was a surreal scene: The official border was bustling, with everyday people, cars, and big trucks crossing legally in both directions across eight lanes of traffic and a pedestrian walkway.

But beneath the official port of entry crossing, a group of about a hundred migrants could easily be seen crossing illegally by wading across the Rio Grande, which at this location and at this time of year was only about a foot deep. As they huddled together, the migrants prayed in gratitude to Our Lady of Guadalupe, the Patroness of the Americas, for having delivered them to the United States. They clutched their few belongings, waiting to hand whatever identification they had over to the Customs and Border Patrol officers. These officers sorted the people into lines: single men, single women, families, and a few lone children. Nearly all were Venezuelan, fleeing the poverty created under the dictatorships of Hugo Chávez and Nicolás Maduro. They had walked across the forbidding Darién Gap, a snake-infested tropical jungle on the border between Colombia and Panama, where South America and North America connect. From there, they made their way through Panama, Costa Rica, Nicaragua, Honduras, Guatemala, and Mexico before finally reaching the US border.

I approached the migrants and asked why they had left Venezuela. Many exclaimed they had no hope there, and had to escape for a better life for them and their families. I felt sorry for them as fellow human beings but I also knew that their pain and suffering would in all likelihood continue.

We left the migrants, climbed into waiting government SUVs, and crossed into Juárez, Mexico. We were driven along the border to the US consulate for what is commonly referred to as a "stakeholder" meeting. This particular meeting was attended by me, my staff, Mayor Leeser, the mayor of Juárez, the governor of the state of Chihuahua, their respective staff members, a large group of law enforcement and border agents, and representatives from the private sector on both sides of the border. We were also joined by a highly effective US congresswoman named Veronica Escobar, a Democrat who represented most of El Paso and much of the area around it, including Fort Bliss, the second-largest Army installation in the United States.

We sat around a horseshoe table in a nondescript room inside the consulate, little placards identifying each of us by name. As the US ambassador, I sat at the head of the table and chaired the meeting. The main focus of our conversation was the modernization of the border and the migrant crisis. Nearly everyone at the table weighed in.

We used the word "crisis" freely and often in this meeting (and in many others), even if at that time the White House refused to acknowledge it as such. It was plain to those of us present that this was indeed a crisis. To claim it wasn't one not only strained credibility, but also disrespected the men and women tasked with guarding the border, the people trying to follow legal pathways for entry, the business owners and local leaders who had to deal with this situation day in and day out—and not least the migrants themselves.

The meeting was fruitful. We agreed to work together to improve infrastructure at the border crossings along the nearby section of the Rio Grande, and we resolved that we would push both of our federal governments for more support and real solutions.

There was one more stop that day before my staff and I hopped on a plane west to San Diego: a local migrant shelter. I had been to centers like this before up and down the border. They were large, warehouse-like facilities whose main function was to further sort migrants into categories beyond the triage that happened right at the border.

In some of these shelters there were hundreds of people. Some—like single men—were gathered up to be returned to Mexico by bus or plane; others, who were sick or had tested positive for COVID, were being held in the medical facility; those who had criminal records were put in cells to await either deportation or prosecution; and some were being given the much sought-after "NTA" paperwork—the "notice to appear." These migrants would be released into the United States until the courts could determine if their asylum claims were legitimate, though these cases could take months or even years to be decided.

Unlike the unbridled joy we saw on the faces of the Venezuelans crossing the Rio Grande earlier, the people in these shelters were overwhelmingly disoriented and sad. For them, the spell had broken. The realization that their dreams would not soon come true hit them hard. It was heart-wrenching to see so much misery and exhaustion, even on the faces of young children and their mothers. Some cried as they told me of appalling horrors—robbery, rape, and extortion—they'd endured while traveling along the migrant corridor.

During my visit, I reflected on the selfless courage and generosity of religious leaders and volunteers like Sister Norma Pimentel in McAllen, Texas, a Mexican American Catholic nun who gave all she had to help suffering people up and down the Texas–Mexico border. It angered me that selfish, cowardly politicians in Washington and Latin America did not match the courage of these religious leaders and volunteers.

I also felt sorry for the men and women of the CBP, as they masked their anger and frustration and dutifully did their jobs. They were being asked to do an extremely difficult and exhausting task, under ever-shifting rules, and with a dearth of support or resources. The words spoken two nights earlier in Nogales rang in my ears: "Nobody cares about what's happening here."

That night, my staff and I flew to Houston to make a connection to San Diego, where we repeated the process all over again—visiting stakeholders, crossing the border to Tijuana, meeting mayors and other politicians and business leaders, visiting migrant shelters and walking along the border. Just to the east of the San Diego–Tijuana Port of Entry, the California state and local governments had recently spent about half a billion dollars modernizing the US side of the border with a planned new port of entry called Otay Mesa East. I met there with California officials including Lieutenant Governor Eleni Kounalakis and Baja California Governor Marina del Pilar, as well as Mexican and US officials. Nothing was happening yet on the Mexican side, but I committed to work with both governments to try to make Otay Mesa East an example of our two countries' most modern border crossing.

From San Diego–Tijuana, I made one more trip, again by helicopter. At the request of US Senator Mark Kelly, a colleague and friend and a famed astronaut and decorated military leader, I flew out to see what could be done with the huge spike in migrant flows in Yuma, Arizona. I was accompanied by CBP officials as well as Consul General Tom Reott, a thirty-year foreign service officer who had been sent to Mexico by Trump during his first administration. Tom was now posted to Tijuana and managed the relationship between California and the Mexican states of Baja California and Baja Sur. Like Congresswoman Escobar in El Paso, Tom had a clear vision for what had to be done to modernize the border, get migrant flows under control, clean up the Tijuana River, and jointly modernize the ports of entry.

After a short flight toward the east, we reached the Yuma Sector, which starts at the Imperial Sand Dunes in California and extends for 126 miles to the Pima County line, where the mighty Colorado River crosses into Mexico. Unlike the borderlands I'd flown over before, Yuma was green from above, its seemingly countless fields brimming with leafy lettuces of all kinds (Yuma is often referred to as North America's winter vegetable capital). As we flew over this landscape, the CBP official with us pointed to sewage tunnels the smugglers used to cross migrants into the United States, to more sections of torch-cut border wall, and to other gaps due to the halt in construction. Tom and I talked about the need to close these physical openings, and to establish "mirror patrols" on both sides of the border, groups of Mexican and US law enforcement officers who would work together to prevent people from crossing. These are logical solutions, but they were not being effectively implemented by the Department of Homeland Security or by the Mexican National Institute of Migration.

At one point, we landed to speak with the CBP agents on the ground. Just like everywhere else I'd visited, these officers were trying in vain to stanch the flow of migrants across the border. And like everywhere else, these CBP officers were not happy with Washington and what they regarded as a lack of support. They were universally polite and appreciated that I had come to see them and the reality of the border, but their refrain was a common one: "Nobody cares."

I told them I cared. I thanked them and promised I would work relentlessly to find solutions to these long-standing challenges. However, I couldn't help but feel as though for those of us on the front lines of the border, we were the proverbial tail trying to wag the dog in DC.

From Yuma, I flew by helicopter back to San Diego, where I caught a commercial flight on Aeroméxico to Mexico City. Flight delays kept me from arriving at the ambassador's residence until 3:00 AM, but that time allowed me to reflect on my latest tour of the border. There was no denying it: The border—a dynamic 1,954-mile-long stretch of land through some of the most geographically perilous parts of the country, a divide that saw nearly $2 billion of trade every single day—was antiquated, under-resourced, underdeveloped, insecure, and broken. In this, Trump had been correct. And if President Biden wanted to lead from a position of strength, then, in my view, we had to do something about it. There was no other choice.

30

DEATH FROM THE GUATEMALAN BORDER

December 9, 2021, was my ninetieth day in Mexico. At first, it was like every other day: busy and full of meetings.

Built in the 1960s, the embassy complex was a bland, five-story concrete cube on Paseo de la Reforma. (A $1 billion modern complex, which would be dedicated in 2024, was still under construction a couple of miles to the northwest.) The rooms reserved for the ambassador were on the fifth floor, overlooking an inner courtyard. They consisted of a waiting room, a conference room, the deputy ambassador's office, and my personal office.

Though this zone was not quite a SCIF—a Sensitive Compartmented Information Facility, commonly found in US government buildings—no outside electronics were allowed in any of these rooms. Every day, I would enter the building from the street, pass the armed soldiers guarding the complex, salute the "Post One" Marines dressed in their green fatigues, and take the elevator upstairs. After keying through a secure door, I would leave my personal cell phone and iPad, as well as my government-issued phone and iPad, in a designated drop-off area. Only then could I enter my office. Once inside, the flow of information was strictly controlled. Whenever I wanted to check my personal emails or texts or see what was going on in the wider world, I had to step out to use one of my devices.

I did just this in the midafternoon of December 9. There were a few nonurgent texts from Hope, who was in Denver, and a few personal messages from colleagues in Washington—but one WhatsApp message stood out. It was an urgent request from the office of Mexico's foreign affairs secretary, Marcelo Ebrard. A tragedy had occurred that day in the state of Chiapas, and Secretary Ebrard wanted my support and that of the United States.

I checked the news. In the southeastern city of Tuxtla Gutiérrez, about 140 miles from the nearest border crossing between Mexico and Guatemala, a tractor trailer carrying more than 160 Guatemalan migrants had crashed. At that moment there were no solid numbers, but dozens were dead and over a hundred were injured, some quite seriously. I called the secretary's office and spoke to a member of his staff. Ebrard was wondering if the United States would join a joint Mexican-Guatemalan-US investigation into what had happened. While details were scant, the authorities believed these Guatemalan migrants were being transported by human traffickers from Guatemala all the way to the United States.

This type of migrant crossing typically went like this: A person in Guatemala would pay a coyote roughly $15,000 to be transported out of Guatemala and through Mexico to a set point on the US–Mexico border. Before leaving Guatemala, the migrants were loaded into trailers, and other than short breaks at designated stops, they would stay there for the roughly 1,300-mile trip. This harrowing journey could take a week or more, since the smugglers often had to take circuitous routes to avoid Mexican "filtros," or "filters," designed to catch and turn back migrants.

Once at the US border, the coyotes gave the migrants three attempts at crossing. If they were caught by border agents and sent back, the smugglers tried again a few days later. After the third attempt, any further tries required additional cash payments of several thousand dollars. Altogether, the trip was extremely harsh and full of perils, from harassment and sexual abuse to hunger, lack of facilities, heat exhaustion, and, in this case, death.

Before answering Secretary Ebrard's request, I could have called someone from the State Department or the National Security Council in the White House, apprised them of the situation, and asked for permission to devote US resources to a multinational law enforcement investigation. But I knew Washington. Most of the time, getting permission took weeks or months. With dozens dead and over a hundred injured—and with an active crime scene on Mexican soil—there was no time for that. If I took heat for it later on, so be it.

"Yes," I said to Secretary Ebrard's staff. "You can count on us." Almost as soon as I hung up, I called Bobby Garcia, Mission Mexico's attaché for the US Department of Homeland Security. I asked Bobby to get down to Tuxtla Gutiérrez and start working with Mexican investigators. I would also make the trip, but in the meantime, I wanted his eyes on the situation.

Secretary Ebrard invited me to a meeting with the Guatemalan foreign minister and ambassador to Mexico at his offices in Plaza Juárez, a modern, rust-hued concrete-and-glass tower in Mexico City's Centro Histórico. Secretary Ebrard, a physically imposing blue-eyed man who stood at least six feet, two inches tall, held court. As we conferred, we agreed that we had to get to the bottom of what had happened, to bring whoever was responsible for this to justice, and to do what we could to help the migrants who had survived the crash.

Following our closed-door session, Secretary Ebrard led us to a press room teeming with reporters and photographers. We ascended the dais and the secretary took the podium. He was in his element. Before serving as foreign affairs secretary, he had been a popular mayor of Mexico City—a frequent springboard to the Mexican presidency—and in 2012 had briefly run against Andrés Manuel López Obrador, or AMLO, the left-wing populist who after several attempts finally won the presidency in 2018. President López Obrador had since folded Ebrard into his cabinet.

Secretary Ebrard did most of the talking at the press conference, promising to find out who was responsible for this tragedy. There would be a "national crackdown on human smuggling," he promised. He further added that there would be "no impunity" for the criminal traffickers once they were found.

"No impunity" or "zero impunity" were common refrains from AMLO in his frequent morning press conferences. Mexico is famous for many things: beaches, mountains, food, tequila, art, music—and cartels and corruption. I had barely been in Mexico for three months, and I was not yet qualified to make judgment calls on how successful AMLO or any of his deputies had been at rooting out corruption. But like any addict trying to kick a habit, acknowledging a problem is a necessary first step. And so I was heartened to hear Secretary Ebrard repeat his president's words: "no impunity."

The Guatemalan foreign minister followed Ebrard with some brief remarks of his own, noting that all but four or five of the victims were Guatemalan, and most of them were from the Guatemalan highlands, a physically and ecologically majestic but economically depressed area. I took the microphone last. My message was also brief. I said the United States would work with Mexico and Guatemala to stop these international smuggling organizations who were taking advantage of these migrants and their dreams of finding work and happiness in the United States.

On December 19, I traveled to Tuxtla Gutiérrez, landing late that morning. My staff and I passed through the airport and climbed into an armored embassy car. We were driven half an hour, mostly through the jungle, to our first stop: the hospital treating the survivors of the crash. There, I was greeted by Chiapas's governor, Rutilio Escandón, who was officially in charge of the investigation.

Governor Escandón and I went inside and were greeted by a small team of doctors and surgeons. After changing into yellow scrubs and hair caps, we were taken to the ICU, where many of the survivors were still being treated ten full days after the crash.

Most of the migrants were young men, aged sixteen to twenty-five or so. I wandered freely among them, saying hello and introducing myself as the US ambassador to Mexico. I tried to put myself in their position—injured young people who had been victims of criminal smugglers, and who would soon be repatriated to Guatemala. People who more than anything wanted to get to the United States in the hopes of making a life for themselves. Here they were nursing broken limbs, concussions, lacerations, road rash, and worse.

I asked how they were being treated in the hospital, and to a man they said the same thing: "Fine. With God's help we will be OK."

Whether that meant God's help to find legal ways to enter the United States, to escape the torment of criminal gangs in their hometowns, or simply to heal and get better, I did not know. All I could see were damaged, desperate people with no good options. Rarely had I felt so powerless in my life.

I stepped away from one young man and surveyed the ICU. There were probably a dozen people in there, all in various states of severe injury. Two caught my eye: a young woman off in the corner, the top of her head and one side of her face covered in white gauze, who smiled while snuggling a two- or three-year-old boy.

I turned to the doctor accompanying me and gestured to the woman, asking, "What happened to her?"

"She was thrown from the trailer during the crash. She flew through the air and landed on her head. Part of her scalp got torn off, and she was heavily concussed. We thought for sure she would die. But we got to her quickly enough and pieced her back together. She's tough. I expect her to make a full recovery."

"My God. The boy was with her?"

"Yes."

"What happened to him?"

"It's impossible to know, but he was unharmed. He was running around the crash scene when the police and EMTs arrived, barely a scratch on him. He had lost track of his mother, and for a little while, we didn't know who he belonged to. Her injuries made her difficult to identify, and it didn't help that she was unconscious. Somehow, though, we were able to figure out the two were traveling together. They've been inseparable since."

"Can I talk with them?"

"Of course."

The doctor led me over and introduced the woman, Vanessa, and her son, Damián. I stood next to her bed, introduced myself, and said in Spanish, "I'm so sorry this has happened to you, Vanessa. If there is anything I can do to help you, I will try."

"Thank you, sir," she said.

"How are they treating you here?"

"Good, very good, sir," she said. "It is a very nice hospital. Nicer than back home."

"And how is this little man? Damián, is it?" I asked. He looked at me blankly, seeming distrustful.

Vanessa's face lit up as she hugged him tighter. "Thank God, he is fine." I didn't ask what happened, but she must have sensed my interest. "The coyotes put us on a trailer that was so crowded. We were like cattle in this truck."

Being from the Valley, I knew exactly what she meant. When we transported cattle to auction, we would load every last cow that would fit onto the trailer, not just to be economical, but also to protect the animals—they're less likely to be injured if they're packed so tightly they can't move. The smugglers probably applied the same principle when loading human beings into the back of one of their tractor trailers.

The thought made my stomach turn.

Vanessa continued, "We were so happy that day, sir. I was going to meet my husband. It was going to be the first time I'd seen him in over two years. And this one—he had not seen his father ever. We were excited."

"Where is your husband?" I asked.

"Wisconsin."

"Cold there, especially this time of year," I said.

"I wouldn't have cared, sir."

"What does he do?"

"He works on a dairy farm," she said. "He tends the cows, milking, getting the milk ready. It is hard work."

"I know it is," I said. "I used to milk cows on our ranch." I looked at Damián and smiled at him. For whatever reason, he was suddenly disarmed. He smiled back shyly.

Vanessa peered at him and then looked at me. "That is the first time I have seen him smile since the accident, sir," she said. I tousled his hair. "Gracias a Dios," she said. "We are alive. We are going to be OK."

Who was I to disagree? I could only imagine her excruciating physical and mental pain. Here she was—a mother with her toddler son whom she had probably saved by protecting him with her body when the tractor trailer crashed into the concrete barrier. I wondered what her life had been like or would be like. She and Damián would soon be returned to Guatemala, like all of the other migrants on the truck, both living and dead. And yet she still had faith, she still had hope, that someday, somehow, she would reunite with her husband, and her boy would meet his father.

"You know, Vanessa," I said, "the immigration system we have in the United States is very broken. Very broken. And my hope is that, one day, we'll be able to fix it so tragedies like this can be avoided. Maybe, someday, there will be a way for entire families to make the trip to the United States legally. This shouldn't have to happen. You shouldn't be here, like this . . ." I trailed off. I wanted to beg her not to try again—it was too dangerous; her odds of succeeding were too low. And if she ever did make it, all three of them would likely never have legal status in the United States.

She nodded, but the look on her face revealed nothing. Maybe one day there would be a legal way for her to see her husband, or maybe not. Either way, I could only assume that she was going to keep trying.

I said goodbye to Vanessa and Damián and spent another hour or so at the hospital speaking with more survivors and medical staff. As I left, I pressed $100 from my wallet into a staffer's hand. "We can't help that mother and boy get to the US," I said. "But I want to do something. At least to help them get some clothes and survive. Please make sure they get this." The staffer took the money and slid away toward Vanessa and Damián.

I never saw or heard from either one again.

After leaving the hospital, I met with the team of Mexican investigators, most of them from the Mexican equivalents of the Department of Justice and the FBI. Though it wasn't much more than a formality, I also met with a federal prosecutor known as "Tiburón"—the Shark. He had also headed Mexico's Interpol office, and in the ensuing years, he would work closely with the DOJ, FBI, and other US law enforcement agencies to send Mexican cartel members to the United States to face justice. I felt some hope that with Bobby Garcia and Tiburón at work, we might find the human smugglers behind this crime and bring them to justice. We could not let them repeat this horror.

We were scheduled to return to the airport and fly back to Mexico City, but I was not yet ready to leave Tuxtla Gutiérrez. I needed to see the crash site for myself. I told my guards and driver that even though it was out of the way, we had to make the detour.

By then, Bobby had watched CCTV footage from state-operated cameras along the highway and determined that the truck that crashed had been part of a convoy of three trucks. We calculated that if every trailer were packed full—a safe assumption, since the smugglers only made these trips when their trailers were full—and if each person had paid $15,000, then the smugglers were looking at a payday of over $7 million for only a couple weeks of work.

All three trucks had taken a sharp curve on a road with a high retaining wall along one side. The first two made the turn without incident, but the third was moving too fast and overturned. The trailer opened, and many people were thrown from it, including Vanessa. Bodies, clothing, belongings, parts of the truck, blood, flesh—all got strewn across the roadside. The smugglers were relatively unharmed. They escaped the cab of the overturned truck and made a run for it.

We pulled up to the retaining wall, which appeared to be made of plaster-covered cinder blocks. A small auto repair shop was built into one side of the wall, and workers milled around outside. The scene showed no signs of an official investigation. There was no crime scene tape, no evidence markers, no officers on watch—nothing. I hoped the investigators had done a good job gathering evidence, but this was not an encouraging sign. Additionally, there was still clothing as well as shoes and personal effects littered here and there along the road, which was otherwise quite clean. I could only assume these were remnants of the accident. Another bad sign.

I stood by the wall and took in the scene. Fifty-six people had died right here only ten days earlier. The only signs of their deaths were a few bunches of wilted flowers near the wall, but I wouldn't have been surprised if, after another month or so, a small permanent shrine popped up in this location (one did).

I briefly visited with the men working in the repair shop—"A terrible accident," they said, "a complete tragedy"—and wandered along a nearby unpaved residential street. Aside from the knowledge that so many had died so near here, there was nothing remarkable about it. Just a typical working-class Mexican neighborhood on the edge of a thoroughfare, now forever scarred.

I climbed into my car and told the driver to take us back to the airport. I hoped that the joint Mexican-Guatemalan-US investigation would be able to uncover all that had happened and arrest those responsible. None of them had been identified or taken into custody yet, but the Mexican agents suspected that corrupt government officials in Chiapas may have been involved. Hopefully, there truly would be "no impunity" for them and the people who had perpetrated this crime.

Only time would tell.

THE PRESIDENTS

31

GETTING TO KNOW AMLO

A week after standing at what I always will remember as the wall of death in Tuxtla Gutiérrez, I returned to the Valley for Christmas. The holidays came as a welcome respite. Being around Hope, Melinda, Andrea, our granddaughters, and all of my siblings and their families recharged my batteries. It also gave me some time to reflect on everything I'd taken in over my first hundred-plus days as ambassador.

The broken border, and the things I had witnessed there, weighed heavily on me. Its human toll, which many Americans were often content to ignore or gloss over, was incalculable. I knew that, despite the difficulties, modernizing the US–Mexico border could only benefit the people and the intertwined economies of our two countries. The border had to be fixed, and I knew it could be—if only the governments of both Mexico and the United States would commit to fixing it.

I like to think that I had been effective in setting specific goals and achieving them as Colorado attorney general, US senator, and Interior secretary. I had full faith in my abilities, so those were not the issue. The issue was whether I could marshal the powers inside the Palacio

Nacional and the White House to dedicate themselves to the problem too. That work would have to start right away.

I was more confident where Washington was concerned. I knew how the White House worked—how to get meetings with agencies responsible for the border and with my former colleagues in the Senate. The more pressing question was: Could I get President López Obrador on board?

Here, I was less confident.

Over the course of my first hundred-odd days in Mexico City, I'd had a couple of short one-on-one meetings with AMLO and had seen him in action in several cabinet meetings. AMLO was an impressive and dedicated politician with a remarkable 70 percent approval rating. He was a loquacious and energetic storyteller who was effective and opinionated, and I sensed that he and I had a good shot at getting along. What I wanted most immediately was a prolonged sit-down with him, with as few distractions as possible. This was no small ask.

President López Obrador worked like no politician I had ever seen. He did not employ a chief of staff, preferring to organize his own agenda. He started every day at 4:00 AM, held a national security cabinet meeting at 6:00 AM, and then continued nonstop until late at night, when he returned to his home to sleep for a few hours before doing it all over again. I wasn't sure how he did it.

During my holiday break, I reached out to the Whisperer, a friend and leading businessman in Mexico who knew AMLO well, and asked if he had any advice on how I might arrange a private meeting with him. "You've called at the right moment," the Whisperer told me. "The whole country is closed this week. Let me make a few calls and get back to you."

I thanked him and hung up. The Whisperer called back a short while later to tell me that AMLO was free all morning on December 29. "He has nothing scheduled, and he wants to meet with you. He has been keeping tabs on you," the Whisperer said with a chuckle. "He's been very impressed with your level of activity. He knows you've been all over Mexico."

"It has been a lot of travel," I admitted.

"Can you cut your family time short to come back this week?"

"Yes, I can."

"Great. I'll let him know."

I immediately rebooked my flights on Aeroméxico. A few days later, on December 28, I returned from the Valley to the Mexican capital. The next morning, I got up early, prepared my notes, and headed to the Palacio Nacional.

Once I entered the Palacio, a staffer met me and guided me through Corridor Eight, the route by which all visitors reached AMLO's chambers. We walked silently through the empty hallways. The Whisperer had been right: Everyone was away, and nothing was going on.

The sound of our footfalls echoed in the halls. Mexico City isn't built on secure bedrock but on a vast ancient lakebed, and at least two tectonic fault lines run under its unstable foundation. The ground there shifts often—there have been thousands of small earthquakes and many large ones over the centuries, some quite catastrophic—and the buildings are often deformed as a result. The four-hundred-plus-year-old Palacio complex was no exception. Walking its endless halls could sometimes feel like moving through a funhouse with slanted floors and crooked walls.

President López Obrador, sixty-eight years old at the time, greeted me with a broad smile in the hallway and walked me into his office. The Mexican president's office was larger than the Oval Office but less ornate. It felt more like a workspace than a national set piece like the Oval. He beckoned me to a leather couch and sat in a chair next to me as a staff member brought us coffee and water.

I knew by then that President López Obrador loved to talk, and if you let him, he would carry on nonstop for hours. But what followed was very much a back-and-forth, even if he did speak more than me. Setting policy discussions aside, we began simply by telling each other about ourselves.

Andrés Manuel López Obrador was born in 1953 in the rural southern state of Tabasco, the oldest of seven children. He described his early life as "simple but honest." His family was not rich—far from it—but they were happy. They had a small ranch, and he and his brothers and sisters spent most of their days outside, running around and playing games.

He still owned the family homestead, which he called "La Chingada." When he first told me this, he smiled coyly, and I couldn't help but laugh. "Chingada" is a vulgar Spanish word that in certain contexts can be quite offensive, but here it translated loosely to "Hell's Ranch" or "the Last Place." Coming from limited means in a rural setting, he told me that he had always been attuned to the struggles of ordinary people, which would later form part of the basis for his brand of left-wing populism. "Tabasco shaped me," he insisted that day. His innermost being, it seemed, was inseparable from this place.

As he spoke, I couldn't help but draw parallels to my own life, which I shared with him. "Señor Presidente. As you already know, I am Mexican American. Like you, my ancestors came both from Europe and from the Native peoples of the Americas, and like you, my people have been on this continent for hundreds of years." He nodded appreciatively. "You may not know, however, that I also come from a ranch—in a place known as Los Rincones, nestled in Colorado's San Luis Valley, near the headwaters of the Rio Grande. My homestead is called the Ohkay Ranch, which means 'place of the strong people' to the Indigenous people of the Ohkay Owingeh Pueblo, and like you, I also come from a big family." I explained that up until 1848, my ancestors were Mexican, but that after that year, we became United States citizens under the Treaty of Guadalupe Hidalgo.

"We didn't cross the border," I told him, with an obvious nod to the present-day issues we would shortly discuss. "The border crossed us."

I did not need to explain the historical background of this to AMLO, who knew his history well. He understood that the Mexican-American War was the source of many of our two countries' current problems. The border we live with today is a direct vestige of this war—it was broken then, it remains broken now.

"Tell me about your ranch, Ambassador," he said to me.

"Well, we raise cattle there and grow hay for our herd and for dairy farms in New Mexico and Texas. I live in the state capital of Denver and my native place near Los Rincones. It's a long drive—two hundred and sixty-five miles, a solid five hours and more in winter when the snow comes. It's in a massive alpine valley, so when you come from the north, you have to come over the mountains through a pass called La Veta, referring to a mineral vein there. It's still another sixty-five miles from La Veta to our ranch, but as soon as I'm on the downhill side of that pass, I know that I am home. I am home among the beautiful rural expanses, the places with more cows than people, where honest, hardworking farmers and ranchers have been from the beginning. That is where my heart is, Mr. President. That is my America."

"It is the same for me at La Chingada," AMLO said. "I can only turn off my mind when I am there, connecting with the trails and the trees. Did I mention that I planted fruit trees there some time ago?"

"No."

"I did. It's not a large ranch like yours, only a few acres now, but we have all sorts of fruits that grow year-round. They are sweeter there than anywhere else."

"I know what you mean," I said.

I felt like we had connected on a real level, not just the transactional basis that characterizes so many relationships in politics and diplomacy. AMLO began speaking again, telling me about his political awakening—how working with Indigenous people had changed his perspective forever, and how he learned to hate the corruption that plagued Mexican politics. He spoke about his first wife and the birth of their children, his wife's untimely death from lupus in 2003, and the death of both of his parents around the same time. He talked about his second and current wife, Beatriz, a born and bred "capitalana," as women from Mexico City are called. "She didn't like La Chingada at first," he said. "She is such a city girl. But she has come around."

And he told me how it felt to finally earn some political success when he was elected mayor of Mexico City in 2000. Though he ran several times, it would take another eighteen years before he became president.

From this point in the conversation, AMLO returned to the subject of history. He saw the people-centered policies of his presidency, as well as the political dominance of his party, Morena—which held both houses of Congress and most of the governorships across Mexico—as a "fourth transformation," or "cuatro T." The first three Mexican transformations, as he saw them, were the presidency of Benito Juárez, essentially Mexico's George Washington, whose Republican forces helped defeat the colonial French occupation of Mexico in the 1860s; the Mexican Revolution, begun in 1910 by Francisco Madero to overthrow the dictator Porfirio Díaz; and the presidency of Lázaro Cárdenas between 1934–1940, which focused on serving the poor, nationalizing major Mexican industries, and creating the modern Mexican state.

AMLO's "cuatro T" focused on reducing poverty by instituting programs that seemed to me to be modeled on FDR's New Deal, investing heavily in education and job training, and decreasing income inequality. He also said his highest priority was rooting out corruption.

After a while, AMLO turned the conversation to the most prominent painting in his office, one of Benito Juárez. "President Kennedy gave this painting to Mexico when he visited in 1963," AMLO said. "He cared about Mexico and the Americas, and he recognized that Benito Juárez was Mexico's greatest president. Juárez saved the republic." AMLO stopped for a moment in apparent deference before continuing. "Juárez was the first Indigenous president of Mexico, a Zapotec man from San Pablo Guelatao in Oaxaca. Your great president Lincoln and Juárez served at the same time. Juárez also lived in the United States when he was exiled, and Lincoln's decision not to interfere in Mexico's war against the French helped our cause. Our politics are intertwined." AMLO then went on for another thirty minutes on the back-and-forth history of Mexico and the United States.

When he was finished, I spoke up. "This is a perfect segue, Mr. President. I would like to talk about our shared border." And so we did.

In all, I spent more than three hours that day with AMLO, and by the end of our meeting, we agreed that we would work together to transform the relationship between the United States and Mexico.

We would develop joint efforts to modernize the border through infrastructure projects and coordination of law enforcement and military action against the cartels. We would develop impoverished rural southern Mexico, including the narrow Isthmus of Tehuantepec. We agreed that a modernized and properly patrolled isthmus could serve as a barrier and filter—a "curtain of security," as we both called it—for migration flows from Latin America before they reached the US–Mexico border. We agreed to work on better managing migration across the Americas, concentrating on treating migrants humanely, creating legal pathways to enter both Mexico and the United States, and addressing the root causes of poverty, corruption, lack of jobs, and criminal violence that had spurred these massive migration flows in the first place. Finally, we agreed that, with Canada, we could create an integrated North American economic powerhouse, one that would benefit all of the Americas and also thwart China's aspirations to dominate the Western Hemisphere.

These were weighty commitments. But I told him I had President Biden's full support, and he took me at my word. AMLO had not traveled to the United States since President Biden had taken office, but he liked Biden, and he believed that he was what he claimed: a hardworking American who put people before billionaires and corrupt actors.

So our collaboration began. We stood, and AMLO escorted me out of his office. Before we parted, I told him something that had stuck in the back of my mind. "Mr. President," I said, "when I was a little boy in Colorado, the white children at school sometimes called me and my friends 'brown trash' and 'dirty Mexicans.' The Mexican American kids were not allowed to speak Spanish in school, and we were made to wash our hands often because we were thought to be dirty. I didn't like this,

I never understood it, and I got in all kinds of trouble for disobedience and was seen as an unruly kid. I didn't know where it all came from until I was older, until I was in college."

I paused and stared at the portraits of Mexican presidents on the walls of the Palacio. AMLO had been listening intently. I continued, "I've been witnessing the fallout from our nations' troubled relationship for my whole life. I hope that, in time, our work together can also help our people better understand and respect one another—and help Americans and Mexicans better understand themselves. I hope that someday, all of our peoples, including the Indigenous peoples who have been on this continent for thousands of years, can better understand each other."

AMLO clearly appreciated my sincerity. "I hope for the same, Ambassador," he said. As we parted, he gave me a gentleman's abrazo and shared two cell phone numbers with me. "Call me with anything, Ambassador, at any time. I hardly sleep. I will answer."

"Thank you, Mr. President."

"Thank you."

And with that I left the Palacio Nacional. I had the full support of AMLO. Now all I needed to do was get on a plane and convince the powers that be in Washington that they had to act. What the United States needed was someone in DC, in the White House itself, pushing hard on these initiatives in our massive federal government.

What we needed more than anything was someone in the White House with a clear authority and an understanding of Mexico and our borderlands.

32

A BORDER AND MIGRATION COMMANDER

Just two weeks later, on January 12, 2022, I flew to Washington for two full days of critical meetings.

First, I headed to the White House for a scheduled sit-down with Jake Sullivan, the chair of the National Security Council (NSC). I had known Jake for several years and liked him. He was wicked smart, unflappable in a crisis, and a committed public servant. Despite being only forty-five years old, Jake had served in government for nearly twenty years, working on various political campaigns, and was a recognized foreign policy expert. He'd graduated from Yale undergrad, gotten a master's degree at Oxford, gone back to Yale for law school, and then clerked for Justice Stephen Breyer.

I entered Jake's West Wing office just down the hall from the Oval. Tall with dirty blond hair, and always neatly dressed like the consummate professional he was, he greeted me warmly. He sat on a worn chair, and I lowered myself into an equally worn chair nearby. I gave him a copy of the migration deck I'd prepared for my meetings. I would leave it with him when we were finished.

"Great to see you, Ambassador," he said. "How's the posting so far?"

"It has been eye-opening and very busy, but I am here to tell you that with the right push, we can fix migration and the border and transform our relationship with Mexico. I had a very good three-hour meeting with President López Obrador right after Christmas. He respects President Biden for his commitments to Mexico and is ready to work with us."

"I'm glad to hear that," he replied.

I noticed him glance at a stack of papers on his desk. "And you, how is your work going?"

His clear blue eyes met mine, and with a serious tone he said, "I just know that Russia is going to invade."

He was referring to Russia's buildup of troops along the borders of Ukraine, which US intelligence had determined (correctly) was an all-but-certain prelude to a Russian invasion. This situation was quite justifiably at the forefront of every US foreign policy official's mind, including Jake's. As the NSC chair, Jake managed a portfolio that involved the entire globe, including Russia, Ukraine, China, Taiwan, Iran, the Middle East, Europe, and many other places. He had a lot to worry about; his was a weighty and serious position.

After we finished discussing Russia, I went through my presentation deck with him. I told him about a framework that, in my view, would bring the border and migration under control.

While the NSC played a major role in Mexico—thus, my meeting with Jake that day—they often left this issue to their counterpart, the Domestic Policy Council (DPC). The DPC's portfolio covered migration and the border, among many other things.

In my view, the overlapping mandates of these two offices resulted in unnecessary confusion. Was the border a domestic security issue or a national security issue? Of course, the answer is that it is both.

Jake was receptive to my proposal and was especially interested in creating a "curtain of security" along the Isthmus of Tehuantepec in southern Mexico. I then got around to my most important ask. "To get this done, we need someone here in the White House to work exclusively on this. What we need, Jake, is a border and migration 'czar' who can focus on this Herculean challenge full time, all the time. We need someone who has the clear authority and respect to command the whole of government to act with urgency on the border and migration."

As Jake knew, the word "czar" is often used as shorthand for someone who has been appointed by the president to oversee a single issue. Going back decades, we have had industry czars, drug czars, climate czars, cybersecurity czars, and many others. There have been multiple border czars since 2000, but regardless of which president appointed them, none were able to actually fix the border.

"The Mexican government is primed to help us," I continued. "I'm prepared to do my part to ensure they uphold their commitments. But for this work to succeed, I need a counterpart here, in the White House, working every day to coordinate the interagency." "Interagency" is an inside-the-Beltway term for the interplay of the alphabet soup of departments, agencies, and sub-agencies across the United States government—DHS, NSC, DPC, CIA, GSA, CBP, DOJ, FBI, DOD, DOC, EPA, and on and on. "We need multiple parts of the government to respond simultaneously, and someone needs to be here to keep them on the same page. The jurisdictions are too diffuse to be left to the agencies themselves. We need someone like Thad Allen or Jeff Zients to be this new czar and make sure things get done," I said.

Jake nodded. I didn't have to explain what either of these two men had achieved. Admiral Thad Allen of the US Coast Guard had been appointed by President Obama in 2010 to oversee the response to the Deepwater Horizon oil spill, the massive environmental disaster in the Gulf of Mexico that we tackled together when I was Interior secretary. And Jeff Zients had been appointed by President Biden to be the COVID czar. During the first three months of Biden's presidency, Zients was able to move vaccination rates for seniors from around 8 percent to over 80 percent. His efforts literally saved hundreds of thousands if not millions of lives.

"I'm with you," Jake said. "But you have to talk to Ron about that. Ultimately, it's his decision." He was referring to Ron Klain, the president's chief of staff.

"I'll pay him a visit, then."

"You should. Tell him you have my support. And as far as the president is concerned, I'll relay what we went over today and share this deck with him. Thank you so much, Ambassador," he said. "This is important work." He then rose from his chair and graciously saw me out of the room.

I stepped into the hallway. The West Wing can be a crowded and sometimes claustrophobic place, but I had spent a lot of time there over the years, and I knew how it worked. I didn't have an appointment with Ron, but if I said hello to his receptionist and asked to see him, there was a high probability I could get a few minutes with him.

I walked down the short hallway toward the Oval Office. The chief of staff's office, which is right next to the Oval, was deceptive in its simplicity. It consisted of a desk and computer, a conference table, and a dozen or so chairs. It is not an exaggeration to say that in this sparsely decorated room, some of the world's most important decisions are made.

Luckily, Ron's receptionist told me that he was in and would be available in a few minutes. "Can I get you something to drink?" she asked.

"No, that's fine. I'll just wait here."

As I casually chatted with the polite young staffers outside Ron's office, I reflected on the political aspects of this situation. Unless the broken border and migration system were fixed, they would become huge political liabilities for President Biden. Everything he had stood for in winning the presidency was at stake. As I had learned from battles in the Senate, migration and the border had become the third rail of American politics. The president's chief of staff needed to understand the imperative of having a leader in the White House prepared to engage fully with the policy and the message around the border and migration.

A short while later, Ron opened the door and smiled. "Ambassador, hey. I heard you'd be here today. Come in."

I followed him inside. I pulled another copy of my presentation deck from my briefcase and passed it to Ron. I'd not had a lot of interactions with him, but given that we had both spent many years in the trenches of presidential politics, I felt I understood him.

I gave Ron the same pitch I'd presented to Jake, ticking through some of the current jurisdictional problems. "The NSC and DPC have disparate authorities, agendas, and constituencies. The DPC asserts that immigration and the border are domestic matters. The NSC is reluctant to step on DPC's toes. On the other hand, the NSC effectively has one person to run all of the Western Hemisphere." This was Juan Gonzalez, a man I would come to know well over the next two years. "I've heard people describe his job as like *Home Alone*—the movie—because he has virtually no help and no authority to direct action. He and his minuscule staff have to deal with democracy issues and dictatorships and upheaval in Nicaragua, Cuba, Venezuela, and Haiti. Juan is good, but he doesn't have the authority or bandwidth to fix the border and migration."

Ron listened intently. I continued, "The State Department authorizes permits for all the border projects, but General Services is responsible for getting the work done. The Department of Homeland Security is responsible for securing the border and handling migrants, but they're chronically under-resourced. What I'm saying, Ron, is that here in DC, no one is in charge of this crisis on the border. We need somebody like Thad Allen or Jeff Zients to take charge here."

The president's chief of staff appeared to agree with my assessment, even if he seemed careful to avoid using the term "crisis." He said he monitored the numbers at the border daily and had designated a few coordinators to focus on migration-related problems, but those people hadn't worked out. I suggested appointing someone with political stature and knowledge of Mexico and the Congress, like former senator Chris Dodd or Federico Peña. Federico was Mexican American and had been raised in Brownsville, Texas, right on the border. As Ron knew, Federico had also been mayor of Denver and had served as the secretary of both the Transportation and Energy Departments under President Clinton. Ron said he would "seriously consider" my request. We shook hands and I left the White House.

From there, I went to the State Department, where I met with Secretary Antony Blinken and the State Department officials handling the Western Hemisphere and Mexico. I told them about my meeting with AMLO, the opportunity before us to fix the border and migration, and the need for an effective coordination and communications strategy to diminish the flow of asylum-seeking migrants to our border. The secretary seemed supportive. He said he would continue to place a priority on Mexico and would make frequent trips there.

From the State Department, I went to the Depression-era building known as Main Justice to meet with Attorney General Merrick Garland, Deputy Attorney General Lisa Monaco, and other senior Justice Department officials engaged with Mexican matters. As the chief law enforcement officers of the United States, their main concerns were cartel activity, fentanyl smuggling, gunrunning, and human trafficking.

Then I went to the Department of Homeland Security (DHS) to meet with Secretary Alejandro Mayorkas. I knew there was long-standing institutional distrust between DHS and the State Department. On the surface, they played nice with each other, but things were messier in practice. Each department had responsibilities at the border, but neither took full responsibility. More often, these two massive governmental departments tended to blame the other for migration and border problems, which just resulted in more gridlock—and a lot of bureaucratic infighting and frustration. That history drove right at my point: The border and migration crisis required someone in charge to soothe and circumvent egos and make the interagency apparatus function well. Of course, Secretary Mayorkas had no authority to appoint such a person; all I could ask for was his support and that of his embattled department.

Once again, I made my pitch, which included a discussion of the infrastructure projects along the border that the US and Mexico should jointly undertake. Secretary Mayorkas said, "Ken, of course I share your concerns, and I think working with Mexico on border projects is important. But I don't think we can do much until the migration flows are brought under control."

"Ali, I have been to the border a lot lately. It has hardly changed over the past two hundred years, and it is broken. We need to bring it into the twenty-first century.

"We need barriers, yes, but we also need modern ports of entry, community infrastructure projects that give the people on both sides something to rally around and share, water infrastructure, rail infrastructure, and transportation. When this is all modernized, it will open the door to joint patrols on both sides, to joint special operations against the cartels. It will cut down on human smuggling, and prevent deaths like those in Tuxtla Gutiérrez. It is not either-or, Ali. We can do both."

I added that this effort would require a "whole of government" approach that was outside of his scope, since the authority to make these decisions rested exclusively with the president and the White House. He agreed on that point.

But he was also insistent that my holistic approach to the border wouldn't happen with the current migrant flows. He repeated, "We don't have the resources, Ken. And that's not to mention the complete inability of Congress to find real and lasting solutions through a comprehensive immigration bill."

"We must try to do both at the same time," I responded. "I am more than happy to help with Congress. I know the people there. I know we can do this."

I left the secretary's office with his commitment that he would also make as many visits as he could to Mexico.

As a former senator, I had full access to the Hill, where I would meet with lawmakers whenever I visited Washington. This trip was no exception. I met with my friends Colorado Senators Michael Bennet and John Hickenlooper, but I also spoke with colleagues like Assistant Minority Leader Dick Durbin from Illinois, Senator John Cornyn from Texas, Representative Michael McCaul from Texas, and with the forty members of the Congressional Hispanic Caucus. In all these meetings, I gave an overview of our efforts in Mexico and the need for Congress to focus on solutions to the border and migration. If a comprehensive immigration law could ever pass in Congress, it would be more durable and meaningful than anything the president did on his own.

When I left Washington to return to Mexico City, I was confident I had made progress, even if I still struggled against bureaucratic ambivalence. This being Washington, I hadn't expected my casting about for help to be snag-free, but things were poised to move forward.

33

THE STATE OF THE UNION

For the rest of that month and all of February, I resumed my grinding schedule in Mexico. I met with AMLO, with Secretary Ebrard, with Attorney General Gertz, with Security Secretary Rosa Icela Rodríguez, with the Mexican secretaries of Defense and Treasury, with governors and mayors and NGOs. We discussed security, migration, energy policy, infrastructure, law enforcement, the cartels, corruption, and transportation.

AMLO and I continued to work together to bring attention to developing the Isthmus of Tehuantepec. Two modern seaports were already under construction on either side of the isthmus, and combined with a proposed railroad across the isthmus, they would not only bring economic benefit but also create a modernized barrier that human smugglers and drug traffickers would have to cross; it would be a state-of-the-art gauntlet that would expose many of them to capture.

I traveled back to the north, stretching myself and my staff thin, as we yo-yoed from one end of the border to the other: Matamoros and Brownsville, Laredo and Nuevo Laredo, El Paso and Juárez, Nogales, Tijuana and San Diego—and back again. I even joined AMLO for a couple of days on one of his border tours. We started in Tijuana, where AMLO had agreed to ensure the Mexican government would do its part in completing the massive, billion-dollar transnational crossing project called Otay Mesa East. AMLO promised to start the work and to complete the project by 2024, which was a tall order, but when both the American and Mexican sides were done, he wanted to inaugurate it with President Biden. It would be our shared border's most modern and high-tech crossing point.

AMLO, Secretary Ebrard, and I then flew in a Mexican military helicopter to Nogales. We surveyed the border there and discussed modernizing the rail crossing that links the Union Pacific Railroad to Ferromex, Mexico's largest rail network.

It was a busy time.

Then, on March 1, President Biden gave the annual State of the Union speech in Washington.

I watched it from my living room in the ambassador's residence, switching back and forth between CNN and Fox. I had sent a letter to the president with my recommendations for his speech. I was confident he would get these issues right, but I was still heartened to hear the words from the president himself as he stood before Congress and the American people.

"If we are to advance liberty and justice," he said, "we need to secure the border and fix the immigration system. We can do both. At our border, we've installed new technology like cutting-edge scanners to better detect drug smuggling. We've set up joint patrols with Mexico and Guatemala to catch more human traffickers. We're putting in place dedicated immigration judges so families fleeing persecution can have their cases heard faster. We're securing commitments and supporting partners in South and Central America to host more refugees and secure their own borders.

"We can do all this while keeping lit the torch of liberty that has led generations of immigrants to this land—my forefathers and so many of yours. Provide a pathway to citizenship for Dreamers, those on temporary status, farmworkers, and essential workers. Revise our laws so businesses have the workers they need and families don't wait decades to reunite. It's not only the right thing to do—it's the economically smart thing to do. That is why immigration reform is supported by everyone from labor unions to the US Chamber of Commerce. Let's get it done once and for all."

As he said these words, I sat in my chair holding a copy of the speech and a highlighter. I drew bright yellow hashes across all of these words, folded up the paper, and put it in an envelope. On the outside, I wrote, "President López Obrador." It would be hand-delivered to him the next morning.

President Biden was on board. I was confident the border and migration czar was forthcoming. I leaned back in my chair and listened to the rest of the speech, a smile on my face.

We were on our way.

34

POTUS COMES TO MEXICO

By November 2022, Mission Mexico was deep in preparation for what would become one of the most significant diplomatic events of my tenure as ambassador. The North American Leaders' Summit, scheduled for January 8–10, 2023, in Mexico City, would bring together the leaders of the United States, Mexico, and Canada. It had been nine years since a US president had visited Mexico. That, of course, was President Obama, who'd visited in February 2014. Trump never went during his first presidency and, as of this writing, has not visited in his second term, either.

The closest Trump came to an official visit was in late 2016, just a couple of months before his first election, when he met with then–Mexican President Enrique Peña Nieto. The meeting had been thrown together at the last minute, and Trump's main talking point was that if he won, he would build a wall to physically divide our nations and borderlands—and that Mexico would pay for it. Peña Nieto blanched, later tweeting that Mexico would never pay for such a thing.

The visit was regarded as a failure and was loudly denounced in Mexico. Trump didn't care. Only hours after meeting with Peña Nieto, Trump flew to Phoenix, Arizona, to deliver an inflammatory speech in which he claimed that Mexico would "100 percent" pay for the wall and that "anyone who is in the United States illegally is subject to deportation." He also said he would create "within ICE" a "new special deportation force."

As I often remarked in my many speeches in both Mexico City and Washington, it took ninety-nine years following the Mexican-American War for a US president to visit Mexico City. During WWII, Mexico and the United States became indispensable allies. They fought side by side in the Pacific, and many braceros came to the United States as a labor force to help on the home front. To honor this, President Harry Truman visited Mexico City in 1947, enthusiastically declaring before millions of Mexicans that our two countries had entered a new era of relations based on friendship and respect.

President Biden's visit would take place in this tradition of respect. Yes, this was a trilateral summit that would include Canada, but it was also a bilateral summit, as Biden would meet AMLO first, just the two of them, before they were joined by Canadian Prime Minister Justin Trudeau. It was a big deal.

From my many personal conversations with AMLO, I knew that he also viewed this as a historic opportunity. But one major issue threatened to derail everything: AMLO wanted President Biden to land Air Force One at one of his brand-new infrastructure projects, the $4.1 billion Felipe Ángeles International Airport—or AIFA, as everyone in Mexico called it. But the US Secret Service had never used this airport, and therefore AIFA wasn't cleared. It was simply too new. The Secret Service insisted that, as a matter of protocol, the only place they could land Air Force One and the other presidential aircraft was Benito Juárez Airport. For AMLO, this was unacceptable.

"Ken," AMLO told me that December, "AIFA represents the new relationship between our nations. More Americans come to Mexico than any other nationality. AIFA is clean, honest, and built by our own military, not corrupt contractors. If President Biden lands there, it will demonstrate that he understands what we're trying to build together."

I attempted to explain the US government's way of "doing" things—the layers of bureaucracy, the risk-averse nature of the Secret Service, the practice of sticking with known quantities—but he stood firm. AMLO believed he had bent over backward to cooperate with the United States on migration, on fentanyl, on trade issues; in his mind, it was as if the United States was telling him they didn't even trust him to build an airport.

I took up the issue yet again with the White House, asking Jake Sullivan to intervene. Fortunately, he must have taken it directly to the president, who cut through the red tape: Air Force One would land at AIFA.

And so, on the evening of January 7, I waited with AMLO and his right-hand man, Daniel Asaf, on the tarmac as Air Force One descended through the clear Mexico City sky. We watched as the massive white and blue Boeing 747 touched down smoothly and taxied to the edge of the red carpet that had been rolled out for the US president.

The president doesn't just hop off Air Force One. There's a string of other things that happen first. Staff and reporters exit through the rear of the plane, the Secret Service descends from the front to inspect and clear the area, and the Beast—a custom-built armored Cadillac that is flown in on a separate Air Force transport plane—is pulled up alongside Air Force One to receive the president. As I waited with AMLO, he remarked about how formidable the Beast was in comparison to his own simple white touring van.

I'd ridden in the Beast on several occasions, and while it is impressive, it is not the most comfortable ride. With eight-inch-thick armor plating, three-inch-thick bulletproof glass windows, and a modified truck chassis underneath it all, the Beast weighs in at around twenty thousand pounds. Inside, you can feel every bump in the road, and it doesn't exactly sail around corners.

Finally, President Biden appeared at the top of the jet stairway. As he descended, AMLO's face lit up. The two men came together and shared a warm handshake. "Señor Presidente," AMLO said as Biden reached the tarmac. "¡Bienvenido a México!"

"It's good to be here," President Biden replied with his trademark congeniality. "Your airport is beautiful."

"Mr. President," I said, "it's wonderful to see you."

"Ken," Biden said. Then, turning to AMLO: "How's the ambassador doing?"

"He is a very busy ambassador. He has been all over Mexico!" AMLO said.

Biden nodded approvingly, then said to AMLO, "Come on, take a ride with me in my car."

AMLO beamed. "Con gusto. ¡Vamos!"

It's not unprecedented, but it is exceedingly rare, for anyone other than the president and his staff and cabinet members to set foot in the Beast. For one, it's a national security issue. The president can't let just anyone inside the vehicle that is designed to transport and safeguard the most powerful person in the world. But beyond that, it is private. And private is not always good when it comes to heads of state hanging out with each other. In this case, Biden seemed not to mind the privacy; besides, they would be joined by a translator.

A Secret Service agent held the door open, and both presidents climbed in, followed by the translator. The door closed, and the Beast pulled away. My senior policy advisor, Zeppa Kreager, and I climbed into another vehicle and followed the presidential motorcade for the long ride to the hotel. I later learned that President Biden and AMLO mostly discussed infrastructure, a topic both men loved and believed in wholeheartedly as a means for lifting up their people. (Biden also answered a lot of curious questions about the Beast.)

The motorcade wound through the sprawling metropolis to the InterContinental Presidente Hotel located just off Paseo de la Reforma. The presidential delegation had taken over the entire InterContinental—there were no other guests. Security was everywhere. Secret Service agents, Mexican federal police, and military personnel created concentric circles of protection around Polanco, the bustling Mexico City neighborhood where the hotel stood.

The following morning, January 8, I said goodbye to Hope and rode in my armored SUV to the hotel for a "prep meeting" where President Biden would be briefed in advance of his meetings with AMLO and Canadian Prime Minister Justin Trudeau.

I passed through the hotel's security checkpoints and went upstairs to a windowless conference room. The room had been swept repeatedly for recording devices by US security experts and had been deemed safe. As in the official section of the embassy, everyone who entered the conference room had to leave their cell phones and other electronic devices outside, where they would be held under guard by the Secret Service. I handed mine over to the agent on duty and entered.

The room was unremarkable—a long conference table that seated about sixteen people, generic hotel furniture, and a small side bar with coffee, water, fruit, and breakfast pastries. Over the next fifteen minutes or so, everyone assembled in advance of the president: Secretary of State Antony Blinken, Attorney General Merrick Garland, Homeland Security Secretary Alejandro Mayorkas, Commerce Secretary Gina Raimondo, Climate Envoy John Kerry, Special Advisor for the Americas Chris Dodd, National Security Advisor Jake Sullivan, Deputy Chief of Staff Jen O'Malley Dillon, NSC Director for the Western Hemisphere Juan Gonzalez, a few NSC staff members, and me.

President Biden walked in a few minutes late. He said hello to everyone, sat, and said in an authoritative tone, "OK, what've we got?"

Sullivan began. "Mr. President, we thought it would be useful in preparation for your meeting with AMLO to hear from people who've been on the ground in Mexico. Ambassador Salazar has been doing excellent work getting to know AMLO and keeping our relationship moving forward."

"Looking forward to hearing from you, Ken," the president said.

Sullivan turned his attention to Secretary Blinken, who took the floor to touch on the broader agenda for the summit. His remarks were brief, and then Kerry spoke. I was reminded why he had been such an effective secretary of State. He was passionate about the unexpected progress we'd made on climate change and shared how Mexico had surprised everyone by embracing renewable energy and carbon reduction in ways that few had anticipated.

"Mr. President," Kerry said in his distinctive baritone, "we have a real opportunity here. AMLO understands that Mexico's future depends on clean energy, and they're ready to partner with us in ways that could not just transform North America but serve as a model for the world."

Kerry was followed by Chris Dodd, the former US senator from Connecticut who had been installed a month or so earlier as a presidential advisor for the Americas. His remit included Mexico, all of Central and South America, and the Caribbean. Dodd, who'd spent two years with the Peace Corps in the Dominican Republic in the late 1960s, spoke fluent Spanish—his command of the language was better than mine—which was a great help in his work. He delivered his report with characteristic eloquence, saying that a real opportunity lay before us if we could only give sustained attention to the hemisphere.

"Mr. President," he said, "these countries don't need a lot from us. They just need a little bit of attention. An occasional phone call, a presidential visit now and then, or someone in the White House they can confide in—that would go a long way. That's the kind of thing that will make the difference between partnership and neglect."

I couldn't have agreed more. For nearly a year, I'd been asking the White House team for a border and migration czar, and Chris Dodd had seemingly been brought in to help. But as effective as I knew he could be, he had not been empowered with the authority to make real progress. And even after a lot of bureaucratic wrangling, he had only been given the assignment on a part-time basis. Meanwhile, Vice President Harris had been put in charge of getting at the "root causes" of the migration problem, which meant addressing poverty and corruption in places like Guatemala and Honduras. But sadly, her designation in this position was having no effect on migration flows.

I spoke next. I walked the president through my assessment of AMLO: his strengths, his limitations, his obsessions, his blind spots. I highlighted the progress we'd made on our nations' commercial relationship, telling him, "In short order, Mexico will be our largest trading partner, with over two billion dollars of goods and services crossing our border every single day." I described our joint efforts to address the rivers of guns and fentanyl flowing between our countries, and the successes our two countries had in capturing notorious cartel figures like Rafael Caro Quintero and one of the Sinaloa Cartel leaders, Ovidio "El Ratón" Guzmán López.

"And of course, AMLO is willing to work with us on the border and migration, but the challenges are enormous." I told the president how every morning, my staff and I reviewed the previous day's migration numbers. In December 2022, they were still very high, but we'd made a lot of month-over-month progress reducing the flow of Venezuelans in particular, as well as Mexicans and Hondurans. I accentuated the positive, attributing our recent success to collaborations with AMLO's government. "We can bolster these enforcement initiatives," I stated, "by supporting Mexico in some of AMLO's most important infrastructure projects in southeast Mexico and along the border. He sees these investments as Mexico's economic future—and many of them also will function as effective 'curtains of security' for the United States.

"We are making real progress, Mr. President," I concluded. "Mexico is a ready partner."

Secretary Mayorkas went next, followed by Secretary Raimondo. Sullivan then explained that the president had to meet with his traveling staff to deal with other issues of the day, and we were dismissed. As President Biden rose to leave the room, he announced, "This was the best meeting I've ever had on Mexico and the Americas. We need to do this regularly. I'd like to meet with this group once a month to make sure we all stay on task." He looked around the room at each of us as well as Deputy Chief of Staff Jen O'Malley Dillon and Juan Gonzales. "I'm serious about this. Set it up. Make it happen." Then the president exited the room.

Everyone was elated. Here was the president of the United States, committing to pay sustained, high-level attention to Mexico and Latin America—exactly what those of us who worked in the region had been pleading for since the beginning of the administration. In Chris Dodd's case, he'd been hoping to get this level of attention for *decades.* I'd been doing the same since my discovery of Kennedy's Alliance for Progress at Colorado College.

The next day, January 9, was devoted to bilateral meetings at the Palacio Nacional—the first formal meetings of the summit. January 10 would be the trilateral meeting between the United States, Mexico, and Canada. During the bilateral, I witnessed AMLO at his most gracious and Biden at his most engaged. These were two men who believed in the people who had elected them and who believed unfailingly that government could be a force for good in those people's lives. And they were here, together, to further that belief with action.

In one notable exchange, AMLO remarked, "We cannot fix the migration challenge with walls." Instead, he pointed out, they needed to build real opportunities for real people.

The following day's trilateral meeting at the Palacio went equally well. The three leaders made formal joint declarations on climate change, supply chain resilience, and migration management. All the right words were said, all the right commitments made. As the meeting concluded, the only wrinkle I experienced was a personal one: Hope had come down with a painful case of shingles. I wished I could be with her, but there was no way for me to get away from my official duties. Thankfully, the embassy medical staff was able to take care of her.

After the five-hour trilateral meeting, the only thing left to do was convene with President Biden to ensure follow-up on the summit's commitments and to prepare the president for his first and final press conference in Mexico.

But someone had decided that this briefing would only include President Biden's inner circle—and not Chris Dodd, or John Kerry, or me.

At first, I thought this was a mistake. Surely, we should be included in the briefing that would prepare President Biden for the most important press conference of his presidency on the Americas.

I felt as if a switch had been thrown within me. Yes, the summit so far had the appearance of being perfect. But throughout, I harbored a kernel of doubt that made me wonder whether I should put my faith in this White House team to deliver on President Biden's commitments, especially since I had been asking for a border and migration czar for nearly a year, yet none had materialized. That very day, I had met with John Kerry and Chris Dodd to outline the need for someone in the White House to be in charge of the border and migration. They agreed with me.

Struggling to contain my emotions, I looked for my friend Juan Gonzalez, the National Security Council's much-beleaguered Western Hemisphere director. I found him sitting in one of the Palacio's grand patios, near a room that served as a holding pen for Biden's cabinet members and their staff. I wasted no time telling Juan pointedly that I needed to see the president before he took the podium.

Juan could see how angry I was. He looked at the ground as he said quietly, "I'm sorry, Ambassador, but I'm not in control of who's in the room with the president."

I took a breath. "Juan. If this were a presidential delegation in Beijing, your counterpart and the US ambassador to China would both be present to brief POTUS before he spoke to the *Chinese press*! This is wrong, Juan. We both know it." I took a deep breath. "Let the president know I am going to resign."

All color left Juan's face. "With respect, sir, I think that would be a mistake."

"Juan, you do what you need to do, and I'll do what I need to do."

I left Juan and went into the press conference's waiting room, where I found a quiet corner. I grabbed a pen and took out a blank piece of ambassador stationery from my briefcase. "Dear Mr. President," I wrote, "It is with great regret that I must tender my resignation as your ambassador to Mexico . . ."

Once I'd finished the letter, I read it and reread it. Then I signed my name across the bottom in blue ink. I folded it up and stuck it in my jacket pocket. After the press conference, I would hand my resignation letter to President Biden. I hoped that if I did, our government would get the message and finally realize the harm in their neglect of Mexico and the Americas.

Just then, a Palacio staff member appeared to inform us that the press conference would begin shortly. I stood with everyone in the room and followed the group to the Palacio's largest and most ornate courtyard.

I found a seat and texted Hope that I had some important news. She would be disappointed, of course, but I also knew that she would be happy to have me back home. For a few moments, I daydreamed about my future: being with my family, taking care of Hope, helping my daughters and granddaughters, and of course, returning to the Valley. With any luck, by the end of the week I'd be driving one of my family's John Deere tractors down Road M, no suit, no tie, a worn pair of cowboy boots on my feet and a rumpled straw hat on my head.

A few minutes before the press conference began, a red-faced White House staff member hurried over to my seat. "Ambassador Salazar?"

"Yes?"

"The president has asked to see you."

"Now?"

"Yes, sir."

I stood, gathered myself, and strode quickly behind the staffer as I was led back through the Palacio's halls, past the Diego Rivera murals, past the guards and protocol officers, to the small conference room where the president waited. The staffer ushered me in and closed the door. President Biden and I were alone.

"Hello, Ken. How are you doing?" he asked in that familiar voice. "Jake said you wanted to see me."

"I'm OK," I said. I spread my notes out on a nearby table. "I'd like to go over my talking points with you about AMLO and this press conference." Standing shoulder-to-shoulder, I ran through the key points I felt he should address. And then I said, "I also need to recommend something specific." He nodded, looking at me intently. "We need someone in the White House to oversee the border, migration, Mexico, and the Americas. No one is in charge now. We need a border and migration czar, like President Obama had with Thad Allen on the oil spill and you had with Jeff Zients on COVID. Someone focused exclusively on this crisis, with the authority to coordinate and direct action across agencies in Washington and communicate the message with one voice on these issues. With all due respect, Mr. President, if we are to succeed, it is urgent that we have someone like this in charge."

The president thought for a moment. "That's a good idea," he said. "It makes sense. Even with so much else going on in the world, it is still crucial for us to make progress here. Let me see what I can do."

"Thank you, Mr. President. We can get this right, but we don't have time to waste." We shook hands and parted ways as he straightened his tie for the press conference. I walked back alone, my boot heels echoing in the long corridors.

It hadn't gone down how I'd wanted. It had taken my statement to Juan that I intended to resign to get a meeting with President Biden to let him know about the necessity for a migration czar to oversee the policy and messaging of his White House. Nevertheless, I had delivered my advice, and President Biden seemed to agree with my recommendations. I decided to carry on and not resign. It would have sent a message, yes, but it would also set back much of the hard work Mission Mexico had undertaken on so many issues, including the border and migration.

I returned to the press conference. While Biden, AMLO, and Trudeau took to their podiums and delivered their remarks, I moved my resignation letter from my jacket pocket to a pants pocket and quietly wrote a separate letter, simply thanking President Biden for coming to Mexico.

The press conference ended, and the leaders were led out to their motorcades. In the bustle, I found Jake Sullivan and gave him my thank-you note, requesting he deliver it to the president. "I won't be able to come to the airport," I explained. "Hope is not well, and I need to check in on her. I've been ignoring her all day." He said he understood and assured me he would pass the letter to the president later on Air Force One.

As the presidential motorcade departed, I informed my staff that I'd be late for the post-summit festivities, the so-called Wheels Up Party that followed any presidential visit to a foreign country. This marked the end of eighteen-hour days, sleeping in hotel rooms, eating poorly at odd hours, and managing a million and one details so that everything went smoothly. Everyone involved deserved to let loose.

I did too, but first, I wanted to see Hope.

I found her upstairs in the bedroom at the ambassador's residence, still in considerable pain but putting on a brave face. After I made sure she was doing OK, she checked in on me too.

"How did things go?" she asked.

"Mixed," I said, sitting on the edge of the bed. "Biden and AMLO had good chemistry. The meetings went well. But . . ."

"But?"

"But I'm not sure this administration knows what they're doing. I'm not sure they understand or care about how important our countries' relationship is, how fragile it is."

Hope reached for my hand. "You're doing everything you can, Ken. All you do is work."

I was silent.

"Ken," she said firmly, "you can't do this by yourself. At some point, Washington has to step in too."

After our conversation, I took fifteen minutes or so to freshen up before heading downstairs. I was utterly spent, but as ambassador, I had to put on a happy face and lead the hundreds of embassy and administration staffers in celebration.

By the time I made it downstairs, nearly two hundred people had gathered. There were drinks, food, and a DJ, and the mood was celebratory. It was warm enough, even in January, that people had spilled out onto the terrace and into the gardens.

Putting one foot in front of the other, I worked the crowd, thanking people individually and sharing stories from the past few days. I didn't tell anyone how close I'd come to resigning, or how, even after such a successful visit, I harbored continuing doubts about the lack of organization and messaging at the White House.

A short while later, someone outside pointed toward the sky and exclaimed, "There it is!"

Air Force One flew directly over the ambassador's residence, as if President Biden himself were thanking all of us and waving goodbye.

Everyone broke out in a loud cheer. Here we were, US citizens and Mexicans who had worked together to make history happen, watching the president of the United States disappear into the sky above Mexico City.

THE WARNING BELLS

35

THE CRISIS DEEPENS

"The future of our bilateral relationship will be determined in the next ten weeks."

I wrote those words in my journal in early October 2023, ten months after President Biden's only visit to Mexico, sitting at my desk in the ambassador's residence as a passing rain shower streaked the windows. At that moment, migration flows at the border hovered at around eight thousand encounters a day. This was far too high—CBP was only meant to handle a maximum of around four thousand daily migrants at the southern US border.

The problem had become so acute that Congress, with fervent behind-the-scenes encouragement from the White House, led by Assistant to the President Steve Ricchetti, finally seemed poised to act. Three senators—James Lankford, an Oklahoma Republican; Kyrsten Sinema, an Arizona Independent; and Chris Murphy, a Connecticut Democrat—were in the midst of negotiating a border security package that would be part of a larger supplemental spending bill. It was still early, but all signs pointed toward progress. Steve Ricchetti was effective and credited by many as the behind-the-scenes player who had delivered on President Biden's successful legislative agenda. Now he had finally been tasked to help solve the border crisis with Congress. If the supplemental bill passed, President Biden would sign it. Asylum laws would be reformed and the Department of Homeland Security would instantly have more resources to help at the border.

We only had until the end of the year to get everything right. Once the calendar turned to January 1, 2024, it would be all politics, all the time—not only in Washington, but in Mexico City as well. In June, Mexico would hold its own national elections. AMLO would be out, since he was term-limited, and while it was assumed his anointed successor, Claudia Sheinbaum, would prevail, this was politics. Nothing was a sure thing.

Ten weeks to show we were on track. Ten weeks to prove that the US–Mexico relationship could be transformational rather than transactional. Ten weeks before Trump's anti-immigrant rhetoric could find its perfect weapon in a worsened border crisis.

I hoped that the team now in place in Washington would be able to make progress. Following his visit to Mexico in January 2023, President Biden named Dr. Liz Sherwood-Randall, his Homeland Security advisor, as his personal emissary on migration. Since then, she'd made seven visits to Mexico City, and I'd arranged to have her meet with AMLO nearly every time. AMLO liked her, and she him.

At AMLO's request, the White House also designated Amos Hochstein, the president's international energy envoy, to help with Mexico's infrastructure projects on the isthmus as well as the two ports of the transoceanic corridor.

In early October, Liz and Amos arrived at the embassy to prepare for another round of meetings with AMLO and his cabinet officials. Liz arrived first. She was always a commanding presence—tall, blonde, confident, and impeccably put together. Then in her mid-sixties, she'd known Biden since she was a graduate student, one of those Washington figures who measured influence and experience in decades rather than election cycles.

"The president is counting on us to deliver," she said to me, settling into a chair at the conference table. This was her standard opening, a reminder that she spoke for President Biden directly. "We urgently need to deal with migration flows at the border."

Amos entered from the exterior office, where he'd been making important calls on other matters around the world. His remit was truly global, and I could only imagine what daily fires he had to put out. I'd known Amos, a fiftyish man with raven black hair and a bright smile, since he'd joined the Biden team. He was one of the few people in the administration who had a lot of experience in global energy markets, including renewables as well as oil and gas.

"I know we have to deal with migration, Liz," I said. "But everything's connected. Migration, border infrastructure, economic development, security. It's all one package."

"The president understands that," she said.

Liz was smart and absolutely loyal to the president. But she had been given only limited authority to carry messages and convene meetings; she couldn't force the agencies to implement the president's decisions. Importantly, she seemed to have been given zero authority over the messaging on migration or the border. It was above her pay grade, so to speak, and that was precisely the problem. For reasons I couldn't comprehend, we still did not have a border czar and no crisis-messaging strategy on migration and the border at the White House.

"AMLO's getting frustrated," I told them. "We've pushed hard for joint border modernization instead of a massive border wall, and Mexico has made this a matter of national priority, investing billions. Just look at Otay Mesa East in San Diego. The Mexican government is now pouring hundreds of millions of dollars into that crossing on their side. But when AMLO asks for us to deliver on Otay Mesa East, we can't even get the White House to make it a priority. The excuse is that projects like these take endless years to review and complete. That shouldn't be the case if the border and migration are truly a matter of national security. It's no wonder AMLO sees our efforts as just bureaucratic lip service."

Liz interjected, "But Ken, the president has made it clear that *migration* is the priority."

I couldn't believe I was having this conversation *again*. "You can't separate them, Liz," I said. "When we fail on infrastructure promises, AMLO questions our commitment to everything else. He's spending billions—on the isthmus, the gas refinery, and border projects like Otay Mesa. These are his legacy projects. When we don't match their energy, he feels disrespected."

Amos looked up from his notes and added, "Speaking of the isthmus, I hear AMLO wants Biden to come to the opening ceremony in December."

"That won't happen," Liz said quickly.

I grimaced. "I didn't presume it would," I said. "Don't worry. I'll go to all the ribbon cuttings. But it would mean a lot if the United States also sent a cabinet-level delegation to show our support."

I hoped that our high-level meeting already scheduled with AMLO three days later on October 5 would finally move the ball forward. On that day, we convened at the Palacio with AMLO and Secretaries Blinken and Mayorkas. Secretary Blinken spoke about root causes, migration, and fentanyl, and Secretary Mayorkas spoke about the pride he'd taken in helping protect Dreamers through the Deferred Action for Childhood Arrivals policy back in 2012. He then earnestly stressed that we were doing our best in the United States, but at that moment, we needed AMLO to help reduce the increasing number of migrants arriving at the border.

"As you know, we're working with Congress on asylum reform," Mayorkas added, reading from his notes. "And we're seeking tens of billions of dollars to strengthen border security in the forthcoming supplemental spending bill. But we need your help in stopping migrant flows."

AMLO listened politely, but I could tell from his expression that he was frustrated. When Secretary Mayorkas finished, AMLO repeated his usual refrain about addressing root causes of migration through development, and about his vision for a North American partnership modeled on the European Union. Biden's officials listened politely.

After the session broke, I pulled Secretary Mayorkas aside in the hallway.

"Ali, the messaging is all screwed up," I said. "We can't just talk about what Mexico has to do to keep migrants from reaching our border. We need to talk about development, about creating opportunities so people don't have to leave their home countries. And we have to let people know that when they arrive at the border, they will be returned immediately. There is no White House–driven message on any of this, Ali. It's all screwed up!"

He looked at me with exhausted eyes while his staff waited behind him. "Ken, I have a lot on my plate already. I'm about to be impeached for all this border stuff. The Republicans have it out for me."

"I know. And I'm sorry. They're just using you to score political points."

"I'm doing the best I can, but I have to catch my plane," he said as he turned to his staff and left the Palacio.

Secretary Mayorkas *was* doing the best he could, I knew. But his best was constrained by political realities that had nothing to do with solving actual problems. Later, in February, House Republicans would vote in favor of his impeachment, making him only the second cabinet secretary to face that indignity. Even though Secretary Mayorkas was not convicted in the Senate and would serve out his term, his authority was already severely diminished.

I spent the last week of October in Washington, racing between Senate meetings, trying to build support for the supplemental security bill, and pushing anyone who would listen to support Mexico's infrastructure initiatives. I met with Anita Dunn, one of the president's senior advisors, urging her to craft a strong and effective communications strategy. I also sat down with Steve Ricchetti and exchanged notes, and with Natalie Quillian, a deputy chief of staff, who had been given the assignment of marrying domestic immigration politics with the realities at the border. She and Steve had the support of the president and Jeff Zients, who had replaced Ron Klain as chief of staff. But Steve and Natalie had been brought in too late. Still, there was no one in charge of the crisis messaging at the White House.

From the White House, I went to the Capitol. I once again met individually and in small groups with Senators John Cornyn, Chris Coons, Chris Murphy, James Lankford, Susan Collins, Kyrsten Sinema, and others. In the Senate Foreign Relations Committee room, I briefed a large bipartisan contingent of senators on everything going on in Mexico. They sympathized with our many challenges, but I sensed they were all acutely aware of the political third rail of migration and the border. Nevertheless, they expressed hope that something might change for the better.

I then flew from DC to Denver to spend a short but desperately needed thirty-six hours with Hope and our girls before flying back to Mexico City.

October became November. Mexico City overflowed with Day of the Dead icons and masks and posters. The start of the dry season arrived, with its increased smog and pollution. And everywhere you looked, you'd see cempasúchil flowers, a type of marigold that splatters streets and window boxes and gardens with oranges and yellows and assaults the nose with its sickly-sweet smell.

And on top of all this, the sound of the warning bells—in my ears, at least—heralding yet more bad news from the border.

During a morning briefing in early November, DHS Attaché Bobby Garcia pulled up the previous day's charts. "We're seeing a major uptick, Ambassador," he said, his usually steady voice rising with growing concern. "We're headed toward nine thousand encounters a day if we can't get a handle on this."

We were witnessing a worst-case scenario. "The buses aren't running as regularly to southern Mexico," he explained, referring to the charters the Mexican government hired to relocate migrants from the border to the deep south. "And Mexico's repatriation flights are flying less and less." He paused. "The Mexican migration director told me it's all due to budget issues. They've run out of money. The migration director asked if you could help by talking to AMLO. No one seems to be able to move him, even though these exploding numbers are alarming."

"You're right, this is bad. I'll try to talk to AMLO and his team and explain the urgency of funding their commitments."

"Yes, sir. Please do. Otherwise, this is all going to blow up, Ambassador," Bobby said.

Budget issues, I thought as Bobby and I parted ways. I knew what that meant. AMLO was racing to complete all his signature infrastructure projects before his term ended in September 2024. These were the achievements that would define his presidency for posterity. Meanwhile, the unglamorous work of managing migration—paying contractors to run buses, funding repatriation flights—was getting squeezed out.

It was like watching a slow-motion car crash while everyone argued about who was driving.

I looked at the calendar. My ten-week window was rapidly closing. What more could I do to get Mexico and the United States to solve this crisis?

That's when it hit me: I needed to bring AMLO to APEC.

36

APEC

The Asia-Pacific Economic Cooperation (APEC) forum, to be held in San Francisco later that month, would bring together President Biden, AMLO, Xi Jinping, and many other leaders from across the Pacific Rim. It might be the last chance before the elections for Biden and AMLO to meet in person and get principal-level sign-offs on all that had to be done right away.

The only problem was, AMLO didn't want to go.

I'd anticipated this. He'd boycotted President Biden's Summit of the Americas in Los Angeles in 2022, even though I'd spent many hours trying to persuade him to attend. He refused, but finally agreed to send Secretary Ebrard to make all the necessary commitments on behalf of Mexico. But APEC was different—this was about North American economic integration and competing with China.

So I offered AMLO a high-value card: a personal meeting with President Biden in San Francisco. "President Biden specifically wants to see you," I told him one day in his office at the Palacio. "Since your term is almost over, this could be your last chance to sit with him in person."

AMLO walked to the window overlooking the Zócalo. He asked when the United States would be finished with its side of Otay Mesa East and when we would begin to support his legacy projects for "el rincón olvidado"—the "forgotten corner" of southeastern Mexico, as he called this region. And he repeated his common refrain that the United States was not investing in the development of Latin America like JFK had done in his Alliance for Progress. I could hear in his voice what he wasn't saying: Was the United States actually committed to modernizing the border and developing curtains of security along the Isthmus of Tehuantepec, or were they all just empty words?

He had me there. Otay Mesa East and the isthmus project, as well as the broken border with Guatemala, were emblematic of our entire problem: Mexico racing forward with crucial infrastructure projects while the United States remained mired in bureaucracy and broken politics. AMLO had even sent his most powerful cabinet members to Washington with me asking for help on the isthmus project, but he'd gotten few tangible results. It appeared to be the same old story again and again. The United States would dismiss Mexico, and Mexico would not trust the United States to do what it had promised.

Old wounds. Deep waters. Blurred lines along the borderlands.

"I'll raise it again with the president," I said, trying hard not to betray my weariness with my own government. "But I would still like for you to reconsider about San Francisco, Mr. President. Your presence would mean a lot to me and President Biden, who holds you in the highest regard."

It was worth a try. At that point, I'd garnered a reputation among AMLO's cabinet for persuading AMLO when they could not. AMLO was famously stubborn—when he made a decision, no matter how big or small, it was final—but for whatever reason, I'd been able to get him to change his mind now and then.

"Thank you, Ambassador," he said, as both an expression of gratitude and an indication that my time was up. I rose, donned my cowboy hat, and left his modest office.

Two days later, Daniel Asaf called me at the embassy. "The president is happy to accept President Biden's invitation to come to San Francisco." I breathed a sigh of relief.

As we worked to arrange AMLO's APEC logistics, the migration flows at the border continued to spiral out of control. By November 15, the day I flew to San Francisco, Bobby Garcia's morning briefing was apocalyptic.

"Over nine thousand encounters yesterday," he reported. "Mexico's National Institute of Migration says the contractors haven't been paid in three weeks. The buses have stopped running entirely. Things are all headed in the wrong direction, Ambassador."

After this, I hopped in an embassy car to the airport and called Treasury Secretary Rogelio Ramírez de la O. The secretary, who had a PhD in economics from Cambridge, was a friend and I could always speak candidly with him. "Mr. Secretary," I said, "Mexico needs to get those contractors paid. We need the buses and flights running again. The situation is now critical. I assume you've seen the numbers at the border."

"I have, Ambassador, and I agree. But we do not have the budget for it. The president's priorities are clear," he replied calmly. "The Maya Train opens next month. The isthmus railroad is nearly complete. AMLO believes these projects will change Mexico forever. I will work to try to find the money, but AMLO must approve it."

"But migration could destroy both our presidents' legacies," I said solemnly as I pulled up to the airport. "Please reinforce the funding crises with AMLO." Secretary de la O agreed to do so.

I landed in San Francisco that evening. Only two US ambassadors had invitations to this gathering of world leaders: myself and Nick Burns, the ambassador to China.

Liz Sherwood-Randall waited for me at San Francisco International Airport so we could share a car to the city center. We went straight to the Fairmont on Mason Street, a five-star hotel in a beautiful neoclassical building that would have looked right at home in Washington, DC. Liz got out, expecting me to exit as well. But because I'd been added to the delegation so late, I didn't have a room there.

"Where are you staying, then?" she asked, clearly surprised.

"The Holiday Inn at Fisherman's Wharf," I said.

"Oh," she said, a bit awkwardly.

"I haven't even picked up my credentials yet," I said.

"Understood. I'll see you tomorrow, then."

"Yes. See you tomorrow."

The Holiday Inn wasn't quite what I expected. San Francisco was in the midst of a well-documented homelessness crisis, and in an effort to clean up the city while hosting so many dignitaries, the city had made arrangements to temporarily house many of the people who usually lived on the streets or in local parks. And wouldn't you know it, the Holiday Inn at Fisherman's Wharf had been designated as one of the places to house these folks.

That first night, walking down the hallway to my room, I encountered one of the hotel's temporary residents—a middle-aged man with weathered features and clothes that had seen better days.

"Hello," I said.

He looked surprised that someone had acknowledged him. "Evening, sir. You here for the big conference?"

"Something like that."

"They moved us here three days ago," he said. "Cleared up the whole area near the Moscone Center. Can't have the Chinese president seeing how we really live, right?"

"No, I suppose not," I said.

I slept fitfully that night, not because I was uncomfortable with the setting or my hotel-mates, but because of the gravity of the upcoming conference. A lot was riding on the next couple of days.

The following morning, I woke early, got ready, and walked through San Francisco's eerily empty streets. A security perimeter extended well beyond the convention center and the Fairmont, and the shops nearby were closed, the usual street life entirely absent. Police stood at every corner. It felt less like a major US city than a movie set, carefully staged to hide what real life typically looked like around here.

I reached the Moscone Center, where most of the meetings and press conferences were slated to occur, and picked up my access credentials. Then I waited for the Mexican delegation to arrive.

I'd been in near-constant contact with AMLO's people since leaving Mexico City. Because AMLO hadn't committed to APEC until the last minute, every aspect of their trip was hasty and chaotic. Most of them didn't speak English, and they had to scramble for hotel rooms, throw together meetings with other leaders, and figure out how to get badges for everyone before the conference began. Throughout that morning and early afternoon, I was in frequent contact with Mexico's new foreign minister, Alicia Bárcena (Marcelo Ebrard had stepped down to run for president against Claudia Sheinbaum). She'd received her credentials, but most of AMLO's other cabinet members had been left out.

I felt bad for them and tried to help. This was a major delegation, representing a prime US ally, and since APEC was taking place in the United States, we had to take care of them and make them feel welcome. I worked with my staff to secure the credentials they needed to get into the convention center, and when I met them that afternoon outside the Moscone Center, they greeted me with warm smiles and abrazos. They were happy to see me, and I was happy and proud to see them in the United States.

I escorted them inside and gave them a brief orientation. Like most convention centers, the Moscone Center is sprawling and Byzantine, with hidden meeting rooms and out-of-the-way lounges. I took them to the main staging area, where the various officials went their separate ways. Finally, I accompanied AMLO's cabinet members to the Leaders' Lounge, where only those with the highest-level clearances were allowed to enter.

We quickly found AMLO inside. He waved us over, and the cabinet members and I sat. As we chatted, Xi Jinping strolled past with his entourage. The Chinese leader's eyes swept the room, cataloging who was talking to whom, measuring US influence in real time. I briefly wondered how many actual spies were in the Moscone Center at that exact moment.

"The Chinese are very interested in Mexico and the isthmus," AMLO said quietly, as President Xi disappeared into another meeting. "They see what we're building. They want to finance the industrial parks and the ports."

"All the more reason for us to be full partners," I replied.

AMLO smiled. All I thought was, *China doesn't have politburo elections every two years like we do in Congress. A lot easier for them to finance projects all around the world.* Maybe AMLO thought something similar.

That evening, I arranged for Liz, AMLO, and me to meet at AMLO's hotel—a session that wasn't on any official schedule. For about ninety minutes AMLO lectured us about his vision for North American integration and how the United States was not meeting our commitments. Liz and I agreed with him that we needed to work together on this aspirational vision for the Americas, but we tried to move the conversation back to the migration crisis.

Overall, it was a good meeting. Afterward, I said to Liz, "We needed him to let off some steam before meeting with President Biden tomorrow. If he feels heard tonight, maybe he won't grandstand with POTUS."

The next morning, November 17, I walked from Fisherman's Wharf to the Fairmont, went inside, and met President Biden's inner circle in a small conference room. Jake Sullivan and Secretary Blinken were already there. Biden would meet with AMLO later that day, and Jake asked if Liz and I could brief the president.

President Biden entered a short while later, looking fresh and ready for the day. After a round of the usual pleasantries, Liz spoke for a few minutes and then turned the briefing over to me.

"Mr. President," I said, "here's what's going on right now with Mexico." I walked him through our progress on all fronts, including security, the binational relationship, and trade. Concerning the border, I said, "The situation is painful, Mr. President, and we need AMLO's help, especially in funding Mexico's migration control." Everyone in that room knew the numbers were exploding. Trump and the GOP were already making a lot of noise about the border, and I could see that this weighed on the president. The fact that the border security bill in Congress was moving forward helped matters, though; it looked certain to pass, and a bipartisan immigration law would be an extraordinary achievement.

I then turned to infrastructure. "AMLO needs to see real progress on our infrastructure and development commitments—Otay Mesa East and the isthmus especially. They've become a symbol of whether we're serious about partnership or not."

President Biden nodded, turning to his team, and said, "We'll make sure we're moving on that."

Following the briefing, we moved to a room in the Moscone Center where President Biden and AMLO would hold a press conference before they sat down together privately. The two men warmly greeted each other as the press corps poured into the room. Cameras clicked as President Biden and AMLO sat in a pair of lounge chairs that had been set up to emulate an Oval Office meeting.

During the press conference, both leaders praised our partnership and shared values. They discussed migration, fentanyl, and infrastructure. AMLO didn't criticize the US, and President Biden stayed on message. It was progress. I felt confident that if I could return to Mexico City and push one more time for AMLO to find the money to help with migration, he would come through.

The delegations filed out, and the press moved on, but I stayed seated, writing up an action plan. When I looked up, the room was suddenly empty—except for me and President Biden.

I got up and said, "Mr. President!"

"Ken!" he exclaimed, turning to me. "How'd that go?"

"Excellent, I thought. Thank you. If we follow through, AMLO will surely help us on migration flows and the border."

"Good," he said. He pulled out a handkerchief and wiped his nose. The gesture seemed to trigger something, a moment of candor I didn't expect. "This is a tough job," he said quietly. "I wouldn't be running again if it wasn't so important. The other guy has to be stopped. He's just so . . ." His voice trailed off. "If only there were someone else."

The words hung between us for a moment. Joe Biden was the president, but I also considered him a friend. I wasn't going to argue with him or give him any unsolicited advice, but I wished I could help him. In that moment, I felt a small measure of the weight that he carried, day in and day out.

"We will get the border under control," I said. "It won't be your Achilles' heel." He gripped my shoulder. "Mr. President, do you remember that fundraiser in 2020 at my house in Denver?"

"Yes. You and Hope put on a great party."

"The media and most Democrats counted you out then. But you kept going because you felt in your soul that the nation and everything you had worked for was at risk. You will do it again." As I said the words, I hoped I was right.

He didn't say anything for a moment, then looked at me and simply said, "Thanks, Ken."

"You're welcome, Mr. President." I gave him a hug and exited just as his staff reappeared.

The moment was over. But that glimpse of doubt, of exhaustion, of a man pushing himself through another campaign because he genuinely feared that Trump could win and that only he could beat him—that would stay with me for a long time.

The rest of APEC was seamless. AMLO was one of only two leaders to secure a bilateral meeting with President Biden, the other being Xi

Jinping of China, arguably the world's only other superpower. Mexico was finally being respected, and the United States was finally attempting to make good on its promises.

January was a little over a month away. With a little luck—and with a new bill supporting border enforcement about to pass in Congress—the United States and Mexico would be on their way to putting the past behind them and the future before them. The transformation of our border was nearing a point of no return, one that would propel both countries forward and benefit the entire Western Hemisphere.

37

THE IMMIGRATION EMERGENCY

By early December 2023, migrant encounters at the southern border surged to ten thousand per day. And not just from Mexico, Guatemala, and Honduras, but from all over the globe. The word was out: If you wanted into the United States without a visa, then the US–Mexico border was your spot. Haitians, Cubans, Venezuelans, Peruvians, Salvadorans—even Chinese and the occasional Russian—were walking, busing, flying, and sailing into Mexico and then making their way to the border to either risk an illegal crossing or claim asylum.

This surge turned an existing crisis into what I can only call an emergency. Eleven months before the US election, it had the potential to be politically devastating for President Biden. But even more than that, it was a human catastrophe on an industrial scale. These people were more than statistics; they were human beings risking everything to make this perilous trip. Migrants were crossing the high seas, jungles, and deserts. They were falling off freight trains in the Sonoran scrublands and sometimes dying by the side of the steel tracks. Children were being separated from families. Women were being sexually harassed and raped.

Families were paying their entire life savings to unscrupulous coyotes. On the US side of the border, CBP agents were focused on processing the overwhelming number of migrants, effectively shutting down legal commerce at several locations. And communities along both sides of the border were overwhelmed, their resources stretched beyond breaking, with cartels rushing into the lawless breach.

In my meetings that December with Mexican officials, I kept repeating the same phrase: "You need to fund the migration control program." I said it when I went to the ribbon cutting for a new international airport in Tulum; I said it in Mérida when AMLO inaugurated the Maya Train. But AMLO had spent Mexico's budget on his legacy projects. There was no money left.

The irony was bitter. The isthmus project was meant to be part of the solution to the migration crisis. If we could create a modern security corridor along this relatively narrow belt, we could intercept smugglers and migrants long before they reached the US border. Instead, AMLO's priorities had contributed to the very crisis the isthmus project was partially designed to prevent.

Nevertheless, as a demonstration of US support for the project, I accepted AMLO's invitation for the inaugural train journey across the isthmus in December 2023. During that trip, I planned to repeat my appeal to AMLO about funding the agreed-upon migration controls.

In early December, I hitched a ride on a Mexican Navy flight from Mexico City to Salina Cruz on the Pacific coast of Oaxaca and then traveled to the train depot. A crowd had gathered for what felt like the beginning of a presidential whistle-stop tour.

The celebration began in a large pavilion where hundreds of officials, business leaders, and dignitaries had assembled. I chose a seat in the front row as AMLO arrived with the secretaries of the Navy and Army, the governor of Oaxaca, and a parade of cabinet ministers. After a few speeches about transforming Mexico's economy, we boarded the gleaming train that would carry us north to the Atlantic.

At the head of the train was a modern silver locomotive, and behind it were around half a dozen passenger cars that looked like high-end Amtrak train cars. AMLO's presidential car was the first one behind the locomotive. He boarded it, along with the Defense secretary, Luis Crescencio Sandoval, and the secretary of the Navy, José Rafael Ojeda. They were clearly positioned alongside AMLO to emphasize that this was a military project under naval command.

Joining them were some of Mexico's wealthiest and most powerful business leaders, including the influential Carlos Slim. He understood the importance of Mexico's relationship with the United States in the context of global economics and was a strong advocate of my mission.

I was placed in a car with an assortment of invited guests—the Canadian ambassador, the Danish ambassador (a Danish company had promised to invest $9 billion in a clean hydrogen project along the isthmus), and a handful of other dignitaries. Behind our car was one for various staff members, another car teeming with press, and two cars for the people who worked on the train, who served meals and drinks and made sure everyone was comfortable.

The train pulled out of Salina Cruz with a ceremonial whistle, beginning what would be a nine-hour journey across the narrow Isthmus of Tehuantepec. It would take this long not because the 180-mile journey was difficult, but because AMLO would stop at half a dozen towns and villages to do what he liked to do most: be among the people. In his view, this project was as much for the benefit of these poor southern communities as it was for shipping magnates or immigration law enforcement officials. The train would bring economic activity to these forgotten places, and, it was hoped, would provide more Mexicans with more reasons to stay in Mexico instead of trying to get into the United States. It was a multipurpose project.

I always marveled at AMLO's willingness—no, his absolute joy—to be among throngs of Mexicans. Typically, when he ventured into the world, he would sit in the passenger seat of his unarmored white van, his body man Daniel Asaf dutifully at his shoulder, and move carefully through crowds of hundreds and often thousands of supporters. He'd roll his window down and shake hands, give awkward hugs, kiss babies, accept gifts, and sign autographs. His was a tactile presidency. It was unlike anything we've seen in the United States in decades, since JFK was killed in 1963 and his brother Bobby was killed five years later on the campaign trail. After that era of political assassinations, which arguably culminated with the attempt on President Reagan's life in 1981, the movements and interactions of presidents have been tightly controlled and choreographed.

Not so for AMLO. Perhaps because over 70 percent of Mexicans supported him (an incomprehensible level of support for a US president), he was willing to take the risk. But I suspect that even if he were less popular, he still would have done it. He loved the people and the people loved him.

For the first leg of the train journey, I sat at the window and took in the passing scenery. The seaside town of Salina Cruz soon gave way to dense jungle and low, hilly passes. I couldn't help but appreciate AMLO's feat. The railroad track had been laid over a century ago, but AMLO had modernized it and created new depots. Once the deepwater ports were complete at either end of the isthmus, it would be transformed into a piece of transportation infrastructure that might compete with the Panama Canal.

We made our first stop about an hour into the journey. I got out and mingled with the crowd, watching as AMLO emerged from his presidential car in his white guayabera shirt and khakis—nothing fancy—looking every bit the "man of the people" he claimed to be. The crowd cheered. Music played over a PA system. As local officials greeted him, the celebration quieted a little. Speeches were made, and AMLO chimed in with a few words at the end, basking in the adulation. He was in his element.

The train whistle blew and AMLO wrapped up. Before I knew it, we were all aboard and headed north again. I returned to my assigned car and chatted some more with the Canadian and Danish ambassadors. At some point during our conversation, our car's AC broke, and within only fifteen minutes or so, the car became stiflingly hot. It was December, yes, but we were in the tropical jungle of southern Mexico, where it never gets especially cool. Eventually, I stood and excused myself, saying, "I'm going to get some fresh air."

That was part of my motivation. But beyond getting some cooler air, I wanted to see what else was happening on the train—and maybe see if I could finagle myself onto AMLO's car to discuss the emergency at the border.

Fortunately, only our ill-fated car had its AC fail that day, and so I stayed cool as I walked up and down the train. At the rear of the train, I checked in with the servers and dining car staff. In another car, I chatted with various members of AMLO's cabinet. I also stood in between cars all alone, enjoying the tropical air that flowed through the breezeway.

When I got to AMLO's carriage, however, I hit a wall. I couldn't go any further without permission. But I didn't need permission to loiter, so I did. Not long afterward, Daniel Asaf emerged. He was always friendly, and I had been impressed by his ability to keep up with AMLO's unrelenting pace.

"Want to see the rest of the train, Ambassador?" Daniel asked with a grin. "Let's go up front."

Sure, why not? Daniel led me quickly and unceremoniously through AMLO's car to the diesel locomotive. The engineer welcomed us into the cab, where we witnessed the massive engines at work as they pulled the train across the Isthmus of Tehuantepec. It was quite the experience. I could feel the power of the machine coursing up through my feet and legs and into my torso.

I spent fifteen minutes or so up there with Daniel and the engineer, talking about the technical aspects of the project and watching the countryside roll by. Then Daniel led me back to the presidential car, where he casually cut me loose. Technically, I wasn't supposed to be there, but so what? I was the US ambassador to Mexico.

I took a seat at the far end away from AMLO and chatted with Daniel. After a short while, AMLO noticed me and called me over.

"¿Señor Presidente, cómo está?" I asked, approaching him.

"¡Embajador!" AMLO said with a warm smile. I sat across from the president. Daniel moved to stand next to me.

At the same moment, Carlos Slim appeared next to AMLO, and they rekindled a conversation about baseball, AMLO's favorite sport. AMLO engaged wholeheartedly. After all, if the isthmus project were to have lasting success, then he needed to keep people like Slim happy.

After a few minutes, I leaned toward AMLO. "Señor Presidente," I began, "congratulations. This is a truly strategic and important accomplishment."

AMLO's face lit up. "Thank you."

I knew he'd appreciate it, and so I said, "This project connects to everything both Lincoln and Juárez envisioned for the isthmus. Your success with this corridor is of major historical significance. ¡Felicidades!"

AMLO smiled and nodded in agreement.

I then took a chance: "But Señor Presidente, I also really need to speak with you about getting the migration issue under control—"

His demeanor changed immediately. He waved his hand and said, "Look, Ken. We got this. We got this." When AMLO wanted to discuss something, he could talk for hours, but on topics he wanted to avoid, he had a way of shutting down the conversation. Migration wasn't what he wanted to dwell on during his victory lap.

He could tell I was not happy with this, so he added, "We have the program ready, Ambassador. Don't worry." And then he turned back to Carlos Slim. AMLO's focus was entirely on this moment, this achievement, this vision of Mexico as a modern economic power connected to global trade routes. For him, the migration emergency seemed to be a manageable problem that could wait until after the celebration. Ten thousand migrants a day may have been overwhelming our shared border, but right now, AMLO was literally riding the rails of his dreams.

Clearly, my time was up. I rose, reminded AMLO that a US delegation would be in Mexico City for a meeting right after Christmas, and thanked him before retreating to the rear of the car. I chatted with a few more business leaders before rising and heading back to my assigned car. The AC there was still broken, but now the windows were open. I sat and listened to the train clack along the rails. The Danish ambassador described the revolutionary hydrogen facility his countrymen were planning to build along the isthmus. Wind farms producing thousands of megawatts would generate the electricity needed to create clean hydrogen fuel for ships and trains. It would be the cutting edge of energy technology, more revolutionary even than solar and wind.

Several stops and many hours later, the train finally reached Coatzacoalcos on the Gulf of Mexico. By then, it was dark. I bid farewell to my traveling partners and reunited with my security detail, which had been shadowing the train all day long on the road that paralleled the tracks. I greeted my guards, and we drove to the airport and boarded a Mexican military plane bound for Mexico City. As we flew northwest, I recorded the day and my encounter with AMLO in my journal.

During the Christmas lull, on December 27, Secretary Blinken and Secretary Mayorkas came to Mexico City to meet with AMLO once again. The main topic of discussion was the emergency at the border. This time, AMLO agreed to help. Migration enforcement throughout the country and along the border had already started and would continue through 2024. Migrants would be taken off trains and buses and detained on roads heading north. Repatriation flights would resume.

Then, on January 4, 2024, President Biden also took action, issuing an executive order that made significant changes to asylum rules. Almost immediately, the numbers began dropping. From over ten thousand encounters a day in December, the numbers fell to under six thousand for January, and each week saw a downward trend. We'd turned the corner.

Once Congress passed the supplemental spending bill, the numbers were sure to fall even more. It looked like the border and immigration emergency could be under control and might be nonissues in November.

38

POLITICS INTERVENES

Almost three years earlier, on Inauguration Day 2021, President Biden had acted swiftly to fulfill his campaign promises. He announced a flurry of orders to accomplish an about-face on the Trump domestic and foreign policy agendas. As for border and migration, he halted the construction of the border wall, ended Trump's practice of breaking up children and families, and called immediately for comprehensive immigration reform.

But the message received by potential migrants and their human smugglers was different. Given US asylum laws, all migrants had to do was get to the United States border, claim asylum, and wait for their day in court, which could take months or even years. With no enforcement message and an overwhelmed asylum system, our shared two-thousand-mile-long border became irresistibly attractive for anyone fleeing poverty, violence, or persecution in their home country. Legal pathways took years. Organized criminals and smugglers understood all of this, turning the hopes and dreams of regular people into a cruel profit-making machine.

There were attempts to communicate the US position, but in the end that's all they were: attempts. For instance, in June 2021, Vice President

Kamala Harris went to Guatemala City and warned, "I want to be clear to folks in this region who are thinking about making that dangerous trek to the United States–Mexico border: Do not come. Do not come. The United States will continue to enforce our laws and secure our border." She then added, "If you come to our border, you will be turned back."

Strong words. Only no one believed her. The migrants kept coming, and they kept claiming asylum. Yet the border was not "open," as the GOP loved to claim. Including the COVID-era Title 42 expulsions, which permitted the government to turn people away immediately on public health grounds, President Biden had deported around 3.6 million migrants since taking office, far more than the roughly two million people deported by Trump during his entire first term. But the border was certainly broken, and the asylum system was at the root of that. It needed urgent reform.

Which is exactly what the bill being drafted in Congress intended to address.

By mid-January 2024, the Lankford-Sinema-Murphy bill looked certain to pass in the Senate. Just two days before the vote, more than twenty GOP senators were on board. Nearly all the Democrats were also yes votes, placing it well north of the sixty-vote threshold to clear a filibuster.

Its fate in the House was less certain. But a bipartisan coalition had emerged there, led by Representatives Veronica Escobar and Maria Salazar, and it looked like the bill could succeed. If it did, President Biden had promised to sign it. Following this, the migration numbers would likely hit historic lows.

On February 8, 2024, the Senate convened and cast their ballots.

The bill, which was part of a larger emergency funding bill that would send money to Ukraine, Israel, and other global hot spots, failed by a vote of forty-nine to fifty. Only four GOP senators, including Senator Lankford, could bring themselves to cast a yea in favor.

Why? Because over the preceding forty-eight hours, Donald Trump, then a private citizen, personally intervened to kill the legislation. He wanted the border crisis to continue. He needed the chaos, the human suffering, the political vulnerability it created for President Biden and congressional Democrats. And so, a shadow president called the shots—and cowardly elected Republicans fell in line.

The asylum system would not be fixed. The Department of Homeland Security would not get more desperately needed resources. The border crisis would continue. And Biden's faith in Congress, especially the Senate, would prove to be a critical political miscalculation.

Nevertheless, due to President Biden's executive order on asylum and Mexican cooperation, by spring encounters at the US–Mexico border had fallen to around four thousand a day. In my opinion, this was still too high. The sirens of the election year were everywhere.

During those first months of 2024, we worked desperately to bring down the migration numbers even more before they could affect the election. Liz Sherwood-Randall flew to Mexico City regularly, and I attended meeting after meeting with AMLO and Liz. Each time, we pressed the same themes: stronger implementation of migration controls, the need for migrants to apply for asylum in their home countries rather than at the border, and the urgency of creating curtains of security across Mexico and Latin America. AMLO was on board, but he was sensitive to his own country's upcoming election. Claudia Sheinbaum was far ahead in the polls, but that did not mean her victory was a sure thing.

The Mexican presidential election would be held on June 2, making it difficult for Mexico to take more enforcement action at the risk of being seen as doing the bidding of the United States. President Biden could have taken further immediate executive action to impose heavy restrictions on the border. But AMLO would view this as a unilateral action taken by the United States that would have flown in the face of our commitments to address these issues together. This was the first time in our shared history that the United States and Mexico were working together on migration, and President Biden couldn't risk blowing that up by acting unilaterally before the Mexican elections.

On April 28, I was patched into a call between the two presidents. After a few pleasantries, President Biden got straight to the point.

"The migration numbers are too high, Mr. President," President Biden said. "We have done a lot, but we need a more aggressive effort. I've asked Ambassador Salazar to share the data with you, as well as my opponent's ugly attacks about the border. And states like Texas are trying to take immigration into their own hands." He was referring to Governor Greg Abbott's increasingly theatrical border stunts, like putting concertina wire in the Rio Grande and busing or flying migrants to Democrat-run cities like Chicago, New York, and Boston. President Biden was sensitive to the electoral situation in Mexico, but he was also asking AMLO to do more. He conceded that AMLO had reason to say that the United States was not doing enough to address the root causes of migration or the border, a fact that embarrassed him. "If reelected," he said, it would be his focus.

"*If* reelected" . . . This statement said it all.

Here we were in April 2024, less than seven months before the US election, and the president of the United States was stating that the Americas and the issues of migration and its causes would be his priority—*if* he won a second term. I grimaced. In my view, transformative action on the Americas and migration should have been undertaken from the beginning on moral grounds, on national security grounds, and on economic grounds. But even if the White House couldn't see that, why had this agenda not been undertaken on political grounds?

AMLO listened to President Biden and promised to help drive down daily migrant encounters. And for his part, President Biden pledged to take additional action immediately following Mexico's elections to further bring down the number of migrant encounters at the border.

They had decided—the two presidents together. AMLO concluded the call with a gesture of support, telling President Biden, "My goal is that migration and border issues don't affect the outcome of your elections in the United States."

By May, the desperation in Washington reached new heights. Many Democratic voters wanted a different candidate, one who they felt might have a better chance at beating Trump. Unbelievably, despite all Trump did on January 6, 2021, and throughout his first term, he looked increasingly viable.

In an attempt to put Republicans on the back foot, Senate Majority Leader Chuck Schumer decided to resurrect the Lankford-Sinema-Murphy immigration reform bill as standalone legislation, hoping to force Republicans to vote against border security at the height of election season. But that didn't work: The vote on May 23 was even more lopsided than the first go-around. It failed forty-three to fifty and was dismissed by even some Democrats as political theater. Senators Lankford and Sinema voted against their own legislation, and Lankford termed it "a political messaging exercise" rather than a serious attempt to address the issue. Lankford would later tell a *New York Times* reporter that the White House had waited too long. If they had only acted before the calendar turned to 2024, before Trump had won primaries in Iowa and New Hampshire, then the bill could have succeeded. But that's not what happened.

This vote confirmed that any kind of meaningful, bipartisan legislative action on the border was now impossible. Trump's control over the Republican Party was all but complete. The American political system remained utterly broken where it concerned the border, an issue that demanded—then and now—bipartisan cooperation.

On June 2, Mexicans went to the polls. Claudia Sheinbaum won in a landslide, becoming the country's first female president-elect. Two days later, on June 4, President Biden issued an executive order on asylum restrictions and migration number triggers that effectively controlled the border. Daily encounters in June suddenly fell to below three thousand.

On June 10 and 11, Liz and I met with President-elect Sheinbaum and her team. The meetings were productive and optimistic. Sheinbaum was impressive. She was committed to continuing AMLO's cooperation on migration while bringing her own administrative competence and scientific background as a trained climate scientist to the presidency.

If President Biden could survive this political crisis, President Sheinbaum would be an ideal partner for permanently transforming the relationship between the United States and Mexico.

HEARTBREAK

39

THE DEBATE

On June 27, Senior Policy Advisor Zeppa Kreager met me in the living room of the ambassador's residence to watch the first Biden–Trump debate. Zeppa had worked with President Biden for eight years while he was vice president, and she was fiercely loyal. We settled in, hoping for a strong performance like the one he'd had in 2020 against Trump. Instead, we both knew almost instantly that this would be different.

The president rambled and appeared confused, even from the moment he walked on stage. His voice was hoarse, his delivery halting. After a few minutes, Zeppa rose from the couch and walked to the far side of the room, as if she wanted to get away from the television. "This is not his best day," she said softly. The debate continued; the president didn't recover. It was a painful ninety minutes.

Finally, it ended. The post-debate punditry confirmed that we had witnessed one of the worst all-around debates in modern history. Many talking heads who normally supported the president turned on him, and none of them appeared to feel good about it. Some asked why this had been allowed to happen. Some speculated that the president might have been sick.

There was wide consensus that Trump had also been awful—he lied, he threw in constant non sequiturs, he refused to answer direct questions—but it didn't matter.

I turned off the TV and said to Zeppa, "Maybe the president will recover for the next one. We both know he can be much better."

"I hope that's true," Zeppa said. "But we have our work cut out for us." She didn't have to say more. While it was possible Biden could best Trump in a subsequent debate, there was no guarantee another would even take place. Trump had won simply by showing up, and as the clear victor, he now had no incentive to agree to any follow-up encounters.

As I struggled to find sleep that night, I kept coming back to our new political reality. All of President Biden's accomplishments, including the things we were now achieving along the borderlands, would be overshadowed by this debate.

Early July brought another flurry of Mexico City visits from US administration officials, as well as from a bipartisan congressional delegation. I arranged to have them meet AMLO and President-elect Sheinbaum. These folks all had the same mission: reassure Mexico that the strides our countries had made were not fleeting and that we would continue to make them regardless of America's political turmoil. Each delegation was "positive and optimistic about the United States–Mexico relationship," as I noted in my journal. But privately, everyone was worried about November.

By Thursday, July 18, it was rumored around the embassy and in Washington that President Biden would withdraw but still serve out his term.

If that happened, no one knew how the Democrats would proceed. Dropping out this late in a presidential race had no modern precedent. Lyndon Johnson had announced that he would not seek reelection in 1968, but that had been in March, giving a divided Democratic Party the chance to run a primary and, ultimately, coalesce around a new candidate, Hubert Humphrey. Although that race was scarred by the upheaval of the Civil Rights Movement, the tragic assassinations of Martin Luther King Jr. and Bobby Kennedy, and violence at the Democratic National Convention in Chicago, the Democrats rallied around Humphrey as their standard bearer.

It's worth remembering the pain the country endured at that time. I remember it well—especially the assassinations, the violence that erupted in their wakes, and the funeral services that were attended by so many. The country was in mourning that year.

This time was different. There seemed to be three options: run a rushed but open primary, wait until the convention so the state delegations could choose a candidate, or rally behind Vice President Harris.

I sincerely hoped it would be option number one.

40

THE FESTIVAL OF GUELAGUETZA

Three weeks after the presidential debate, I visited Oaxaca with Andrea and Selena. We'd come for the multiday Guelaguetza festival, one of Mexico's most spectacular cultural celebrations, in which Oaxaca's sixteen official Indigenous communities and its Afro-Mexican community showcase their ancient traditions through parades, dancing, food, and music. I'd been invited there as a guest of honor by Oaxacan governor Salomón Jara—an Indigenous Zapotec person himself and one of Mexico's most prominent state-level politicians. Visits like this, which I'd made to all thirty-two Mexican states, always brought me joy, and it was a true honor to witness the greatness of the Mexican people, their history, and their culture. With all the turmoil in the Biden administration, the festival came as a welcome distraction.

And what a distraction! There were hundreds of thousands of people in the streets singing, dancing, eating, and celebrating. As we walked along, people offered us food and souvenirs, and several times I had to turn down tequila from gallon bottles. The colors were overwhelming, but in a good way—bright reds, deep blues, golden yellows, all on display as people paraded around the streets, overflowing with joy and pride. Andrea and Selena marched alongside me and Governor Jara as he led the inaugural parade, passing buildings painted in brilliant colors that glowed in the afternoon sun. It was the kind of festival that could make anyone fall in love with Mexico and her people, and being there affirmed all my positive feelings about our neighbor to the south.

But distractions are just that: shiny objects that pull one's attention away from what is really going on. I was genuinely happy in Oaxaca; I was also genuinely distressed. I had no inside information, but I intuitively knew that Joe Biden would end his campaign.

That evening in my hotel room, I sat alone and grabbed a pen and paper. I drew a line down the middle, forming two columns. At the top of one column, I wrote "Stay," over the other, "Resign."

The arguments for staying were substantial. I could complete the mission through 2024, regardless of who won the election. I would be in Mexico for Claudia Sheinbaum's historic inauguration as North America's first female president. I could work with her and her team to establish a US–Mexico agenda through 2030. Most importantly, I could continue to take care of the 3,300 Mission Mexico employees who had worked so hard to transform the relationship between the United States and Mexico.

The reasons to resign were also substantial. If I left, I could return home to my family and the San Luis Valley; I could use my position to advocate for neglected and forgotten groups in the United States; and, with the goal of healing the relationship between the United States and Mexico, and at potentially great political risk, I could call out the few people with real authority who never took the border, immigration, Mexico, or the Americas as seriously as they should have or promised they would.

I put the piece of paper on my bedside table and went to sleep. For some reason, that night I slept better and longer than I had in months. It was like something inside of me had shifted.

The next morning, with the sounds of that day's celebration already building in the streets below, I realized that I should do more than resign. I needed to complete the mission, and there was only one way to do it.

I should run for president.

I jumped out of bed and grabbed my diary. I flipped to an open page and began writing. My slogan would be simple and clear: "Make America United Again." The three planks of my campaign would be to secure America, save the planet, and end our wars.

I would pledge to strengthen the border and support our police, providing them with the resources and protection they needed. I would emphasize that we needed a real border, with enforceable migration laws, because our country could not exist without borders—but I would point out that these measures did not need to come at the expense of our relationship with Mexico, the Americas, or Hispanic Americans. Quite the contrary. I would argue with conviction and evidence that having a strong border would *enhance* all of these relationships. I would insist that we needed to create a durable binational security treaty with Mexico to fight the cartels and stop the flow of fentanyl and guns. I would also focus on further integrating our economies for the benefit of workers and consumers on both sides of the border.

I would repeat the refrain I'd uttered so many times as ambassador: "Sin seguridad, no hay prosperidad"—without security, there can be no prosperity. This philosophy would not only apply to the border, the cartels, and our partnership with the Mexican government, but also to our own communities, big and small; our schools; our houses of worship; and our capital buildings and institutions. In order to truly exercise their freedom, people must first be and feel safe.

The second plank of my campaign would extend beyond securing the United States: I would insist that we confront climate change. In truth, this was part of being safe. If the United States could take the lead on blunting and eventually reversing the ravages of climate change, then we wouldn't just make the United States and Mexico safer—we would make all people everywhere safer.

Finally, I would work with our allies to end the wars in the Middle East and Ukraine. I would promise to join with Arab leaders to eliminate Hamas while leveraging our relationship with Israel to make them stop the indiscriminate killing across Gaza and the West Bank. I would continue President Biden's work of containing and pressuring Putin to end his illegal invasion of Ukraine, sending the strong message to the Kremlin that they could not do anything like that again.

Beyond these three main planks, I would pledge to strengthen forgotten Americans by bringing them forward into the national conversation: rural people of all races and religions, poor people from across the country, Native American people, Black and Asian people, women, Hispanic people, and so many others. As president, I would also pledge to involve white people—and white men in particular—since it is simply not possible to solve our nation's biggest problems without bringing everyone together. Some would call this "identity politics," but I've always called it a unity agenda. We all live here; therefore, we each need to understand and respect each other regardless of race, national background, or gender. I would state it plainly: An inclusive America is worth living in and fighting for. Diversity is our superpower.

I wrote all of this in under thirty minutes. I put my pen down, my mind and heart racing. Did I have a shot? I had no idea. Not many voters outside of Colorado knew who I was. But I wasn't sure that I cared. This was the world we lived in. This was reality. We had to deal with it. And at that moment, I thought I could be the one to do it.

I closed my diary and locked it in the hotel room's safe. No one could see this prematurely. Then I showered, dressed, and joined Andrea, Selena, and Zeppa for breakfast. But all the while, the wheels in my mind turned.

Throughout that Saturday, I made a few discreet calls on my personal phone and did some research. What were the filing requirements for entering the race, what were the Federal Election Commission procedures, what were the protocols for resignation? I began mentally assembling my brain trust. Jim Kelly, my longtime friend and mentor in

Colorado; Tom Strickland, whom I'd known since the 1980s and who had been with me at Interior; Al Yates, a chemical physicist and former president of Colorado State University; and Stephanie Valencia and Rosemary Rodriguez, the founders of the largest Latina organization in the country.

Of course, the primary endorsement I needed was Hope's. When I called her that night and asked if she was willing to endure all that my running for president would subject her to, she said, "I'm not sure, but I'll always support you, Ken. We've been on this path for a while now. No point in getting off." It wasn't a full-throated "Let's do this!" but it was the truth. She'd understood long ago that she had married a politician, not just the lawyer-rancher I originally aspired to be when we met.

Saturday came and went with a blur of meetings and further cultural events in Oaxaca, all of which kept me busy.

On Sunday, July 21, I woke early. That night, I hadn't slept very well. To clear my mind, I decided to go for a morning jog.

As usual, I was joined by my security detail. We navigated the quiet morning streets together. The city was in a peaceful lull between celebrations, and cleanup was underway in preparation for the final day of the festival. Shopkeepers hosed the sidewalks in front of their stores, sanitation crews swept the gutters and emptied trash receptacles, and café owners put out fresh baked goods and other treats.

After I'd jogged for a couple of miles, I returned to the hotel for breakfast. That morning, we'd all be going to mass at the Cathedral of Our Lady of the Assumption in Oaxaca.

Wherever I went in Mexico I would meet with the Catholic bishops and priests to learn about them and the reality of life facing their flocks. Over 90 percent of Mexico's 130 million citizens identify as Catholic. In Cuernavaca, in the state of Morelos near Mexico City, I would meet often with Monseñor Ramon Castro Castro, a theologian who helped lead Mexico's twelve thousand Catholic priests in their quest to serve the Mexican people. Monseñor Castro Castro was a charismatic leader known for speaking out about violence and corruption. He was particularly vocal about two Jesuit priests who had been ruthlessly killed at their church's altar in Chihuahua's rural Tarahumara Mountains.

These two murders stood as stark examples of how Mexico's priests exist at the nexus of life and death. They know how dangerous the streets are, how active the cartels are, how contented or fearful or frustrated the people are. In every corner of Mexico, they bury the dead and comfort families when their loved ones are killed or disappeared. They learn about their congregants' stark realities in the confessional.

The response from the government was often less than inspiring. Typically, when AMLO met with church leaders, he would only report on his security successes without talking frankly about the threats priests faced. I was clear that I felt that without security there could be no prosperity, and I had been vocal about the murders of priests and consistently raised security concerns about them with AMLO's security chief.

Now it was my turn to meet with the archbishop in Oaxaca. Like virtually all Mexican cathedrals, his church was both grand and worn, not least because it was nearly five hundred years old. We were greeted there by the archbishop, an intelligent-looking man in his seventies with kind eyes and weathered hands. As mass began, he introduced me to a packed congregation: "Es un honor tener aquí con nosotros al estimado embajador Ken Salazar, embajador de los Estados Unidos en México." I stood and bowed, folding my arms over my chest as if I were embracing everyone there. The congregation broke out with heartfelt applause. My heart was with them. I imagined many of the people there were praying for God to grant them a good job and good health, and to keep them safe from the dangers lurking in their communities.

The mass was beautiful and reflected the diverse Indigenous communities that call Oaxaca home. Like the many devout people around me, I felt contemplative as I listened to the archbishop's words. And as I contemplated, I felt the weight of what I was considering. The people here trusted me. They saw me as someone who understood their struggles and their hopes. Would I be sacrificing that trust—to say nothing of the trust of my own countryfolk—if I followed my nascent political ambition and abruptly left Mexico to run for president? Or was this ambition about service, about the mission I'd been on, about understanding, and, ultimately, about engendering even more trust? I couldn't be certain.

Following the service, an usher approached and said the archbishop was ready to meet with us. As we were escorted to a small room behind the altar, I realized this meeting might provide me with the spiritual guidance I needed.

The archbishop greeted us with a smile and warm embraces. "Thank you for hosting us today, Your Excellency," I said in Spanish. "Your church is beautiful and your sermon was powerful. Thank you."

"I'm glad to hear that, Ambassador Salazar," the archbishop said.

I asked him what I asked of most bishops I encountered: "Tell me, how are things here? How are the people in Oaxaca?"

"They are surviving," the archbishop said. He told me thoughtfully about the suffering he witnessed every day—about the migrants on the dangerous trail north; about families torn apart by violence; about church officials and parishioners alike living in fear of the cartels. We both knew that Oaxaca was in the crosshairs of the migration challenges plaguing Mexico and related security issues. But the archbishop spoke with hope about the future: "There are always good paths forward even though they may be difficult to discern at the moment."

"I agree," I said. "I care deeply about the security of priests and the people you serve, and I hope that my work may one day help clear those paths."

The archbishop placed his right hand on his heart and said, "I've read and heard you speak about this many times, Ambassador. Thank you for doing so."

The archbishop then turned to Selena, asking about the flower in her hair. After he had spent a few minutes talking to my family and Zeppa, I asked if I might have some time alone with the archbishop.

He gave each of them a hug and they walked back into the cathedral's soaring nave.

Suddenly it was just me and this Catholic archbishop I'd never met before this weekend. "Archbishop," I began, my voice quieter now, "forgive my bluntness, but I find myself at a crossroads. I'm weighing my options as we speak, and I would deeply value your guidance."

The archbishop leaned forward slightly, his expression growing more serious. "Please continue," he said.

"I have served as ambassador here for three years. I've worked tirelessly to build bridges between our countries and address the challenges we share. I have worked to remind people on both sides of the border of our shared history and intertwined destiny. But I'm increasingly concerned that neither of our governments appreciate the greatness of our respective peoples, or the importance of working together as sisters and brothers for the good of both nations."

I paused, trying to find the right words for what I was about to say.

"I'm contemplating resigning my position and returning home to seek higher office. I know this might sound prideful. But I don't think it's that. I believe I could better serve my country in a different capacity. But I'm torn between my duty here and returning home." For whatever reason, I couldn't just come out with it: "I think I should run for president."

It is my experience that the best spiritual leaders excel at reading between the lines—and they are also masterful diplomats. The archbishop was silent for a long moment, his hands folded across his stomach, his eyes studying my face. When he finally spoke, his voice was gentle but firm.

"Ambassador," he said, "God will guide you to make the right decision. I have no doubt of this." He paused, then continued with what felt like a small sermon, delivered just for me in that quiet room. "I think of the prophet Jeremiah, who lived five hundred years before Christ. Jeremiah spoke of a future of peace, tranquility, and hope, even during the darkest times. He understood that humans face a fundamental choice—between love and peace on the one hand, and discord and division on the other."

The archbishop's voice grew stronger as he continued.

"This choice is too often based on power and greed, which is antithetical to the message of Christ, the message of all the prophets, and the message of all religions that speak of faith, hope, and goodness." He looked directly into my eyes. "You are a man of faith, Ambassador Salazar. I can see it in how you speak about serving others and about your concern for the suffering of your people and ours. For there is no difference between our two peoples. And so I know that faith will guide you to the right decision."

He then placed his hands on my shoulders in a gesture that felt like a benediction. "Whatever you decide, know that you have served with honor and integrity. Trust in God's plan for your life."

"Thank you, Your Excellency," I said.

He blessed me by making the sign of the cross over my forehead, and we said farewell.

As I returned to my family and colleagues, I felt both more conflicted and more resolved than I had all weekend. The archbishop hadn't told me what to do, but he'd reminded me of who I was and what I believed in.

41

THE PRESIDENT'S DECISION

That's when I saw Zeppa. She approached holding a pink Post-it. Even before she reached me, I saw the tears forming in her eyes.

"Ambassador," she said quietly as she passed me the note, "I just got word. The president has officially decided to suspend his campaign." I took the note. It read, "POTUS is out."

I felt a profound sadness. Yes, President Biden and, more fundamentally, his team had disappointed me where Mexico and the Americas were concerned. In my view, their inability to confront the border crisis had been a major factor contributing to his weakened presidency—and now he had decided to leave the race. Eight months earlier in San Francisco, the president told me that he had a duty to run to beat Trump. Now all of that had dissipated into thin air.

But in that moment, as I held that pink Post-it, what hit me hardest was that Joe Biden was a friend and that he was in pain. I can't imagine what it must have been like to concede to his detractors that he could not or should not go on. This was a man who'd already lived through so much—a man who'd lost a wife and a child to a car accident; a man who'd lost a grown son to brain cancer; a man whose sole surviving son had been an addict and had just a month prior been convicted of federal gun and tax violations by President Biden's own Justice Department.

This must have been one of Joe Biden's most trying episodes—and he'd had his share of those.

I knew that the president might endorse Vice President Harris as his replacement, but in my view, that would be a mistake. A big part of our nation's political turmoil had to do with migration and the border, and Trump would continue to attack her ruthlessly on this issue. She had been placed in charge of getting at the root causes of migration, but many felt she had been ineffective. Maybe she hadn't been given enough authority; maybe she thought these problems were intractable; maybe she thought that taking responsibility for such a difficult problem was political suicide, that doing so would cut off her avenue to the highest office in the land. I don't know. But for whatever reason, she had been unable to help with the border and migration crisis, even though she'd sat next door to the Oval Office for almost four years.

By the time I got to the Oaxaca airport, President Biden had tweeted that he was endorsing Kamala Harris.

I thought perhaps I should still run for president. I believed in the cause to which I had dedicated myself as Colorado's attorney general, as a United States senator, as the secretary of the Interior, and now as ambassador to Mexico. But more than that, I was committed to a vision of America that was antithetical to Trump's: diversity as strength, not weakness; a belief in understanding our past, not erasing it; the imperative to address the climate crisis, not dismiss it as a "hoax"; and the duty to proudly lift up *all* forgotten Americans, including Mexican and Hispanic Americans, instead of beating them down.

The next day in Mexico City, I called my family, closest friends, Democratic operatives, and others who would need to be part of any serious presidential campaign. But their response was swift and unanimous:

The party was closing ranks around Vice President Harris. There would be no open primary or contested convention. No matter how frustrated I was with the president and Vice President Harris, no matter how much I believed I could offer different and more effective leadership, there was no path to victory.

And so my dream died as quickly as it had been born.

42

THE LAST MEETING

Two days after President Biden decided to end his campaign, on Tuesday, July 23, AMLO and I met at the Palacio. In advance of that meeting, I had drafted a letter he could send to President Biden. It recounted all the progress our countries had made, and it set forth a vision for the future of North America and the Western Hemisphere. I believed we were moving forward, especially on trade, supply chains, and clean energy initiatives. And it would be an important written commitment from the Mexican president to the United States. If Kamala Harris won, it would be the template that would define our joint agenda through 2030 and beyond. If she lost, it would at least establish a vision for the future of the relationship between the United States and Mexico.

I arrived at the Palacio Nacional in midmorning, the draft letter folded neatly in my inside jacket pocket. As always, I was met in Corridor Eight and escorted to the president's chambers. There, I was met by Daniel Asaf.

"Señor Embajador," he said, "the president will see you shortly. He's just finishing something up."

I waited in the windowless antechamber, decorated with Mexican landscapes and books written by AMLO. I sat and reread my letter. It was good. I hoped AMLO would adopt some or all of its language in his outreach to President Biden.

After twenty minutes, Daniel said AMLO was ready to see me.

I stepped into his office and found him at his desk, pen in hand, a few sheets of handwritten paper scattered in front of him.

"Ah, Embajador," he said with a warm smile, rising to offer me a handshake. "Please, sit. I have been writing something for President Biden."

I suppressed a chuckle and said, "I brought something as well." I pulled my draft letter out and handed it to him. "I thought you might want to consider this letter for your message to the president."

"Why don't you sit and read it to me," AMLO said. As I did, he listened intently, nodding now and then. When I finished, he said, "This is very good, Ken. Thank you. I should sign it and send it to President Biden."

"That would be great, Mr. President," I said. "Thank you."

He then read me his letter. It was gracious and forward-looking, acknowledging President Biden's "courageous decision" to drop out. He and I had often discussed what he called "the indispensables," those who clung to power because they believed only they could lead their people, like Nicolás Maduro in Venezuela or Daniel Ortega in Nicaragua. He believed there had been too many "indispensables" throughout the history of Mexico and Latin America, which invariably had led to massive amounts of corruption, poverty, and lack of opportunity for regular people. And with conviction, he stated that he was not among the indispensables.

As I listened, I couldn't help but feel great appreciation for AMLO. Even if he could be ideologically rigid and stubborn, I liked him. And despite all our disagreements and his frequent attacks on my government's policies, AMLO understood the importance of the relationship between our countries. He somehow believed that Mexico was finally ready to try its hand at trusting the United States.

When he finished reading his letter, I said, "This is excellent. The president will appreciate your words."

AMLO folded his letter carefully and handed it to me. "Please deliver this with my personal regards," he said. "Tell him that Mexico remains committed to our friendship, regardless of politics. I will review your letter and send it later in the week."

I tucked AMLO's letter into my jacket pocket, knowing I was carrying more than just words on paper. AMLO and I exchanged abrazos and I went on my way, hopeful that Kamala Harris would prevail, and that Trump would not be able to destroy everything we had worked for.

I did not know then that I would never meet with AMLO again.

43

THE END OF THE MISSION

Two days after this meeting with AMLO, the Sinaloa Cartel chapito Joaquín Guzmán López kidnapped his uncle Ismael "El Mayo" Zambada García in Culiacán, Mexico, boarded a plane, and flew to an airstrip in New Mexico.

This development was a milestone for me. It capped an active period of law enforcement cooperation against the international cartels. Less than a year earlier, in September 2023, the Sinaloa Cartel leader Ovidio "El Ratón" Guzmán López had been extradited to the United States to face justice, just like his father, El Chapo, before him.

The extradition of El Ratón had been a major success for Mexico and the United States, and the Sinaloa Cartel could not sit idly by. Their chief assassin, or "sicario," Néstor "El Nini" Isidro Pérez Salas, was intent on finding those who had outed El Ratón. In an act of vengeance, El Nini kidnapped and tortured eight suspected informants, brutally killing each, and then dumped their bodies on the border between Sinaloa and Jalisco. Attached to their corpses were notes that read, "This is what happens to snitches."

Mexico initiated an all-out manhunt for El Nini, which the US supported. A little over a month later, on November 22, 2023, El Nini was captured in Sinaloa. For six months, he sat in a Mexican prison as we worked with Mexico to bring him to the United States. By May 2024, the window for El Nini's extradition was closing rapidly, since his legal team was seeking an injunction that would keep him in Mexico. If that happened, as many assumed it would, El Nini would either escape prison or continue to run the Sinaloa sicarios with impunity from his cell. We had to deliver him to the United States.

On May 24, 2024, a US Marshals Service plane was scheduled to pick up El Nini in Mexico. It was supposed to arrive late that night, but it had mechanical and pilot issues and was still grounded as the clock ticked past midnight. We began to worry that it wouldn't arrive at all. At around 2:00 AM on May 25, the lead DOJ lawyer on the case called and asked if I could reach out to the head of Mexico's FBI, the Agencia de Investigación Criminal. We needed to prepare for Plan B. This would involve the Mexican government flying El Nini to the border, where US officials would pick him up and drive him across—a much riskier operation.

Fortunately, the US plane took off, touching down in Mexico just before dawn. El Nini was escorted on board by Mexican officers and officially accepted by US marshals. He was placed in custody and flown to Chicago, where he would join El Ratón to face justice.

Both governments were pleased with the extradition and said as much in their public statements. I believed this was the exact type of joint operation our countries should routinely undertake as we sought to deliver greater security for people on both sides of the border. Only by working hand in hand with Mexico could we have struck such a blow at the leadership of the Sinaloa Cartel.

In this context, the surprising arrests of Joaquín Guzmán López and El Mayo at the end of July 2024 were something both Washington and Mexico City should have been proud of. Guzmán López would not have kidnapped his uncle and brought him to the United States if we hadn't put so much joint pressure on the cartels. I saw this as a categorical victory for the United States and Mexico. It proved that our joint security efforts were working.

Sadly, AMLO did not see these arrests in the same light. Instead, he saw them as a betrayal. US Attorney General Merrick Garland and I assured AMLO through an official communication that it was "not our plane, not our pilot, and not our operation," but AMLO was apparently offended by what he perceived as a violation of Mexican sovereignty. He never spoke to me again.

On that day, I went from someone AMLO saw as a friend to someone he felt he couldn't trust. I was persona non grata in Mexico City. One of the most important assignments of my life, serving as US ambassador to Mexico, was suddenly over.

In the end, this breakup wasn't about arresting cartel leaders, border encounters or the human toll of smuggling, or this policy failure or that lack of messaging: It was about the fundamental breakdown of understanding and trust.

Both countries would likely pay the price for that breakdown, long after the votes in the US presidential election had been cast.

PART VII

THE URGENT MOMENT

44

TRUMP'S PROJECT OF ERASURE

When the ballots were finally counted in early November 2024, what many feared came to pass: Donald Trump won. This was shocking. His first term had not been smooth sailing. He had been impeached twice, including for his actions on January 6, 2021, when he encouraged a mob to storm the US Capitol on the false notion that Joe Biden had "stolen" the 2020 election. Regardless, Trump would return to the White House. And we would soon learn that this time he would not be constrained by Congress, the Supreme Court, his staff, federal agencies, or other US institutions that had been built up over decades and even hundreds of years. Trump would be unbound.

Not long after the November election, Andrea, Selena, and I were invited to a party at the hillside hacienda of one of Mexico's most prominent business leaders, a man I'll call Paco. He welcomed us and several other guests into his home on a lazy Sunday afternoon to enjoy local cuisine and listen to a mariachi band he'd hired for the day. While Andrea mingled and Selena played with a couple of miniature horses in the central courtyard, Paco took me on a stroll through the stone corridors of his countryside getaway. The halls were decorated with Mexican paintings and Indigenous art on pedestals, and at one point he stopped in front of an oil painting of a building I'd been in many times.

"Do you recognize this?" Paco asked.

"Of course. It's the Palacio Nacional." I leaned closer. "But it has an American flag flying over it, not a Mexican one."

"This was painted after the war in 1848," Paco explained. "The US soldiers occupied the Palacio Nacional, took down our flag, and hoisted your country's flag in its place. With jubilant celebration, they showed Mexicans that the United States had succeeded in its war of conquest. Every time I look at this painting, I think of our pained relationship with the United States. Many Mexicans would prefer to destroy this painting. The memory of this moment is a deep and unforgettable scar in their minds."

"So much distrust and pain flows from that war," I said. "If the United States is to continue its march toward a more perfect union, then we can't forget our history—including the painful history of Mexico, Mexicans, and Mexican Americans."

"I completely agree," Paco said. "Somos familia." We are one family.

◆◆◆

Unfortunately, Trump doesn't appear to value relationships of mutual respect with any country in the world, including Mexico. For him, the shared history and heritage of the United States and Mexico appear to be one target among many of his project of erasure.

This stands in stark contrast to Trump's predecessors from both parties, perhaps most notably President Harry Truman. In March 1947, less than two years after the end of World War II, President Truman traveled to Mexico City. He was the first US president to visit in nearly a hundred years—the first since the Mexican-American War ended and the Stars and Stripes flew over the Palacio Nacional.

During his visit, Truman was greeted by President Miguel Alemán and millions of cheering Mexicans. Truman toured the Palacio, the cathedral on the Zócalo, and many other cultural sites. During an unscheduled visit, he laid a wreath at the Monumento a los Niños Héroes at the Castillo de Chapultepec. This was a memorial for six teenage Mexican cadets who had fought to the death to defend the Castillo against the United States Cavalry as it entered Mexico City in 1847. One cadet even wrapped himself in the Mexican flag and leapt to his death to protect it from being captured by Americans.

When President Truman was asked why he'd paid tribute at this site, he replied, "Brave men don't belong to any one country. I respect bravery wherever I see it."

Ramon Ayala, a Mexican engineer, would later say of that day, "One hundred years of misunderstanding and bitterness wiped out by one man in one minute. That is the best neighbor policy."

The United States and Mexico are great nations that deserve the other's respect. As I've tried to show throughout this book, we have a long shared history, some of which is good, some bad, some in between. Whatever anyone may say to the contrary, we are integrated geographically, economically, and culturally. The United States cannot be secure if Mexico is unsafe, and Mexico cannot be secure if the United States is unsafe. Neither country can flourish if the other is falling apart.

Before contested borderlands separated our countries—before there were migrants, guns, drugs—there were just people. They crossed the desert or the Rio Grande whenever they felt like it to work the land, visit family, celebrate feast days, graze cattle, and simply be people who lived in one place that, because of war and politics, is now divided into two. That's what the borderlands are today: a single place that has been split in two.

Throughout my life, it has been my mission to heal this division by advocating for further integrating our economies, our security apparatus, our cultural inheritances, and our beautiful desert landscapes. Expanding our ability to move *legally* back and forth across our shared border is an important part of this mission.

For me, this mission has also always been interconnected with a second mission: to celebrate and not demonize our diversity here at home. When I talk about diversity, I don't just mean diversity of race, gender, or religious faith (or lack of it). I also mean diversity of opinion, of knowledge, of ideas.

The United States is a child of the Enlightenment. We are perhaps the only nation in history to be founded on ideals, not creed or tribal identity. Indeed, the colonies broke free from the dominant "tribe" of monarchical England because of these Enlightenment ideals: that people should be free of tyranny; that government should be accountable to those they serve; that all people have inalienable natural rights; and that no one person or governmental entity may place unreasonable restrictions on those rights. For 250 years, these ideals have awed and inspired both free people and enslaved people, the poor and the wealthy, the desperate, the idealistic, the inventive, and the industrious. They are the ideals that have led directly and through great struggle to more freedom for more people, from Black Americans to Irish Americans to Italian Americans to Latino Americans to Asian Americans to LGBTQ+ Americans to Catholic Americans to Jewish Americans to Muslim Americans to women and many more in between. This mutable and expansive brand of American freedom has also inspired the people of other countries to be freer and to fight for their own inalienable rights.

These ideals uphold the notion that there is no single kind of American, but rather that any kind of person can be one. The United States' promises are not given only to a certain type of person. If they are, then our country becomes something else, something older, something less ideal and more tribal. It is not a democracy. And to quiet some naysayers, I want to be clear that I am not suggesting that anyone can come to the United States and become a citizen. What I am saying is that there is no limit on where a US citizen can come from or what they should look like.

Precisely because there are so many different kinds of Americans, our country is a richer and better place. To me, it is clear that true diversity leads to unity, not division. The evidence of this unity is everywhere, from our music to our food to our innate pluckiness to our love of the open road. Only one country in the history of the world could create jazz and rock and roll and bluegrass, or Tex-Mex and chicken-fried steak, or the Ford Model A and the Tesla Model Y.

Looking back on my career, I believe my time at the Interior Department had been the most impactful in my fight for an inclusive America. Together with President Obama, we told many forgotten American stories. We formally recognized the experiences of Native Americans, Latino Americans, Asian Americans, and women suffragists. We helped tell the story of American slavery, of the fight to end it, of the struggle for Black civil rights that began well before the Civil War and that came to a head—at least in terms of lawmaking—in the 1960s. We told these stories as part of our effort to unify the nation in all its complexity and diversity.

In October 2009, we secured the permit to finally build the Martin Luther King Jr. Memorial on the National Mall. It took two years to construct, and President Obama dedicated it on October 16, 2011. As I made my introductory remarks that day, I looked at Barack and Michelle Obama, and at the civil rights icon John Lewis, knowing some of what they and their families had overcome. I thought about how Americans of all backgrounds had stood on the shoulders of figures like Dr. King and the many others who had fought for both their inalienable rights as human beings and their legal rights as persons living in the United States.

In 2026, this dedication would not be possible. Instead of working toward diversity, Donald Trump and his administrative agents have undertaken an active campaign of erasure. It is whitewashing. It is an attempt to make America something it isn't.

I don't believe they would ever permit, build, or dedicate a monument to any Black civil rights leader, not even one of Dr. King's stature. Nor would they do any of the other things we did to commemorate Black Americans or the complexity of our nation's history. They would not organize and dedicate a monument at Fort Monroe or Honouliuli; they would not recognize Harriet Tubman or the Underground Railroad; they would not honor the struggle for women's equality on the

National Mall; they would not memorialize the Buffalo Soldiers in Ohio or the United Farm Workers in La Paz, California.

Instead, Trump and his cohort would prohibit the telling of this history, preferring to erect monuments to white supremacists and segregationists. Using a disingenuous trick, they have returned the names of Confederate officers and soldiers to prominent military bases. They fired many non-white and female officers across the military branches, including the chairman of the Joint Chiefs of Staff, one of the most highly decorated officers in the entire US military. They removed signs that explained our great but complicated history from national parks across the country. They dictated the end of DEI—diversity, equity, and inclusion—on the grounds that only their definition of merit counts.

Perhaps they reasoned that since many people had voted for Obama, and Americans had elected him as president—twice!—affirmative action was no longer needed. Or perhaps it was too much for Trump and his followers to see the success of Barack Obama and people like me, whose doors of opportunity had been opened because of the Civil Rights Movement. Perhaps they decided to try to close the door on Americans like us because they do not view us as true Americans. Whatever their reasons, history will prove them wrong.

Of course, Trump's project of erasure is not limited to issues of race, gender, or cultural background. He has erased funding for medical research. He has erased Congress's willingness to hold him to account. He has erased due process for many migrants and even some citizens. He has erased the idea that he and his family and friends cannot reap personal profits from his presidency. He has erased norms that constrained all of his modern predecessors.

To take just a few examples: He now uses government websites to display partisan messages lambasting "Radical Left" Democrats. He conducts political rallies on military bases and warships in front of captive audiences of US soldiers and seamen. He has demolished the East Wing of the White House without consulting Congress or submitting any proposals to the public for review, all to make way for a gargantuan ballroom. He has redesigned the iconic national parks pass to feature his face alongside George Washington's, with the slogan "Make America Beautiful Again"—as if the national parks are any place for politics, as if the lands of the United States are not already beautiful.

Trump and his administration have erased, in a very short time, the notion of shared government, of checks and balances, of accountability, of a constitutionally constrained executive. His project of erasure is a vile effort to subjugate and hobble the messy strength of our democratic pluralism. This is precisely what he and his enablers are ultimately trying to erase: our democracy.

When I was stationed in Mexico, I would often jog or walk through Bosque de Chapultepec, the "lungs" of Mexico City, a green space nine times the size of New York's Central Park. It is full of trees and deep ravines, a spotlessly beautiful place. I often passed the Niños Héroes monument President Truman had visited in 1947, but I also frequented the monument to the Aztec Eagles, Mexico's 201st Fighter Squadron.

On July 25, 1944, three hundred members of the Mexican Air Force arrived for instruction at a US airbase in Laredo, Texas. Calling themselves the Aztec Eagles, these soldiers trained for six months before deploying in the Pacific, where they flew ninety-six missions against the Japanese. Five pilots were killed in action.

Whenever I visited that monument, I thought of the thousands of Mexican Americans who served and died in World War II, including my uncle Leandro. In Texas, Mexican American soldiers who had been killed in action were refused burials in certain graveyards for the simple reason that they were Mexican American. Even in death, and after great sacrifice and heroism, they were still subject to discrimination.

As I reflect on all of this, I can't help but think about how un-American Trump's project of erasure is. I am reminded of the sharply contrasting vision I quoted at the beginning of this book, President Ronald Reagan's farewell address from January 1989:

> The past few days when I've been at that window upstairs, I've thought a bit of the "shining city upon a hill." The phrase comes from John Winthrop, who wrote it to describe the America he imagined. What he imagined was important because he was an early Pilgrim, an early freedom man. He journeyed here on what today we'd call a little wooden boat; and like the other Pilgrims, he was looking for a home that would be free.
>
> I've spoken of the shining city all my political life, but I don't know if I ever quite communicated what I saw when I said it. But in my mind it was a tall, proud city built on rocks stronger than oceans, wind-swept, God-blessed, and teeming with people of all kinds living in harmony and peace; a city with free ports that hummed with commerce and creativity. And if there had to be city walls, the walls had doors and the doors were open to anyone with the will and the heart to get here. That's how I saw it, and see it still.

President Reagan's vision for our nation sounds like the perfect prayer for our future. Yet Trump and his followers have abandoned this vision. Instead, they are saying that people like me and countless others do not belong in our country.

To them, I say: Tell Daniel K. Inouye and the heroes of the 442nd they don't belong. Tell the Tuskegee Airmen they don't belong. Tell the Navajo Code Talkers they don't belong. Tell the Mexican American soldiers who were killed in World War II they don't belong. Tell my uncle Leandro he didn't belong. Tell the women who have served in all our wars—and have only now risen through the ranks to become leaders of our military commands—that they don't belong.

To these madmen and -women who have intentionally blinded themselves to history, I say: You are destroying the best hope for America. Diversity is our superpower. You should be ashamed of your project of erasure.

45

A NEW NORTH AMERICAN ALLIANCE

This project of erasure must be stopped. Just like we must defend diversity as our superpower, we must also fight for what I call a "New North American Alliance."

Imagine . . .

What if we had modern and secure borders that people could cross safely without having to stop for hours and wait in fear for themselves and their families?

What if the United States, Mexico, and Canada patrolled our borders together, conducting joint cross-border raids against criminal smugglers, drug cartels, and gunrunners?

What if we supported communities all along our borders, most of which are forgotten rural places that suffer from the same depredations as poor communities in Appalachia or the Rust Belt?

What if we created curtains of security *and* prosperity across southeast Mexico and Central America that hobbled smugglers, drug distribution networks, and arms dealers?

What if the United States, Mexico, and Canada took a chance on vocational and university student exchanges so that students from all three countries could learn together and share the richness of our cultures?

What if we truly integrated the supply chains of North America so we weren't dependent on adversaries on the other side of the globe?

We must fight for this now. For the sake of our national and economic security, we must embrace an alliance among our three countries, which share over seven thousand miles of borderlands. With the support of a president and Congress, the United States could lead in creating a durable legal framework for this continental alliance.

We could enshrine the New North American Alliance in enforceable laws and trilateral treaties built on mutual respect for each nation's sovereignty. It would have chapters on strong borders, defense and security, orderly migration, and integrated supply chains. The aim would be simple—to create an economic and democratic powerhouse for the continent of North America that can serve as an example to the rest of the Americas and the world.

President Kennedy foresaw some aspects of this New North American Alliance in his Alliance for Progress, when he proclaimed it "a vast cooperative effort" focused on "satisfy[ing] the basic needs of the American people for homes, work, land, health, and schools." Kennedy implored republics across the Americas to "transform the 1960s into a historic decade of democratic progress."

In 2006, forty-five years after Kennedy announced his Alliance for Progress, I walked around the White House gardens with his brother Senator Ted Kennedy. We had been summoned to 1600 Pennsylvania Avenue to work with President Bush on the border and immigration. As we walked, I thought about how the Alliance could have prevented the challenges we faced. After all, people would rather stay in their home countries than take the dangerous road north and try to eke out a life in the shadows here in the United States.

I asked Senator Kennedy that day why he thought the Alliance had failed.

He thought for a moment. "My brother was deeply committed to the Alliance," he said. "But sadly, it fell victim to the politics of the Cold War, especially after the Bay of Pigs. Maybe if he had lived . . ." he said, trailing off. I remained silent.

"After his death, no one cared," he said. "They didn't see Latin America the way he did, and the Soviets were exploiting whoever they could politically. No president since has picked up the mantle of the Americas."

"It's shameful," I said.

Kennedy agreed. "This is exactly why the work we're doing on immigration and the border is so important. Perhaps someday in the future we will finally achieve a successful Alliance for Progress in the Americas."

Of course, the efforts spearheaded by Senators Kennedy and McCain on the border and immigration failed, killed by Republican opposition in the House of Representatives. Then as now, the border and immigration were the untouchable third rail of American politics. It is easier and more politically advantageous to maintain the broken status quo, to vilify migrants for problems they did not create, and to continue to disregard and denigrate our neighbors to the south. In my view, that is why we have not seen another Alliance for Progress since JFK's dream died, despite the urgent need for it.

There have been some leaders who have tried, however imperfectly, to create such lasting alliances. President Obama was one such leader. He supported border modernization, immigration reform, and a new relationship with Mexico. While I was Interior secretary, he and I made working with Mexico and Latin America part of my job. We led the creation of a Gulf of Mexico transboundary agreement with Mexico, providing for the development of shared oil and gas reservoirs in the Gulf; we cooperated with Mexico on the restoration of the Colorado

River Delta; and we established a three-million-acre binational conservation area at Big Bend National Park in Texas and in the Mexican state of Coahuila. Importantly, we also endeavored to tell the story of Mexican Americans and other Latinos by establishing monuments and historic landmarks and by holding celebrations of our shared history and culture at the White House. And from the beginning, we focused efforts on taking another shot at comprehensive immigration reform.

In 2013, a bipartisan immigration bill we had worked on with the Senate Gang of Eight, which included my friend Senator Michael Bennet, passed the US Senate by the wide margin of sixty-eight to twenty-three. It would have modernized the border, provided a path to citizenship for Dreamers and certain other undocumented people living in the United States, and added forty thousand border patrol officers to ensure that our border was secure. But once again, Republicans in the House of Representatives killed the bill. They did not want to give Obama a victory. Instead, they held fast to their belief that a broken border and immigration system would propel Republicans to power in the next presidential election.

And they were right. Three years later, in 2016, Hillary Clinton lost the presidential election to Donald Trump. During that election, Republicans gained ground with Hispanic voters, including those in the heavily Mexican American congressional districts on the Texas borderlands.

Since his November 2024 election, Trump has moved even further from the possibility of North American cooperation, embarking on unprovoked and illegal trade wars with most of the rest of the world, including our neighbors to the north and south. His isolationist and racist views of Latin America suggest that any hope for a New North American Alliance appears to be dead, or at least dormant for the time being.

The urgency of a New North American Alliance is as great today as it was during my time as United States ambassador to Mexico. And increasingly, the demographics of the United States require this New North American Alliance. Almost seventy million Latinos are US citizens, most of them Mexican American, and one in four school-age children in the United States right now is Latino. A healthy US GDP depends on the contributions of these people, on bringing them into the mainstream, and on treating them with dignity and respect as fellow human beings. As impactful as the New North American Alliance will be to Canada, to Mexico, and beyond, it begins within our own borders.

This is your America. This is my America. This is our America.

We can—we must—make it so.

EPILOGUE

Keep the Faith

My grandmother and grandfather were both born in 1884 in Colorado. They were married at La Iglesia de San Francisco, just down the road from Los Rincones, in the early 1900s.

By then, the Salazar clan had lost most of the land they'd owned in the mid-1800s, but the family did manage to hold on to the small homestead in Los Rincones that would, decades later, be home to Henry, Emma, all of my siblings, and me. There in the harsh, remote area along the New Mexico border, the winters were bitterly cold, and the growing season was less than ninety days. But they eked out a living, sustained by hard work and their faith in a better tomorrow.

In 1920, my grandparents acquired 160 acres of prairie at a place known as El Punche, about twenty-five miles from Los Rincones. At the time, the federal government was giving away tracts of public land like those in El Punche to encourage settlement in the rural West. My grandparents had dreamed of expanding their small fifty-acre farm, and they hoped to use those 160 acres for grazing their cows and sheep. So they applied for and were given a homestead grant.

Every summer, they would load the entire family into their covered wagon—there were virtually no cars in the Valley in those days—and they would spend weeks at a time in the rustic wood and stone cabin they had built at El Punche. There, they constructed fences and corrals and made other improvements to the land to fulfill the conditions of the land grant.

Although my grandmother gave birth to eight children over the course of her life, only three, including my father, survived into adulthood. The others died before the age of five. One of these was my redheaded, blue-eyed uncle, Willito.

Willito was two years old in the summer of 1920. While Grandpa Juan worked the fields at the homestead, and Grandma Tita took care of the cabin and the children, Willito came down with a fever. His condition rapidly deteriorated, and Tita prayed that he would get better. She carried him and comforted him for endless hours, pacing the floor of the small cabin, and she made sure he drank enough water and ate enough of a cereal called puliadas to keep him going.

At some point, Grandma Tita and Grandpa Juan realized they had to get Willito to the nearest doctor in Antonito—twenty miles and a full day's journey over open country and ragged wagon tracks. With the limitless, unblinking sky overhead and the endless prairie and piñon-covered hills all around, their wagon wheels creaked over the Valley floor for hours. Willito started to sweat profusely. Grandma Tita held him in her arms as the wagon moved slowly forward, the team of horses moving at a fast trot under my grandfather's steady hands. Grandma Tita tried to hold back her tears, dabbing Willito's forehead with a cloth dipped in water. His eyes vacant and expression gaunt, Willito began to call out, "¡Ay, Mama! ¡Ay, Papa! ¡Ay, Dios!" That was all he said, over and over. "¡Ay, Mama! ¡Ay, Papa! ¡Ay, Dios! ¡Ay, Mama! ¡Ay, Papa! ¡Ay, Dios!"

Grandma Tita implored Grandpa Juan to hurry up, but the wagon and the team of horses could only move so fast. As the minutes ticked by, Willito's pleas grew steadily quieter, descending to a faint whisper. "Ay, Mama . . . Ay, Papa . . . Ay, Dios." Then he stopped talking. The only sounds were the rattle of the wagon's wheels along the hard road, the clop of the horses' hooves, and the whisper of a slight breeze.

Willito let out a long sigh and died in Mama Tita's arms. They were only a few miles away from Antonito.

My grandmother was a petite but tough woman. Though she was poor and uneducated in the formal ways of school, she was educated from the real struggles of life, and she was rich in wisdom, resolve, and undying faith in God and her family. I was lucky to know her. She lived in Los Rincones with us—on the same homestead where she was born and where she gave birth to her eight children.

I'd heard the story of Willito's passing many times from her growing up. One day, toward the end of her life, I knelt by her bedside at our home in Los Rincones and asked, "Mama Tita, how did you keep going after losing Willito?"

She looked at me and smiled. "Because I had three children who survived, mi hijito. I had to keep living for them . . . and for you!" She squeezed my hand and continued, "You have to keep the faith. Dios te bendiga. Tanto que te quiero." I kissed her forehead.

You have to keep the faith.

We all do.

ACKNOWLEDGMENTS

Writing *Borderlands* would not have been possible without the encouragement, guidance, and support of my family, our ancestors, the people of the San Luis Valley, and the people and dedicated public servants I met throughout my travels in Colorado, the United States, Mexico, and many special places around the world. Special thanks go to . . .

. . . Las estrellas de mi vida, Hope, Melinda, Andrea, Mireya, Selena, and Amelia, who have had a front-row seat on this journey for over forty-six years since I met Hope. Thank you also to our son-in-law, Blake.

. . . El corazon de Los Rincones, la familia. It all goes back to Dad and Mom, whose values of faith, family, and community inspired our commitment to each other and a patriotism for a diverse and inclusive America. My brothers and sisters, Leandro, Leroy, John, Elaine, Margaret, Elliott, and June, who played and worked together—and still do, which keeps us together forever.

. . . My siblings' partners, Loretta, Michelle, Mary Lou, Edwin, Marvin, Gale, and Ted, who have shown us the true meaning of diversity and commitment to the Valley. And their children and grandchildren—Alegria and Bryan, Alyssa and Steelsen, Rosa Carmen and Kelley, Gabriel and Clorinda, Lucas and Hollie, Jesus and Kaylee, Esteban and Katie, Miguel and Krystal, Deanna and Craig, Michaela and Mike, Lucia and Codie, EJ and Eric, Ezra, Leandro, Emma, Andrew, Nahlia, Nathaniel, Zoe, Zander, Francisco, Isidora, Charlie, JT, Kaydence, Elisa, Wesley, Michael, Mason, Ida, Barrett, Sicily, and Bronx—are a continued inspiration. Special thanks to Gerardo and Alma Rodriguez, Diana, Jesus, Nelson, and families.

. . . The New Mexicans. My mother's family from Cañon de Jemez, San Miguel, Cuba, and Albuquerque, starting with my grandpa Jesus, grandma Isidora, and my aunts and uncles—Tomasita (Joe), Candelaria (Jose), Leandro, Manuel (Delci), Sister Consuelo, Sister Mary Agnes, Epifania (Sisto), Elizaida (Amarante), Gloria (Gilberto), and Cipie (Roger). And to Sisto Sandoval for showing me the big city of Denver. And the entire Henry Salazar family from Espanola and Chamita and its surrounding areas.

. . . The people of the San Luis Valley and their ancestors, the ranchers and farmers, the many friends, teachers, and neighbors who taught me so much, from grade school to high school and continue to do so today. Special thanks to Mike and Celina Espinoza and their children Yanira, Idana, Resa, and Ramon and to so many wonderful families whose names are Medina, Espinoza, Bagwell, Shawcroft, Montoya, Sowards, Robins, Jarvis, Lopez, Cordova, Brady, and Valdez, and so many other great families rooted in the landscapes of the San Luis Valley.

. . . Leaders and spiritual advisors Father Michael Sheeran, Father John Fitzgibbons, Father Kevin Burke, Father Marshall Gourley, Father Pat Valdez, Father Murray Bodo, and Cuernavaca Bishop Ramón Castro Castro.

. . . Colorado College leaders, professors and friends, Lloyd Worner, Kathryn Mohrman, Jill Tiefenthaler, Manya Whitaker, David Finley, Timothy Fuller, Juan Chavira, Rowena Rivera, Claire and Joe Garcia, and my forever friends Mike Espinoza, Tom Autobee, Randy Serna, Dolores Atencio, Pat and Jeanette Garcia, Hank and Sheri Worley, Jack and Judy Pottle, Ted Swan, Matt Solano, Tony Marquez, Marie Casias, Ed Joyce, Daniel Ortega, and Carlos Ortega, and members of MECHA and the Black Student Union.

. . . Michigan Law friends and associates—La Raza and the Black Law Student Association and their members, Dean Terrance Sandalow, Dean Jeffrey Lehman, and Dean Evan Caminker, who led the effort for diversity and inclusion against all odds and won, Professor Yale Kamisar, Broderick Johnson, Joe Sax, Ernest Newborn, Valerie Jarrett, Rick Lopez, Armando Lopez, Natalia Delgado, Lori Keenan, and the Class of 1981.

. . . My friends in higher education at Adams State University, President David Tandberg, Colorado State University Chancellor Tony Frank, and Regis University Presidents and Jesuit Leaders Michael Sheeran, John Fitzgibbons, and Kevin Burke; and the University of Colorado, Presidents Bruce Benson and Todd Saliman.

. . . My friends and respected Native American leaders like Elouise Cobell, Judge Michael Burrage, Chief Gary Batton, Choctaw Nation of Oklahoma, Governor Bill Anoatubby, the Chickasaw Nation, Leonard Burch, long-time leader of the Southern Ute Indian Tribe, Jefferson Keel, Jennifer Weddle, Larry Echo Hawk, Hilary Tompkins, Mike Connor, John Echo Hawk, and Lucille Echo Hawk.

. . . My esteemed friends, Colorado Attorneys General J.D. MacFarlane, Duane Woodard, and Phil Weiser.

. . . My friends and distinguished judges, Federal Judges Carlos Lucero, Christine Arguello, Michael Burrage, Regina Rodriguez; Colorado Supreme Court Justices Mary Mullarkey, Monica Marquez, and Maria Berkenkotter; Colorado Judges Tony Navarro, Terry Fox, John Daniel Dailey, Andy McCallin, Don Quick, and Michael Goodbee.

. . . My esteemed colleagues in the legal profession, including Bill Marsh, Steve Black, Alan Gilbert, Anne Castle, Felicity Hannay, Renny Fagan, Mark Grueskin, Jim Hautzinger, Don Sherwood, Jim King, Norm Brownstein, Steve Farber, Jennifer Weddle, Ted Trimpa, Beth McCann, Karen Howard, Larry Echo Hawk, Hilary Tompkins, Mike Connor, Bob Russel, Tom Downey, Garth Lucero, Jan Zavislan, Josh Widoff, David Robbins, John Kuenhold, Mike O'Donnell, Jim Spaanstra, Manuel Martinez, Steve Chavez, Ralph Torres, Paul Hultin, Malcolm Wheeler, Jeff Reeser, Gary Reiff, Cole Finegan, Dee Wisor, Tom Strickland, Stanton Dodge, Mindy Sooter, Hallie Levin, Stephanie Evans, Anjan Sahni, Joel Green, Bill Lee, Seth Waxman, Jamie Gorelick, Howard Shapiro, Daniel Volchok, Denver District Attorney John Walsh, Natalie Hanlon-Leh, Bob Novick, Ben Powell, Craig Goldblatt, David Ogden, Susan Murley, Barbara McDonnell, Tommy Beaudreau, Yoon-Young Lee, David Bowker, Peggy Otum, Bill Paddock, and David Harrison.

. . . The Colorado Attorney General team who, under our slogan fighting for Colorado's Land Water and People, led the fight to create safer communities in prosecuting gangs, domestic violence and youth violence in Colorado's schools; protected consumers and the elderly from fraud; protected the treasured water and landscapes of Colorado; and defended diversity as America's superpower.

. . . The US Senate team who took the fight for land, water and people to Washington and helped create a comprehensive energy framework, including renewable energy; gave voice to rural America, farmers and ranchers; promoted laws and policies strengthening homeland security and military readiness; expanded veterans' health care opportunities; and protected our military men and women in far flung places around the world including Iraq and Afghanistan.

. . . The Interior Obama-Salazar Dream Team, who took the fight for America's land, water and people to Interior and ushered in an era of energy independence for the nation; proudly served as custodians for our treasured landscapes and planet; directed new initiatives to recognize the heritage of all the peoples of the United States; created new, respect-based federal commitments and relationships with First Americans; and demonstrated through action that diversity is our superpower.

. . . Public servants, colleagues, and friends: Harry Reid and Landra Reid, Daniel "Danny" Inouye, Pat Roberts, Robert "Bob" Dole, Lisa Jackson, Pete Rouse, David Krone, Jim Messina, Mandy Grunwald, Ben Nighthorse Campbell, John McCain, Ted Kennedy and Vicki Kennedy, Jeff Bingaman, Carl Levin, Debbie Stabenow, Dianne Feinstein, Barbara Boxer, Lisa Murkowski, Susan Collins, Olympia Snowe, Max Baucus, Jack Reed, Sheldon Whitehouse, Chris Dodd, John Kerry, Hilda Solis, Jon Tester, Byron Dorgan, Kent Conrad, Lucy Calautti, Pete Domenici, Patty Murray, Maria Cantwell, Pat Leahy, Tom Daschle, Jon Corzine, Jay Rockefeller, Joe Lieberman, Mel Martinez, Mark Pryor, Lamar Alexander, Tom Carper, Tim Johnson, Tom Vilsack, Steve Ricchetti, Denis McDonough, Gary Myrick, Marty Paone, Elizabeth and Smith Bagley, Alonzo Cantu, Adrienne Arsht, Jason Marczak, Neil Herrington, Cecilia

Muñoz, Will Shafroth, David Hayes, Stephanie Valencia, Grant Leslie, Julissa Reynoso, Halle Mayes, Melissa Koenigsberg, Mickey Ibarra, Janet Murguía, Javier Palomarez, Arturo Vargas, and Roman Palomares.

. . . The Presidents and First Ladies: Gerald Ford, Bill Clinton and Hillary Rodham Clinton, George W. Bush and Laura Bush, Barack Obama and Michelle Obama, Joe Biden and Dr. Jill Biden, and Jimmy Carter and Rosalynn Carter. I am forever grateful to them.

. . . My political colleagues and mentors in Colorado: Roy Romer, Mike Stratton, Zee Ferrufino, Ben Nighthorse Campbell, Tim Wirth, Gary Hart, Mark Udall, Ed Perlmutter, Michael Bennet, John Hickenlooper, Jared Polis, Ruben Valdez, Polly Baca, Rosemary Rodriguez, Ramona Martinez, Amanda Sandoval, Debbie Ortega, Federico Peña, Paul Sandoval, Virginia Castro, Richard Castro, Stewart and Shirley Bliss, Wellington and Wilma Webb, Michael Hancock, Ray Kogovsek, Pat Schroeder, Michael Polsky, Pat Stryker, Joe Zimlich, Al Yates, Tom Strickland, Jim Kelley, Cole Finegan, John Kammerzell, Angela Padilla, Rutt Bridges, John Fielder, Tim Gill, Dee Wisor, Chris Romer, Jim Carpenter, Gail Schoettler, Judi Wagner, Barbara Grogan, John Echo Hawk, Lucille Echo Hawk, Jim Polsfut, Mike Dino, Bill Ritter, Bill and Luz-Maria Shearer, Patricia Barela Rivera, and Chris Henderson.

. . . The stellar Mission Mexico team of nearly 3,300 people working tirelessly to transform the relationship between the US and Mexico, along the two-thousand-mile northern border and to the south all the way to the Selva Maya and the Guatemala border.

. . . The *Borderlands* publishing team. Nils Johnson-Shelton, my friend and writing advisor; BenBella Books and its terrific team, inspired and led by Glenn Yeffeth, CEO; Adrienne Lang, publisher; Jennifer Canzoneri, VP of marketing; Claire Schulz, editorial director; Sarah Avinger, art director; Monica Lowry, production director; Susan Welte, sales manager; Alicia Kania, vendor content manager; Madeline Grigg, publishing associate; and Aida Herrera, chief financial and administrative officer.

. . . The *Borderlands* inspiradores, my friends, colleagues, and advisors, whose tireless work together for over three decades led to the flowering of our causes—Ken Lane, chief of staff; Velina Wallick, special advisor; Joan Padilla, scheduler and advance and *Borderlands* project manager; Cody Wertz, communications; Zeppa Kreager, senior advisor; the chairpersons of the effort and my forever friends, Dr. Al Yates and Ann Yates, Jim Kelley and Amie Knox, Stewart and Shirley Bliss, and Shirley Harris; and forever friends Sol and Corine Trujillo, Mickey Ibarra, Henry Cisneros, Rosemary Rodriguez, Federico and Cindy Peña, Lola and Rob Salazar, Linda and Robert Alvarado, Stephanie Valencia, and Romaine Pacheco.

. . . The first readers, my forever friends, who gave me unvarnished, critical, and helpful advice in helping explain the vision of our march toward a more united, less divisive America. Gratitude to Father Kevin Burke, Dr. Al Yates, Jim Kelley, Juanita Chacon, Happy Haynes, Ken Lane, Joan Padilla, Federico Peña, Jack Pottle, Rosemary Rodriguez, Pete Rouse, Arnold Salazar, Alan Salazar, Tom Strickland, Stephanie Valencia, Velina Wallick, Daniel Yohannes, Santiago Guerra, Mark Grueskin, Cody Wertz, Matt Lee-Ashley, Kate Kelly, Zeppa Kreager, Kendra Barkoff, Tim Daly, Chris Henderson, and my siblings and family. Thank you for giving me the courage to write about the joy in the journey and our nation's uncomfortable truths.

. . . The endorsers of this book who are leaders on the front lines for change on the borderlands: US Senator Mark Kelly; US Senator Catherine Cortez Masto; Actress, Producer, Director, Entrepreneur and Businesswoman Eva Longoria; US Representative Joe Neguse; US Representative Veronica Escobar; Luis A. Miranda, President of 5000 Broadway Productions and Chairman of the Miranda Family Fund; US Senator John Hickenlooper; and US Representative Jason Crow.

. . . Mr. Michael Ford and the extended family of Gerald R. Ford for permitting me to re-print in full President Gerald R. Ford's 1999 *The New York Times* opinion-editorial titled, "Inclusive America, Under Attack." This extraordinary opinion-editorial by the former president is as relevant to America today as it was almost 30 years ago.

INDEX

R

S

ABOUT THE AUTHOR

Ken Salazar is a fifth-generation Coloradan whose ancestors have lived in the American Southwest for more than four hundred years. Ken grew up in the rural San Luis Valley, where the Salazars continue to farm and ranch the same lands his family has been working since before Colorado became a state. Most recently, Ken served as US ambassador to Mexico (2021–2025), where he led the US diplomatic mission during a pivotal time for North America. Before this, Ken served as US secretary of the Interior under President Obama (2009–2013), as Colorado's 35th US senator (2005–2009), and as Colorado state attorney general (1999–2005). He devotes much of his time to family and ranching in the San Luis Valley. He continues to be a champion for conservation, civil rights, and an inclusive United States of America.